Government-Nonprofit Relations in Times of Recession

The Public Policy and the Third Sector Series

The Nonprofit Sector in Canada: Roles and Relationships
Keith G. Banting, editor

The Nonprofit Sector and Government in a New Century
Kathy L. Brock and Keith G. Banting, editors

The Nonprofit Sector in Interesting Times: Case Studies in a Changing Sector
Kathy L. Brock and Keith G. Banting, editors

Delicate Dances: Public Policy and the Nonprofit Sector
Kathy L. Brock, editor

The New Federal Policy Agenda and the Voluntary Sector: On the Cutting Edge,
Rachel Laforest, editor

Government-Nonprofit Relations in Times of Recession
Rachel Laforest, editor

Government-Nonprofit Relations in Times of Recession

Edited by Rachel Laforest

Queen's Policy Studies Series
School of Policy Studies, Queen's University
McGill-Queen's University Press
Montreal & Kingston • London • Ithaca

SCHOOL OF **Queen's**
UNIVERSITY

Policy Studies

Publications Unit
Robert Sutherland Hall
138 Union Street
Kingston, ON, Canada
K7L 3N6
www.queensu.ca/sps/

Library and Archives Canada Cataloguing in Publication

Government-nonprofit relations in times of recession / edited by Rachel Laforest.

(Queen's policy studies series)
This collection of papers is based on the 10th Annual National Forum of the Public Policy and Third Sector Initiative conference, held in Toronto, Ont., Nov. 16, 2011.
Includes bibliographical references.
ISBN 978-1-55339-327-6

1. Nonprofit organizations—Congresses. 2. Nonprofit organizations—Government policy—Congresses. 3. Associations, institutions, etc.—Government policy—Congresses. 4. Recessions—Government policy—Congresses. 5. Global Financial Crisis, 2008-2009—Congresses. I. Laforest, Rachel, 1972- II. Queen's University (Kingston, Ont.). School of Policy Studies III. National Forum of the Public Policy and Third Sector Initiative (10th : 2011 : Toronto, Ont.) IV. Series: Queen's policy studies series

HD62.6.G69 2012   361.7'63   C2012-905572-7

CONTENTS

Acknowledgements vii

Chapter 1 Introduction
Rachel Laforest 1

Chapter 2 Muddling through Government-Nonprofit
Relations in Canada
Rachel Laforest 9

Chapter 3 The New Reality of the Government-Nonprofit
Relationship in the United States
Steven Rathgeb Smith 19

Chapter 4 Impact of the Economic Crisis on the Nonprofit
Sector in the United States
John Casey 41

Chapter 5 Not Meeting the Challenge of Change: Government,
the Voluntary and Community Sector, Recession and
the Compact in England, 1997–2012
Meta Zimmeck and Colin Rochester 61

Chapter 6 England's Big Society: Can the Voluntary Sector
Manage Without the State?
Marilyn Taylor 79

Chapter 7 Post-Partnership Ireland: Organizational Survival
and Social Change Strategies in an Era of Economic
Restraint
Gemma Donnelly-Cox and John A. Healy 97

Chapter 8 Citizen Advocacy or Death from a Thousand
Cuts: What Determines the Fate of Third Sector
Organizations in Welfare States after the Economic
Crisis? A View from Ireland's Two Jurisdictions
Nicholas Acheson 113

Chapter 9   The Impact of the Economic Recession on Spain's
             Third Sector
             Carmen Parra   129

Chapter 10   No Connections between Separate Spheres?
             Economic Recession and the Third Sector in
             Germany
             Björn Schmitz   147

Chapter 11   The National Compact: Civilizing the Relationship
             between Government and the Not-for-profit
             Sector in Australia
             John Butcher   165

Chapter 12   Southern Civil Society Organizations in
             Tumultuous Times: Global Recession and its
             Consequences
             Barbara Levine and Evren Tok   189

             Contributors   205

ACKNOWLEDGEMENTS

The production of this book was made possible by the contributions of several people. First, I owe a special thanks to all of the collaborators on this book for their patience, dedication, and assistance throughout this project. The quality of their work speaks for itself. I am especially indebted to Brenda Melles who provided editorial assistance on drafts of the chapters. Chris Cornish also provided assistance and organizational expertise at the Annual Forum of the Public Policy and Third Sector Initiative that preceded this volume. I would also like to thank Valerie Jarus, Mark Howes, the wonderful production team at the McGill-Queen's University Press, for their administrative assistance in the completion of this volume. I am especially grateful to the Social Sciences and Humanities Research Council for their sponsorship of the initial conference. Finally, I want to thank my family for their unwavering love and support.

Rachel Laforest
August 2013

CHAPTER 1

INTRODUCTION

RACHEL LAFOREST

Governments around the world stand at a crossroads. What began as a subprime mortgage crisis in the US housing market, set in motion a global economic recession, the effects of which still resonate around the globe. Faced with an enormous financial burden and new social challenges on the horizon, governments are looking for new institutional solutions that will enable them to do more with less. In many countries, the nonprofit sector has become a key pillar in new administrative reforms. Indeed, most governments recognize that the nonprofit sector is a critical part of their ability to develop and maintain economic strength and social well-being within communities. Yet the kind of supports the sector ultimately receives varies across settings.

This edited volume takes stock of the changes that are currently underway around the world. It discusses how the role of the nonprofit sector in policy is being reassessed and provides a timely analysis of international trends, bringing together in one place works covering a gamut of countries and experiences. By connecting these dynamics, the volume brings context to the complex transformations that have occurred in government-nonprofit sector relations since the early 2000s. These developments are of interests not only for understanding the domestic Canadian scene today but also for the study of government-nonprofit relationships in other countries. In that sense, this edited volume fills a much-needed void by providing a vivid and germane portrait of the nonprofit sector in a variety of public policy arenas.

Government-Nonprofit Relations in Times of Recession, ed. Rachel Laforest. Montreal and Kingston: Queen's Policy Studies Series, McGill-Queen's University Press. © 2013 The School of Policy Studies, Queen's University at Kingston.

The Framework of the Book

This book is the sixth volume to emerge from the Public Policy and Third Sector Initiative in the School of Policy Studies at Queen's University. The Initiative, now in its fourteenth year, is a research and teaching concentration of the School of Policy Studies that focuses on the multifaceted relationships between the public, private and non-profit sectors. The Initiative was established in 2000 with support from the Kahanoff Foundation for the purpose of promoting the inclusion of nonprofit organizations in the process of governing and as a response for the need for research into the growing role of nonprofit organizations in the process of policy making.

The book resulted from the Annual Public Policy and Third Sector Conference, "The Recession and Beyond" organized by the Public Policy and Third Sector Initiative in October 2011. At the conference, more than one hundred international experts, public servants, and practitioners convened to explore and reflect on the distinct characteristics of the new policy agendas being developed in a time of Recession. The conference probed into several questions that are fundamental to this discussion such as:

- What is the place of the nonprofit sector in times of Recession?
- What roles are emerging for the sector in Canada and internationally?
- How can we anticipate the relationship between the state and the sector evolving?

This book builds on this event by bringing together some of the original conference contributors to focus both on the broad picture and on selected country experiences. It offers both a retrospective look on changes to the nonprofit sector agenda during the recession, and a forward looking focus on some of the policy areas where a new role for the sector can emerge. Taken together, the chapters provide us with a deeper understanding of the current state of government-nonprofit relations.

This book is also an opportunity for dialogue on how governments and nonprofit organizations can work together in a time of financial restraint and take forward the lessons learned over the past decade to continue to engage a nonprofit sector which is creative, innovative and collaborative. The aim is to provide a venue to foster knowledgeable debate on this critical and timely topic. In doing so, this book advances one of the basic missions of the Public Policy and Third Sector Initiative, which is to bring together international experts, public servants and practitioners, to discuss common policy problems and solutions and work collectively to develop understanding and promote actions that will lead to effective cross sectoral collaborations. For this reason, this book is written with a broad and diverse audience in mind.

Each of the book's chapters focuses on the government-nonprofit relations within a specific country. In chapter 2, Rachel Laforest discusses how the nonprofit sector has navigated the recession. Canada is one of the countries to have fared relatively well during the recession, however the sector had been subjected to a number of gradual and incremental funding cuts which accelerated when ressources were tight. Because very little forethought was given to the role and place of the nonprofit sector in policy and how these cuts would be administered, she concludes that the nonprofit sector is now in a very fragile state.

In chapter 3, Steven Rathgeb Smith describes government-nonprofit relationships in the US as marked by horizontality and networked collaboration. The 1960s onward cemented the relationship as growth of government funding in the area of health and social care spurred growth in the nonprofit sector. When financial turbulence hit, the US government emphasized greater regulation of nonprofits. Smith attributes the professionalization and self-governance that ensued to these regulatory and financial pressures.

In chapter 4, John Casey examines the state of the nonprofit sector in the US at a more micro level. His chapter details shifts in levels of charitable donations and government funding. While the onset decline in charitable donations caused by the recession seems to have returned to earlier levels, cuts in government funding have had more long lasting effects on organizational practices such has human resources and service levels. His analysis echoes that of Rathgeb Smith concluding that the financial crisis reinforced collaborative relations between the government and the nonprofit sector.

In chapter 5, Colin Rochester and Meta Zimmeck describe how the relationship between the UK government and the nonprofit sector evolved over time leading to the implementation of a Compact – an agreement to strengthen their mutual relationship. The chapter then explains how the weak implementation of the Compact left the nonprofit sector vulnerable to funding cuts when the recession hit and eventually lead to the demise of the government's commitment to partnership. Finally, the chapter examines the organizational impact these broad macro changes have had on the sector, highlighting that the impact has been felt unevenly across the sector, privileging larger, well-established organizations.

Marilyn Taylor, in chapter 6, also examines the UK but focuses the analysis on the political impact of the newly elected Conservative-Liberal Democrat Coalition. She examines the shifting policy agenda articulated around Big Society and its ideological roots, drawing out continuities and ruptures with earlier New Labour Policy. Taylor argues that the newly elected conservative-Liberal coalition have not proposed radical ideas displacing the nonprofit sector in the political landscape. Many of these ideas found their roots early on in Third Way politics. She also ties the Big Society agenda back to Conservative thinking around social responsibility and state intervention in societal matters. Taylor concludes that the contradictions between new funding measures that celebrate civil society and a laissez faire market driven approach to the sector will inevitably lead to an uneven and fragmented sector.

In chapter 7, Gemma Donnelly-Cox and John Healy discuss the impact of the collapse of the Irish economy during the recession on government-nonprofit relations. Given the dire nature of the economic situation in Ireland, all the policy focus has been directed toward economic measures. In addition, the end of the social partnership agreements has reduced the nonprofit sector to an afterthought. Despite these challenges, the chapter details how nonprofit organizations have strategized in this new environment in order to realign their services and activities with national priorities.

Nicholas Acheson's chapter then contrasts the experiences of nonprofit organizations in Ireland with that of Northern Ireland – the former being part of the Eurozone and the latter, not. This comparison illustrates how historical government-nonprofit relations have affected the way organizations understand their own role in the policy process and the narratives that underwrite their strategic choices in the face of the recession. While the rapid demise of the social partnership in Ireland meant that organizations had to reposition themselves quickly and develop an alternative vision to reframe their relationship with government, Acheson argues that the recession was slower to manifest itself in Northern Ireland – where strong horizontal policy linkages had been established between local administrations and nonprofit organizations. As a result, organizations did not develop an alternative narrative articulated around a renewal of mission as they have done in Ireland.

In Chapter 9, Carmen Parra examines the state of the nonprofit sector in Spain, one of the countries in Europe devastated by the recession. Parra explains how the rise of poverty levels caused by unemployment has increased the demands placed on the nonprofit sector. These growing demands have been accompanied by further pressures to increase transparency and accountability given limited resources available to the government. The chapter concludes by examining possible policy solutions that could help the Spanish nonprofit sector navigate the recession.

While it is important to look at countries that have been deeply affected by the recession, to understand how trends in government-nonprofit relations are evolving, it is also necessary to examine countries that have maintained high growth figures and relatively low public sector debt over this period of time. Australia and Germany are a case in point. Both governments remained in a good fiscal position and engaged with the nonprofit sector in a proactive way. Germany stands out as one of the countries in Europe to have successfully navigated the economic crisis. In Chapter 10, Björn Schmitz illustrates how the German government took special measures to enable workers to reduce their work hours as the economy slowed. This enabled the economy to absorb the slow down without rising levels of unemployment. In addition, the government actively sought to protect the nonprofit sector by providing a stable funding source. This enabled nonprofit organizations to be better positioned when the economic situation improved and seize opportunities to expand their role in social services.

Australia is also a country that emerged relatively unscathed from the recession, maintaining very low debt levels throughout. In spite of this, as John Butcher notes in chapter 11, the political environment went through multiple shifts over this period that impacted on government-nonprofit relations. One of the biggest policy transformations was the push towards privatization of social services and the adoption of new public management practices. These measures helped nonprofit organizations increase their market share and solidify their role in service provision. Interestingly, while most initiatives to strengthen government-nonprofit relations through formal partnership agreements, like Compacts, have been abandoned in most countries, Australia has only just begun negotiations to develop such an agreement given the growing recognition of the importance of the sector in the provision of social services.

In the final chapter, Barbara Levine and Evren Tok draw attention to the impact of the recession on nonprofit organizations in developing countries. The global recession has significantly constrained the flow of resources to these organizations that are mainly located in the southern hemisphere. This is an important departure for foreign aid compared to the early 2000s when development assistance was on the rise thanks to the adoption of the UN Millenium Declaration. As in many of the other chapters, nonprofit organizations in the developing world have also been most affected by the shift toward performance measurement. Indeed, many funders began utilizing results-based aid programming in an effort to monitor and obtain greater impacts within communities with fewer resources. The resulting effect has been uneven across the sector.

THE RECESSION AND BEYOND: SOME COMMON TRENDS

As many contributors to this volume attest, it is important to recognize that the shift in political regimes is marked by elements of both continuity and change. Identifying these elements is useful to help those of us grappling to understand how the policy agenda around the nonprofit sector is shifting. From a social point of view, the countries examined in this volume have followed different paths. Governments are faced with tough decisions in the face of fiscal deficits. Some invest in order to create stimulus which will run up larger deficits or adopt austerity measures. Others still focused on becoming competitive. Germany, for example, became an export driven economy. Regardless of the approach taken, some common themes emerged throughout the volume with regards to the state of government-nonprofit relations.

For one, all countries share a preoccupation with the state of public finances. With new fiscal constraints, existing welfare state arrangements, and their financing, needed to be rethought. Regardless of the approach taken, the nonprofit sector was seen as a valuable partner. For some, the nonprofit sector was seen as a pool of untapped volunteer resources that could be harnessed to address social problems. The "Big Society" agenda in the UK and the "Serve America Act" in the US are great examples of initiatives meant to foster volunteering to respond to increasing demands on public services. For others, promoting growth-led investments in the nonprofit sector was seen as a way to marry the pursuit of social and economic value and address flaws in the economy. In many ways, the policy discussion unfolding across countries about the relationship between governments and the nonprofit sector has been more focused on service delivery than on issues pertaining to citizen engagement and policy development that dominated in the 1980s and 1990s.

Secondly, the global shift in policy agendas has been accompanied by a decline in public trust in charities and nonprofits. This has manifested itself in a push toward greater regulation. For example, the US Internal Revenue Services (IRS) has tightened its reporting requirements. In Canada as well, the federal government has dedicated $8 million to ensure that charities provide more information on their political activities and foreign sources of funding. Whether it is through the introduction of performance based contracts or results based management, across the board we can observe a tightening in the oversight of nonprofit organizations. Organizations have been strategic in how they have managed this change. In fact, nonprofit organizations have themselves been pushing greater performance measurement by voluntarily adopting self-monitoring mechanisms such as accreditation and rating systems. This has contributed to a notable professionalization in countries as diverse as Canada, the US, Spain and Australia.

The current economic crisis and the increased competition for public and private funding also encouraged organizations to actively pursue revenue diversification. A general trend across countries has been the rise of growth led investments to encourage entrepreneurship and innovation. As the chapters illustrate, social finance and social impact bonds have rapidly gained favour with policy makers across the globe. In the United States, a Social Innovation Fund (SIF) was established to solve a number of social problems and expand the capabilities and impact of the nonprofit sector. In the UK, the cabinet office has dedicated funds foster social investment and entrepreneurial innovation in the sector as a means to compensate for decreased government funding Germany has also launched a program to support the growth of social innovation projects while Canada is currently looking into the possibility.

These new funding models are transforming the very nature of the nonprofit sector by bringing about important structural and organizational changes. As the chapters in this volume attest, some organizations have expanded the range and geographical scope of their services in order to increase revenue. Hybrid organizations, which pursue a social mission but are structured on business models based on social and financial returns, have been on the rise. As the lines between the public, private and non-profit sector are increasingly becoming blurred, nonprofit organizations have found it increasingly difficult to assert their distinctiveness in the policy arena. The transformations observed within this volume also point to the weakening and in some cases, the closure, of traditional organizations as new social entrepreneurial organizations emerge.

The greater complexity and variety of organizational forms makes one wonder whether the concept of a "nonprofit sector" is functional and masks some of the important transformations underway. These changes go beyond issues of organizational structure, accountability and regulation, they also have important implications with regards to our understanding of democracy. They reflect radically different conceptualizations of the role of the nonprofit sector in policy making. With the chapters in this volume, we can start to identify and analyze how government-nonprofit relations are changing.

CHAPTER 2

MUDDLING THROUGH GOVERNMENT-NONPROFIT RELATIONS IN CANADA

RACHEL LAFOREST

INTRODUCTION

The nonprofit sector is a significant social, political, and economic force in Canada, like in many countries. It is composed of over 161,000 charities and nonprofits, which together account for 8.6 percent of the GDP. In addition, the sector has a full-time equivalent workforce of over 2 million (Hall et al. 2004; see also Statistics Canada 2009). When one factors in the millions of volunteers who donate their time, the sector makes up a considerable, yet distinct, element of the labour force in Canada. This chapter explores the impact of the recession on this important actor in the economy. It examines how government-nonprofit relations had evolved leading into the recession, then presents some data on how the sector has fared after the recession. Finally, the chapter presents some of the future directions for policy reform that may help the nonprofit bounce back.

Contrary to many other countries discussed in this volume, Canada was slow to enter the economic downturn. When the recession hit in 2009, the federal government was in a strong financial position having had budgetary surpluses in previous years, low unemployment rates and net job creation. Thanks to the strength of its banking sector and to effective regulatory oversight, sub-prime mortgages were rare in Canada. Although fragile, growth remained relatively stable in the first year of the recession and economic contraction was less severe than it had been in many other countries. Nevertheless, the federal government had to take measures in order to steer the economy through the recession. It introduced a stimulus plan in 2009 called "Canada's Economic Action Plan" to target investments in infrastructure projects and help with labour

Government-Nonprofit Relations in Times of Recession, ed. Rachel Laforest. Montreal and Kingston. Queen's Policy Studies Series, McGill-Queen's University Press. © 2013 The School of Policy Studies, Queen's University at Kingston. All rights reserved.

market recovery. The federal government also introduced a number of deficit reduction measures. Federal government expenditures, as a percentage of the GDP, decreased over this period from 23.4 percent in 1992 to 14.6 percent in 2013.[1] These have translated into an overall reduction in contribution from various levels of government to the nonprofit sector.

Paradoxically, these funding cutbacks occurred at a time when many of the services formerly provided by governments were being reduced or transferred to the nonprofit organizations, the assumption being that they would have the capacity and resources to take on this additional burden. With little new investment in the nonprofit sector, there is cause to worry about the current state of the sector, its capacity and ability to meet this challenge. How organizations navigate this new reality will likely have an impact in communities, on the quality of services received and ultimately, on the quality of life in Canada.

GOVERNMENT-NONPROFIT RELATIONS IN CANADA

In many countries, the last decade has been marked by significant changes in the goals, funding and governance of social policy. Indeed, many commentators have observed that a new paradigm centered on "social investment" began to take shape in the late 1990s (Lister 2003; Jenson and Saint-Martin 2003; Banting 2006). Canada has been an exception in this regard. Indeed, in Canada, any philosophical underpinnings regarding the role of the nonprofit sector in policy have always been weakly developed, regardless of the political party in power (Phillips 2009). Yet, such a vision is fundamentally important to strengthening the relationship at a macro level because it creates the broad framework through which to interpret the value of the sector to policy. This lack of broad vision for the nonprofit sector is one of the factors that have prevented the federal government from taking purposeful steps toward sustainability and capacity building in the aftermath of the recession. Rather, the federal government's approach can be qualified as one of muddling through, taking incremental steps without much foresight to the overall impact of its interventions.

While the federal government has had a long-standing tradition of supporting the nonprofit sector in the 1970s and 1980s, by the late 1990s it began scaling back funding of the sector. This initial retreat was spurred by the relatively strong opposition mounted by social policy advocates in the face of the federal government's planned social security review and the recognition that most of these actors had been supported by federal grants and contributions in the past. Indeed, in the mid 1980s, the federal government had developed programs through department of Secretary of State that supported the advocacy efforts of organizations representing particular segments of Canadian society such as groups concerned with the official languages, multiculturalism, and women's issues (Pal 1993).

The sentiment in policy circles at the time was that this financial dependency was unsound.

Canada is not unique in its move to roll back the influence of organized interests. Indeed, many other countries such as New Zealand and Argentina adopted a similar stance in the 1980s (Smith 1993, 82-88; Marsh and Rhodes 1992, 257-8). However, for most countries, the powerful interests at the time were unions, not social policy groups. Canada is unique in that the post-war system of representation was constructed around nation-building and social justice issues (Jenson 2006). This legacy has entrenched in the federal government a general resistance towards funding the nonprofit sector to engage in policy advocacy out of fear of recreating similar practices of governance. To this day, the federal government remains reticent to fund organizations through grants because they are unconditional transfer payments and there is no oversight mechanism to ensure that the monies are not used toward advocacy. Rather funding has become increasingly targeted, short-term, and results based (Scott 2003).

While other countries were diversifying the funding instruments used to support nonprofit organizations in the late 1990s, the federal government in Canada had come to rely on two principal funding instruments: contributions and the tax system. The first has presented challenges for nonprofit organizations. Contributions are conditional transfer payments that come with specific terms and conditions to be met. They are most often used as a contracting tool because they are attached to short-term accountabilities. As such they are results oriented focused primarily on providing programs and services. They are often accompanied with a number of stringent requirements and expectations of reporting which can be onerous. When the federal Conservative party was elected in 2006, the financing regime had become sclerotic. The accountability requirements over grants and contributions were so stringent that they were virtually unworkable as the core support for nonprofit organizations (Phillips, Laforest and Graham 2010).

The second, however, provided some flexibility to nonprofit organizations. Given declining government funding, it is not surprising that charitable donations have become even more important as a source of revenue to support the nonprofit sector. Since 1994, the federal government has adopted a number of initiatives to make the tax treatment of charitable donations more generous. Not only has the federal government reduced the point at which the 29 percent tax credit first applied; it has also increased the annual ceiling on eligible donations, and improved tax treatment for the giving of assets. These changes have been gradual and incremental.

One of the biggest changes that has affected the state of government-nonprofit relations in Canada, however, has been the greater centralization of decision making under the Conservative government, and the increased political control exercised through the Prime Minister's Office, has meant that policy changes were adopted incrementally with less a priori rationality with regard to the nonprofit sector (Laforest 2012). In addition, because central agencies, such as Finance Canada, do not entertain a direct relationship with nonprofit organizations in their day-to-day operations, building relationships with them was a low priority. Instead, policies were a tactical and personal response to the governing partisan ideologies rather than a strategic and organizational one. Clearly, the driving belief was that state should have a minimal role in civil society dynamics, aside from encouraging citizens to donate and volunteer. When the recession hit in 2009, relationship building between the federal government and the nonprofit sector was not on the agenda.

THE IMPACT OF THE RECESSION IN CANADA

The revenue of nonprofit organizations in Canada comes from a variety of sources: government funding; philanthropy, which includes charitable donations and foundations; and earned income, which is self-generated revenue through fees and services. The first category, government funding, is the biggest source of revenue for the nonprofit sector in Canada. Indeed, government accounts for 51 percent of nonprofit funding, whereas earned income and philanthropy represent 39 percent and 13 percent respectively (Hall et al. 2004).

Already vulnerable from funding cuts administered by the federal government as discussed previously, the recession further aggravated Canada's nonprofit sector's financial situation. Imagine Canada's *Sector Monitor* is the most recent Canadian study to look at the impact of the economic climate on the charitable and nonprofit sector. Conducted from November 2009 to January 2010, this survey of more than 1,500 leaders from registered charities across Canada found that almost half of nonprofit organizations had difficulty fulfilling their mission (Imagine Canada 2010). More than one in five (25 percent) reported that their existence was at risk because of the economic downturn.

Research conducted across Canada clearly tells the tale of diminished capacity within the sector to respond to growing, increasingly complex and urgent needs in communities. Indeed, at the peak of Canada's recession in mid-2009, more than 800,000 Canadians relied on Employment Insurance (EI) for support, and there are still 1.4 million unemployed Canadians. There is also evidence from many areas of the country that the economic downturn has had a significant impact on things such as domestic violence, homelessness, alcohol abuse, and the like (Co-Operative Housing Federation of Canada 2009; National Coalition for the Homeless 2008). The greatest increase in demand for social services was among children and youth, new Canadians and immigrants, people with mental health issues, and women (United Way Ottawa et al. 2009).

Hence, nonprofit organizations have been important players in addressing these social problems.

While demand for services surged, the funding base of nonprofit organizations was also steadily shrinking in the aftermath of the recession. In a survey of 284 Canadian foundations, Imagine Canada's *Sector Monitor* reported that just over one-third of foundations experienced a decrease in revenues from sources such as investment income, corporate sponsorships, donations and grants, and individual donations (Imagine Canada 2010). Findings at the provincial level echo these numbers. For example, in Ontario, the Ontario Trillium Foundation surveyed 100 nonprofit organizations. One-third of grantees reported been already affected by the downturn by January 2009 (Ontario Trillium Foundation 2009). In response to economic conditions, 41 percent of foundations cut the total value of grants made and 44 percent cut the number of grants made. A total of 17 percent of foundations stopped accepting new grant requests in response to economic conditions, and 7 percent suspended grantmaking. The dramatic decline in the stock market that occurred during the recession has in effect reduced gifts of stock of public companies, which had been a major source of donations for the nonprofit sector in recent years. Furthermore, endowments and community foundations lost millions in the stock market, forcing many to cut or suspend grants to nonprofit organizations.

Earned income has reportedly also been on the decline as a result of the recession. In a survey of 413 agencies, the Social Planning Network of Ontario, 39 percent reported a decline in user fees (2009). Organizations reported that fundraising campaigns have not been drawing in as much money as in the past. The same can be said about special events, bingos, lotteries, and galas – each important sources of revenue for the nonprofit sector. With self-generated revenue and fees and important source of funding for the nonprofit sector in Canada, this does not bode well for their ability to navigate the recession.

The fear of this economic crisis is that we have hit a perfect storm, and increasingly organizations are asking whether they can survive. Ontario organizations expressed considerable concern about their capacity to pursue and sustain their goals and activities within the context of a changing social, political and economic environment. When asked whether their funding for the 2009–2010 fiscal year was secure, slightly more than one-third of agencies were uncertain (Social Planning Network of Ontario 2009). Their main challenge was sustaining operating costs. Both the level and structure of available support are identified as key issues. As well, there are significant human resources concerns, most notably with the ability to retain paid staff and to recruit the types of volunteers needed. Some agencies even reported having to use their reserves to pay for their operations.

Given these changes in funding environment, it stands to reason that charitable giving would be an important revenue source for the sector. As it stands more than half of the $112 billion raised in this sector comes from private funding, a significant proportion through the charitable contributions of individual Canadians (Imagine Canada 2006). Canada currently has one of the highest levels of charitable giving around the world. According to data collected by Statistics Canada, Canadian tax filers claimed $8.3 billion in donations in 2010, an increase of approximately $500 million from 2009 (Imagine Canada 2011).

However, that data obscures another reality – while the total amount of donations made has indeed increased, the number of donors has actually declined, from 30 percent in 1990 to 23.4 percent in 2010. In effect, the base of donors in Canada has been steadily shrinking over the past decade. This trend is further aggravated by the fact that a high proportion of the total amount of charitable contributions is borne by a few individuals. The *2004 Canada Survey of Giving, Volunteering and Participating* shows that 9 percent of donors are responsible for 62 percent of charitable donations. What this data indicates, is that the measure of our societies depends to a large extent on a small proportion of Canadian adults, known as the "civic core."

Another challenge affecting the nonprofit sector is a generational shift in the world of volunteering, and it is compounding the difficulties engendered by declining financial resources. Indeed, 7 percent of the Canadian population does 73 percent of all the volunteer work (Imagine Canada 2004). Together, this small group of individuals accounts for more than two-thirds of all volunteering, giving, and community activities in Canada. These contributory behaviors, which support the public good, are indeed linked. Members of the civic core tend to be older, religious, well educated, in higher status and income occupations, with children 6-17 in the home, and living in communities outside major metropolitan centers. Two of these characteristics are significant if we are to make projections about the future of the donor base in Canada. First, our population is aging – hence the segment of mature donors (those born before 1945), which tend to be amongst the most generous, is rapidly shrinking. Secondly, we are facing a decline of religious belief. This decline may have implications for overall levels of charitable giving in the future as we may loose more of our generous givers.

Because the donor base and the volunteer base in Canada are neither wide nor deep, these trends place the nonprofit sector in a precarious situation. If they remain unchanged, the long-term consequences are a serious depletion of civic resources and a diminished capacity for nonprofit organizations to support the well being of Canadians. Clearly the financial and the volunteer bases of the nonprofit sector have been weakened by the recession and remains fragile in Canada. The federal government has adopted a divestment strategy in relation to the sector that will most likely have important consequences for the development of a social investment perspective on a national scale. Over time, the result of this divestment strategy has been a relatively fragile associational context and a narrowing of the scope for political action.

FUTURE DIRECTIONS: TENSIONS IN DIVESTMENT AND INVESTMENT STRATEGIES

There has been a sea change in the role of nonprofits and charities in Canada over the last 20 years. Canada is far behind other countries in recognizing its role and responsibilities for supporting investment and innovation within the sector. Aside from the capacity issues facing the nonprofit sector, there has been another important barrier to the implementation of a social investment perspective in Canada. The federal government has increasingly been opting out of the social policy arena and divesting itself of responsibility for social policy leadership. The advent of the Conservative government signaled a significantly different model of governance of social policy, coined "open federalism." During the elections, Stephen Harper pledged that this approach would be based on a "renewed respect for the division of powers between the federal and provincial governments ... with a strong central government that focuses on genuine national priorities like national defense and the economic union, which fully respect the exclusive jurisdiction of the provinces" (Harper 2004). Open federalism represents a rethinking of the role of the federal government. The new Conservative government has been content to let provinces address policies that fall within their own jurisdictional powers, which means that the door to federal government engagement with the nonprofit sector is now closed.

The only funding instrument that the Conservative federal government is still willing to examine is that of tax laws in order to facilitate charitable giving. In 2006 capital gains on certain types of gifts of publicly listed securities and ecologically sensitive land were eliminated. More recently, the Conservative government increased the value of the tax credit on charitable giving and increased the ceiling regarding how much net income people can donate. It also allowed the donation of securities and eliminated capital gains on certain types of donations. As a result, Canada now has one of the most generous tax incentive systems.

However, the administration of the tax system does not provide any space for the sector to engage with the state. The objective of these measures is to strengthen opportunities for charitable giving and facilitate the transfer of resources from individuals to organizations. The state is now removed from the equation. The result has been that nonprofit organizations have come to look outside of the state to secure resources through fundraising and corporate partnerships – both of which afford them more flexibility in their use of resources but has proved more challenging because of the recession.

For many observers, the way forward for the nonprofit sector lies in the social innovation agenda (Broadhead 2010). Key foundations have indeed been pushing for social innovation and for a broader array of means of social finance, better access to capital, and more mission-related investment – but they have been pushing the private and philanthropic sector, not the state. Very little has been done so far. However, it is important to note that this dynamic further reinforces a charity-based understanding of civil society in Canada, one in which the state has no direct role with regards to the nonprofit sector. As scholars of the nonprofit sector, we need to be concerned about the impact that this trend may have on the character of the nonprofit sector. For one, it compels organizations to adopt private sector practices in order to adapt to secure resources in the marketplace. Organizations are being asked to provide services and demonstrate value as innovation becomes the key driving focus. Many of the organizations in the nonprofit sector are concerned with social justice and equity issues, they may find it difficult to juggle competing pressures. Finally, and perhaps more importantly, it places the sector further in the shadows of policy debate. If policy makers don't recognize the role of the nonprofit sector for providing voice to marginalized groups, then it can only further mainstreaming policy debates.

NOTE

1.   Federal Government Spending (CANSIM table 385-0032) divided by GDP (CANSIM table 380-0064) 1st quarter 1992: 23.4 percent 1st quarter 2013 14.6 percent.

REFERENCES

Banting, K. 2006. "Social citizenship and federalism: is a federal welfare state a contradiction in terms?" In *Territory, Democracy and Justice: Regionalism and Federalism in Western Democracies*, ed. S. Greer, 44-66. London: Palgrave Macmillan.

Broadhead, T. 2010. "On not letting a crisis go to waste: an innovation agenda for Canada's community sector." *The Philanthropist* 23 (1): 3-26.

Co-operative Housing Federation of Canada. 2009. The Dunning Report: Dimensions of Core Housing Need in Canada. At http://www.chfcanada.coop (accessed 6 June 2012).

Hall, M.H. et al. 2004. *Cornerstones of Community: Highlights of the National Survey of Nonprofit and Voluntary Organizations*. Cat. No. 61-533-XPE. Ottawa: Statistics Canada.

Harper, S. 2004. "My plan for 'open federalism.'" *National Post*, 27 October.

Imagine Canada. 2004. *Caring Canadians, Involved Canadians: Highlights from the 2000 National Survey of Giving, Volunteering and Participating.* Ottawa: Statistics Canada.

Imagine Canada. 2006. *Strengthening the Capacity of Nonprofit and Voluntary Organizations to Serve Canadians.* Ottawa: National Survey of Nonprofit and Voluntary Organizations (NSNVO).

Imagine Canada. 2010. *Sector Monitor.* At http://www.imaginecanada.ca (accessed 16 January 2012).

Imagine Canada. 2011. "Trends in Individual Donations: 1984–2010." *Research Bulletin* 15 (1). Available at http://www.imaginecanada.ca/ (accessed 16 January 2012).

Jenson, J. 2006. "Building Blocks for a New Social Architecture: The LEGOTM paradigm of an active society." *Policy & Politics* 34 (3): 429-51.

Jenson, J. and D. Saint-Martin. 2003. "New Routes to Social Cohesion? Citizenship and the Social Investment State." *Canadian Journal of Sociology* 28 (1): 77-99.

Laforest, R. 2012. "Rerouting Political Representation: Canada's social infrastructure crisis." *British Journal of Canadian Studies* 25 (2): 181-197.

Lister, R. 2003. "Children (but not women) first: New Labour, child welfare and gender." *Critical Social Policy* 26 (2): 315-35.

Marsh, D. and Rhodes, R.A. W. 1992. "Policy communities and issue networks: beyond typology." In *Policy Networks in British Government*, eds. D. Marsh and R.A.W. Rhodes. Oxford: Clarendon Press.

National Coalition for the Homeless (NCH). 2008. *NCH Fact Sheet: Homeless Family with Children.* Available at http://www.nationalhomeless.org (accessed on 14 December 2011).

Ontario Trillium Foundation. 2009. *Challenges and Opportunities for Ontario's Not-For-Profit Sector During Tough Economic Times.* Ottawa.

Pal, L.A. 1993. *Interests of state: The politics of language, multiculturalism and feminism in Canada.* Montreal and Kingston: McGill Queen's University Press.

Phillips, S.D. 2009. Canada's New Government and the Voluntary Sector: Wither a Policy Agenda? In *The Conservative Federal Policy Agenda and the Voluntary Sector: On the Cutting Edge*, ed. Rachel Laforest, 1-27. Montreal: McGill-Queen's University Press.

Phillips S.D., R. Laforest, and A. Graham. 2010. "From Shopping to Social Innovation: Getting Public Financing Right in Canada." *Policy and Society* 29: 189-199.

Scott, K. 2003. *Funding Matters: The Impact of Canada's New Funding Regime on Nonprofit and Voluntary Organizations.* Ottawa: Canadian Council on Social Development.

Smith, M.J. 1993. *Pressure, Power and Policy: State Autonomy and Policy Networks in Britain and the United States.* Hemel Hempstead: Harvester Wheatsheaf.

Social Planning Network of Ontario. 2009. *Hard Hit: Impact of the Economic Downturn on Nonprofit Community Social Services in Ontario.* Available at http://socialplanningtoronto.org (accessed on 13 December 2011).

Statistics Canada. 2009. *Survey on Giving, Volunteering and Participating: public use micro file data, 2007.* Cat. No. 89M0017XCB. Ottawa: Statistics Canada.

United Way Ottawa, Ottawa Chamber of Volunteer Organizations, Volunteer Ottawa and 211 Ottawa. 2009. *From Obstacles to Innovation: The Impact of the Economic Downturn on Ottawa's Social Service Sector.* Ottawa.

CHAPTER 3

THE NEW REALITY OF THE GOVERNMENT-NONPROFIT RELATIONSHIP IN THE UNITED STATES

STEVEN RATHGEB SMITH

Nonprofit agencies are a central and vitally important part of America's public policy agenda and service delivery system. The number of non-profit agencies has more than doubled in the last 15 years reflecting many key trends in public policy and management (NCCS 2012). State and local government increasingly rely upon nonprofit organizations to provide valued public services through government contracts – especially community care for the mentally ill, developmentally disabled, and aged. Federal welfare reform passed by Congress in 1996 encouraged the growth of many nonprofit social service agencies, at least initially. The federal Corporation for National and Community Service (CNCS) provides funding for thousands of "stipended volunteers" through community service programs such as AmeriCorps and VISTA. These programs help support thousands of nonprofits – including well-known organizations such as Teach for America, YouthBuild, and City Year – and have received broad support from across the political spectrum. The Obama administration also established a Social Innovation Fund (SIF) to support innovation and entrepreneurial initiatives through local nonprofits (Allard 2009; Smith 2006; Smith, forthcoming).

The vital role of nonprofit organizations within American public policy fits with the discourse on privatization, devolution, and the long-standing view of the United States as a liberal welfare state regime reliant upon private philanthropy and voluntarism to deal with social problems (Henriksen, Smith and Zimmer 2012; Esping-Andersen 1991). However, this viewpoint tends to mask the extensive direct and indirect government

Government-Nonprofit Relations in Times of Recession, ed. Rachel Laforest. Montreal and Kingston: Queen's Policy Studies Series, McGill-Queen's University Press. © 2013 The School of Policy Studies, Queen's University at Kingston. All rights reserved.

support of nonprofit agencies, especially in social and health services. Indeed, major federal funding programs such as Medicaid are an increasingly important funder of nonprofit social and health care programs.

Yet, government support of nonprofits is now beset by uncertainty. Faced with severe budget problems caused by the recession, state and local governments have slashed spending to countless agencies. Major federal programs face uncertain futures because of concerns about taxes and the federal budget deficit. At the same time, state and local governments are imposing new performance expectations including performance-based contracting and outcome evaluations. These emergent shifts in government policy have also been reinforced by private foundations which face stagnant assets and increased pressure to leverage their funds for positive impact.

Budget cutbacks and new performance regimes have also tended to overshadow the ongoing transformation and diversification of the ways government financially supports nonprofits (Smith 2006; Smith, forthcoming; Salamon 2002). Initially, government financing of nonprofits tended to be in the form of grants and contracts (often with relatively minimal accountability). Increasingly, tax credits, tax-exempt bonds, tax deductions, vouchers, and fees for services are important as forms of government financing for nonprofits. This diversification of funding or "policy tools" tends to mask the extent of public funding of nonprofits and, simultaneously, the increased centralization of government funding at the federal level in many areas such as health and social services. The variety of policy tools has also had important and far-reaching effects on the actual operations of nonprofit organizations. For instance, policy tools such as vouchers and tax credits have facilitated the development of hybrid nonprofit organizations with features of the public and/or for-profit sector, and promoted more cross-sectoral initiatives involving nonprofits, for-profit businesses, and different government agencies.

This chapter analyzes the ongoing evolution of the government-nonprofit relationship in the US within the context of broader trends in public and nonprofit management. The focus will be on community-based nonprofits which represent the majority of charitable nonprofits. In the US, the emergence of new policy tools and devolutionary and economic pressures have promoted greater interest in the development of horizontal networks and collaboration even as government has tried to assert more accountability and authority over nonprofit agencies, especially agencies that are providing public services with government funds.

NONPROFIT ORGANIZATIONS AND PUBLIC POLICY

Government financial support of nonprofit organizations has a long tradition in the United States dating to the colonial period (Salamon 1987;

Smith and Lipsky 1993). Harvard University, the Massachusetts General Hospital and other leading educational and health institutions received public funding in their formative years. Throughout the 19th century and the early 20th century, government funding of nonprofit service agencies continued, although it tended to be most extensive in the urban areas of the Northeast and Midwest. Overall, government oversight tended to be quite minimal. The relatively few agencies receiving public funds were subject to little ongoing scrutiny; indeed government relied upon these agencies themselves (and their boards) to conduct program monitoring.

This basic arrangement continued throughout the early decades of the 20th century. Indeed, in the 1950s the federal government provided extremely limited funding to nonprofit organizations – primarily in a few targeted service categories such as vocational rehabilitation and child welfare – leaving state and local governments very constrained in terms of their ability to fund social services. With extremely limited federal funding, most state and local governments relied upon their own revenues to fund these programs. Nonprofit agencies relied primarily on private donations and modest fees paid by clients (recipients of the service). In any given community, the universe of nonprofit agencies was also dominated by longstanding agencies such as the Salvation Army, Goodwill Industries, the American Red Cross, the Volunteers of America, the Boys and Girls Club, Catholic Charities, and Lutheran Social Services.

This government-nonprofit relationship changed dramatically in the 1960s. The Kennedy and Johnson administrations initiated a wide range of social initiatives at the federal level leading to the rapid establishment and growth in nonprofit community organizations. These included community mental health centers, community action agencies, new child welfare agencies, drug and alcohol treatment centers, domestic violence programs, legal services for the poor, home care, emergency shelters for youth, and workforce development programs. Most of the funding for these agencies and programs was federal, leading to a marked shift away from the voluntaristic roots of the nonprofit sector characteristic of the pre-1960s period. One indicator was the beginning of a long-term decline in the reliance of private nonprofit social service agencies on funds from private donative entities such as the United Way. In the 1960s, many agencies receiving United Way grants often relied upon these grants for well over 50 percent of their much more limited total revenue. With the growth of federal funding, the share of agency revenue from the United Way steadily declined. These same agencies might receive less than 5 percent of their funding from the United Way today. United Way funding has also declined in real terms since the late 1960s. Now, most nonprofit agencies in a given community do not receive any United Way funding, a fundamental change from the pre-1960s era.

The election of Ronald Reagan brought important changes to this evolving pattern of government-nonprofit relations. Under the Omnibus Budget

Reconciliation Act (OBRA) of 1981, federal funding for a wide array of programs was cut and many categorical federal grants were consolidated into block grants. Overall, the Reagan administration hoped that block grants and other policy changes could reverse the rise of federal spending and expansion of eligibility. These policy changes meant that many nonprofit agencies almost immediately lost substantial funding (Smith 2006; Smith, forthcoming).

These changes of government and policy mobilized many agencies and advocates for new sources of funding. Thousands of new nonprofit agencies had been established since the 1960s; these agencies were now vocal advocates of continued public funding. Also, a new constituency existed for expanded services as the growth of federal spending was encouraged by advocates for the poor, disabled, and disadvantaged – many of them family members seeking more services for their relatives and children. State and local government officials were also advocates of new funding since these officials often depended upon nonprofit agencies to provide important services. This new configuration of political interests, as well as rising demand for services, encouraged nonprofit agencies and state and local government officials to seek alternative sources of funds to offset declining federal revenue. One such source was Medicaid, the program created in 1965 as the health program for the poor. Until the 1980s, Medicaid was a very targeted program and funded primarily hospital and nursing home care. But starting in the 1980s, federal policy changes expanded Medicaid eligibility for a wide range of community programs including home care, hospice care, counseling, residential foster care, drug and alcohol treatment, and services for the mentally ill (although the extent of coverage varies from state to state) (Smith, forthcoming).

In addition, other new sources of federal financing enacted as part of the landmark welfare reform legislation of 1996 spurred the expansion of job training, child care, and other social services offered by nonprofit agencies. The overall effect of the rise in federal funding for nonprofit organizations was fiscal centralization, even as the federal government was devolving administrative responsibility to the states. Arguably, the growth of fiscal centralization through Medicaid and other federal programs in service categories such as mental health and child welfare has been facilitated and enabled by nonprofit organizations, especially community agencies. The latter are perceived as legitimate, neutral organizations with community roots.

As noted, the federal government also supports nonprofits through the Corporation for National and Community Service (CNCS) and its AmeriCorps and VISTA programs. Indeed, the Edward Kennedy Serve America Act of 2009 could eventually fund up to 250,000 additional volunteers through AmeriCorps and other federal service programs. Prominent nonprofits such as Teach for America, City Year, the Harlem

Children's Zone, and YouthBuild are just a few of the nonprofits that rely upon AmeriCorps volunteers.

Also, the widespread support for community service dovetails with the extensive interest in social innovation and social entrepreneurship. High-profile nonprofit organizations such as Parents As Teachers, Share Our Strength, Jumpstart, and the Harlem Children's Zone have received well-deserved credit for their innovative programming. These agencies have also received substantial government funding including direct federal grants and contracts. For example, the federal Social Innovation Fund (SIF) has funded many different local nonprofits, especially programs with mixed public-for-profit hybrid characteristics such as workforce development nonprofit that encourages workforce participation by the clients of the program.

CNCS has also supported community service as an expectation and an obligation of secondary and university students. Voluntarism in local agencies also received a big boost from the Bush administration's widely publicized Faith-Based and Community Initiative, through which the administration devoted millions of dollars to faith-based organizations in addressing social problems. One of the key targets of the Bush administration funding was smaller social service organizations that often relied significantly on volunteers and in-kind and cash donations, and had fewer professional staff. The overall goal was to offer faith-based organizations an opportunity to provide more effective services than traditional, more professionalized agencies. The Obama administration continues to support greater engagement with faith-based organizations, although this effort is a much lower profile than during the Bush years.

In short, the relationship between nonprofits and government in terms of funding has changed profoundly in the last 40 years. Prior to the 1960s, nonprofit agencies (except for hospitals and universities) were small and largely reliant on private contributions (especially the United Way) supplemented with client fees; their services were relatively narrow and restricted. Many agencies depended upon volunteers and lacked high levels of professionalism and accountability. The growth of government funding fueled the sharp rise in the number of nonprofit agencies with many agencies, especially in the area of health and social care, now primarily reliant upon government funds. Indeed, nonprofits in some categories such as development disabilities and foster care depend upon government for most of their revenue. Some services such as child care do receive significant amounts of private fee income, while other services such as food banks and emergency shelters receive a mix of government funds supplemented by private contributions (NCCS 2011). Overall, the number of 501 (c) (3) charitable nonprofits has almost doubled since 1999 to just under 1 million (NCCS 2012). Today, nonprofits are crucial to the implementation of public policy and the ability of government to achieve pressing policy goals and priorities, despite the ongoing economic recession.

Even before the current financial crisis, important shifts were occurring in the relationship between government and nonprofit organizations, especially social and health care agencies. First, government contracts with nonprofits are more performance-based. In the initial buildup of government contracting with nonprofit agencies in the 1960s and 1970s, government administrators tended to emphasize "process" accountability, which focused on the outputs and activities of the contract agencies. The advent of the government reform movement of the 1990s encouraged government administrators to restructure their contracts to emphasize performance and outcomes (Osborne and Gaebler 1992; Hood 1991; Phillips and Smith 2010). To varying degrees, many key social service contracts, including welfare-to-work, mental health, workforce development, and child welfare, are now performance-based contracts wherein agencies are reimbursed for services only if they meet specific performance targets (Heinrich and Choi 2007; Smith 2010a). Many private funders such as local United Way chapters and national foundations such as the Edna McConnell Clark Foundation are also tying their grants to an expectation of meeting specific performance targets.

This heightened interest in performance has a number of implications for the governance of nonprofit organizations, including the role of voluntarism within these agencies. First, the shift to outcome evaluation often involves a revolution in management thinking. Agencies need new investments in information systems in order to track outcomes and compile relevant programmatic and financial data. A key ripple effect is the "professionalization" of the administrative and programmatic infrastructure of nonprofits, especially for smaller community organizations that may have roots in local voluntarism. Greater investment in administration and programs can be a severe challenge for these community organizations, given their relative undercapitalization. Also, the resources necessary to comply with performance contracts can raise questions about mission and programmatic focus, since the performance contracts may contain expectations that are at variance with the previous client and program emphases, although some agencies may be able to shape these contract requirements to fit their previous client and program goals. For example, a community agency for youths may have to shrink its counseling program and target youths who meet specific contract expectations in order to meet the performance contract requirements.

The shift to professionalization and performance-based contracting can be especially consequential for nonprofit agencies because such agencies often emerge out of a desire of a like-minded "community" of people to deal with a problem or social need such as homelessness. These individuals create a service agency that regards its mission as logically responsive to their community of interest (Smith and Lipsky 1993). Government, by contrast, tends to approach services and clients from the norm of equity, consistent with the need of government officials to treat groups and individuals fairly. Equity can be interpreted in a variety of ways, but in social and health services, it usually means defining need in order to allocate resources by criteria deemed to be fair. Thus, an agency founded to serve a particular neighborhood or community may be required to expand its geographic reach significantly because government needs to allocate resources across a broader region.

This emphasis on responsiveness may lead the staff of nonprofit agencies to disagree with government, especially on policy matters relating to services, clients, and staff. This clash can be especially pronounced under a performance contracting regime, which can leave nonprofit social service agencies little discretion on the performance targets to be met and may require the agency to shift its focus toward programmatic goals and client groups at variance with their original community of interest (Smith and Lipsky 1993). For instance, welfare-to-work programs might prefer to work intensively with clients from a specific neighborhood or ethnic group. However, many performance contracts for welfare-to-work programs require agencies to meet short-term placement goals in order to be reimbursed for services, greatly reducing the ability of agencies to work with clients on a longer-term, more holistic basis.

The logic of performance contracting also tends to promote market competition among providers; government is supposed to hold agencies accountable for specific outcomes and if they do not meet these outcomes, government will turn to a different provider. Thus the very existence of performance contracting promotes greater uncertainty and more competition from nonprofit and for-profit providers. To the extent that nonprofit agencies are subject to contract termination (for non-performance), then agencies will be understandably more concerned about potential competitors and may adjust their programs and management styles accordingly. Agencies which may not have considered bidding upon particular contracts may do so in a performance contract arrangement as an "insurance policy" in case other contracts are lost. By creating greater vulnerability among nonprofit agencies, market competition can reinforce the vertical, hierarchical relationships between government and nonprofits.

However, some qualifications to the general observation are necessary. First, the fiscal crisis has already reduced public and private revenues for nonprofits, creating less money for nonprofits to use to track outcomes and undertake evaluation. Second, the logic of performance contracting is that government (and private funders and the United Way) will switch providers if performance targets are not achieved. However, the economic

crisis could in both the short and longer term shrink the number of providers in local communities, leaving government with fewer providers,
spurring a reassessment of performance contracting, and providing an
incentive for government to work collaboratively with nonprofits.

Third, the advent of performance contracting and the increased attention to program evaluation and outcomes encourages government and
nonprofit agencies, to varying degrees depending upon the jurisdiction,
to explore ways to achieve accountability through accreditation and self-
regulation. Prominent charity rating services such as Charity Navigator
and Guidestar are forcefully promoting an outcome orientation among
nonprofits included on their websites. The national organization representing nonprofits, Independent Sector, has promulgated a set of good
governance principles for nonprofits including foundations. At the state
level, the Maryland Association of Nonprofits has developed a "Standards
of Excellence" to promote high standards of ethical behavior and good
governance in nonprofits. Further, nonprofit agencies in specific service
categories, such as addiction services, are using accreditation to help support their efforts to enhance their impact and effectiveness. And, greater
interest exists among nonprofits in particular service categories such as
child welfare or drug treatment for cooperation to agree upon standards
of good care and practice. In some jurisdictions, policymakers are also
encouraging or requiring nonprofit agencies to adhere to "evidence-based
practices," that is, practices that have been proved effective through research and field testing (Metz, Blasé and Bowie 2007). The evidence-based
practice movement, like other performance management strategies such as
performance contracting, is an effort to standardize service and reduce the
discretion of service agency workers. Some jurisdictions, such as Oregon,
are requiring evidence-based practice as a condition of financial support,
but meanwhile many nonprofit agencies are voluntarily adopting these
practices in response to evolving professional norms and expectations
and encouragement by government. To the extent that self-regulation
develops, it could mitigate some of the pressure for additional regulation
on performance and promote more collaborative, or horizontal, relationships between government and the nonprofit sector.

Fourth, government and nonprofit agencies providing public services
are often engaged in a long-term relationship (Smith and Smyth 1996).
Thus, despite the pressures of performance contracting and market
competition, both parties have an incentive to work together on performance measures and overall accountability. Indeed, nonprofits often
work through their associations and coalitions to influence government
contracting policy on rates and key regulatory issues. This intertwined
and complex government-nonprofit relationship also encourages movement of staff between the two sectors. Many nonprofit agencies now
have executive directors who previously held important government
positions. Hiring staff with government experience is a very public

acknowledgement that government contracting can be a long-term relationship. Today, nonprofit organizations provide an incredibly diverse array of services, often under very difficult circumstances. Many government contracts are for ongoing services such as child welfare, prisoner re-entry, community programs for the developmentally disabled and mentally ill, home care for the elderly, and workforce development. To be sure, the certainty of funding is often very unclear and unpredictable. Many agencies, especially larger agencies, may experience declines in some contracts and increases in other contracts in any particular year (Allard 2009). However, agencies tend to have long-term relationships with government and are expected to be able to weather the cyclical nature of government funding. As a result, nonprofit organizations need to invest in their staff with the goal of building productive long-term relationships with government in order to be effective and sustainable; staff with government experience can be of great assistance.

Thinking about the relationship with government as a long-term relationship is reflected in other organizational adaptations to contracting. Government contract administrators place great priority on several key management components: sound financial management including regular audits; attention to performance management including the use of current program evaluation models; up-to-date tracking of clients and services; and a good reputation in the local community. In order to meet government expectations on these important priorities, nonprofit agencies with contracts (or interested in obtaining contracts) need to invest in expertise in financial management, program evaluation, and information technology. Over time, then, government contracting tends to profoundly change internal agency dynamics and management style.

The movement of professionals back and forth between government and nonprofit agencies encourages a consensus on programmatic standards in particular service categories. This consensus can become a characteristic of the "contracting regime" whereupon government and nonprofit agencies develop a common set of assumption to guide their relationships. The regime concept – which was originally applied in the field of international relations – suggests that two parties are mutually dependent upon each other so that each party cannot easily exit the relationship. However, an equally important aspect of regimes is that one party is typically much more powerful than the other. In the case of contracting regimes, government tends to be the more powerful partner and is in a position to dictate programmatic and financial expectations even in the face of opposition from their contract agencies (Smith and Lipsky 1993; Considine 2003; Considine and Lewis 2003). For example, a public child welfare department and a set of nonprofit child welfare agencies may develop specific norms about acceptable practice, referral policies, and reimbursement rates. These norms then guide the behavior and strategic management of the government department and the providers. In this relationship, government is able to drive the evolution of these norms given its resources and political influence and the relative absence of alternative funding sources.

Contracting regimes tend to operate based upon a certain level of trust among the two parties, despite this power imbalance. Contracts are often relational and long-term even in instances where competitive bidding is required (Smith and Smyth 1996). This "relational contracting" does not preclude differences of opinion or outright conflict, but it does underscore the stability of many contracting arrangements and the importance of cooperation among the two parties (Deakin and Michie 1997; Ring and Van de Ven 1992; Van Slyke 2009). But this cooperation occurs within a framework established by the more powerful partner. For example, nonprofit organizations may cooperate with government on a contract for community care for the chronic mentally ill, but the standards of care, financial regulations, and outcome measures are still set largely by government. Put another way, a nonprofit agency, by its decision to contract, indicates a willingness to cooperate with government on the implementation of a government program. Consequently, relational contracting (or horizontal governance) does not capture the nature of typical contracting relationships since it implies equity in decision-making among the two parties when in fact, government is the much more powerful partner.

It should also be noted that performance contracting is part of a broader trend in American public policy of greater regulation of nonprofits. The federal Internal Revenue Service (IRS) has for example revised its longstanding reporting forms for nonprofit organizations in an effort to promote greater transparency and greater accountability, especially as it pertains to governance and financial management. State and local governments are expecting more transparency and accountability from nonprofits especially regarding executive and board compensation.

Performance contracting with nonprofit agencies and, more generally, the focus on program outcomes and evaluations is likely to continue to gain prominence in the coming years. Fiscal pressures on state and local government will encourage government administrators to deploy their scarce dollars on their highest priorities and maximize the likelihood of achieving the desired outcomes. Advances in technology have also allowed government and nonprofit agencies to more easily track expenditures, client services, and outcomes. Private donors and funders are also supportive of various performance management strategies. For example, the Nurse Home Visiting program and the Harlem Children's Zone are widely recognized for their positive results and willingness to report their outcomes (Goodman 2006; Grossman and Curran 2004; Tough 2008). Each agency has received concerted support from leading foundations and the Obama administration, including funding for expansion and replication.

Given the emphasis on performance by funders, a central challenge facing nonprofit agencies is to develop the capacity to be able to respond effectively to performance expectations, especially since neither public nor private funders typically provide adequate funding for evaluation in their grants and contracts. Consequently, nonprofits face big challenges in obtaining adequate resources to fund their evaluation and performance-related activities. Whereas larger agencies tend to have more diversified income streams and the capability to use private philanthropic support to fund evaluation, many smaller and newer agencies are at a special disadvantage because of their relative undercapitalization. Technical assistance by government and private funders for these private agencies is thus imperative if smaller agencies are to compete effectively for government contracts and private philanthropic grants. Almost inevitably, though, technical assistance tends to promote greater professionalization within nonprofit agencies, since the advice and support typically involves helping to position nonprofits to meet the higher professional expectations attendant to performance management regimes (Hwang and Powell 2009).

Another manifestation of this changed government-nonprofit relationship is a more competitive environment for public (and private) funding. During the take-off period for government contracting in the 1960s and early 1970s, most nonprofit agencies did not really compete with other agencies for contracts. "Block" contracts with the agency for a certain level of service were the norm. Most contracts were cost-reimbursement contracts that essentially paid agencies for their costs on the basis of the contract terms and budget. Reimbursement was not linked to outcomes, and most agencies recovered their costs (at least as specified in the contract). Little incentive existed for agencies to compete with other agencies since contracts were unlikely to be moved from one agency to another unless egregious problems existed.

In recent years, though, government has shifted away from the traditional contracts that were the hallmark of the initial period of widespread government contracting. Increasingly, new "tools" of government support have come into widespread use, many of them tied to the client of the agency rather than to the producer of services (Salamon 2002). For instance, Medicaid functions like a "quasi-voucher" because eligibility is tied to the client. Thus, agencies are reimbursed for providing qualifying services to eligible clients, and their reimbursement rate is set at a predetermined amount for a specific service. Vouchers for services such as child care and housing encourage this competition for clients. The growing use of tax-exempt bond money for the capital needs for nonprofit organizations including universities, cultural institutions, and health and social service agencies has also introduced more competition for resources. States are typically responsible for administering this bond money and competition among nonprofit organizations for the funds is often very keen.

Greater competition among agencies is also encouraged by performance contracting, which creates the threat that nonprofits could lose their contracts for poor performance (although in practice losing contracts is still relatively rare). The net effect is to increase the funding uncertainty facing nonprofits which also face competition from for-profit firms, although this competition tends to vary tremendously by the service field and location.

The growing support for more client choice in the selection of service providers, especially in service categories such as mental health, developmental disabilities, and chronic illness, is also contributing to this more competitive environment. This movement is evident in the sharp drop in institutional care in favor of more flexible community service options requiring a variety of personal social services such as home care and counseling. Reflecting this interest in smaller, community settings and independent living, the Bush administration in 2003 established the New Freedom Initiative, which provides funding support for more independent living options for the disabled and elderly, including individual funding accounts for them to purchase services such as home care from local community agencies (Center for Medicare and Medicaid Services 2010).

The use of managed care arrangements by government in selected social and health services has created further competition and uncertainty among the affected social service agencies. The basic principle underlying managed care is that government and private insurers can save money by paying a nonprofit or for-profit managed care firm on a per person basis to care for a specified number of individuals, rather than reimbursing providers through traditional fee-for-service arrangements. Thus, the firm has an incentive to control costs because cost overruns will not be covered and the firm can keep any surplus. Initially, managed care was employed in the health-care sector, starting in the 1970s. Then, during the 1990s, many state governments embraced managed care for their Medicaid programs (GAO 2004). In addition, some states and localities created managed care programs for mental health that were "carved out" of the regular Medicaid program (Frank, Goldman and Hogan 2003). In this arrangement, state or local governments might contract with a managed care firm that would then subcontract with local nonprofit and for-profit service agencies to provide services to eligible individuals. Some states have also created managed care arrangements in child welfare (Courtney 2000). As Medicaid has expanded beyond traditional health services to include social services such as community care, counseling, and home care, many nonprofit agencies are providing services to eligible clients through regular Medicaid managed care.

In practice, managed care tends to create a more uncertain and competitive environment for nonprofit social and health care agencies. Previously, agencies had a direct relationship with state or local contract administrators – a relationship that usually involved long-term contracts that agencies could depend on being renewed. The managed care firm, by contrast, is essentially an intermediary entity between the service agency and government. The capitation payment system of managed care means that these firms have an incentive to reduce costs, even if the service demand exists. Overall, nonprofit agencies experience greater uncertainty on their revenues than they did under the old direct contract system.

ORGANIZATIONAL ADAPTATION AND RESPONSE

Greater competition, the diversification of government support, and the economic crisis have created much more overall turbulence in the government-nonprofit relationship. As a result, nonprofits are striving to adapt through a number of different organizational strategies including revenue diversification. The latter can include levying new client fees, selling ancillary services such as technical assistance, obtaining government contracts for services that the agency previously did not provide, and expanding beyond the existing geographic service boundaries of the agency. In particular, earned income has received widespread attention as a source of new revenue for nonprofits (Dees 1996; Alter 2010; Cordes and Steuerle 2009). Some nonprofits have established retail businesses in which clients are also employed or receive training.

Many nonprofit organizations with various hybrid structures mix nonprofit and for-profit elements (Tuckman 2009; Smith 2010b; Smith, forthcoming). For example, the Greyston Bakery in Yonkers, New York, is a for-profit bakery employing disadvantaged workers that has an affiliated foundation that operates various social service programs for the local community. Share our Strength, a national nonprofit focused on reducing hunger, has a for-profit arm, Community Wealth Ventures, to help other nonprofits develop more "market-oriented approaches to social change." The Manchester's Craftsmen Guild, a large multiservice organization in Pittsburgh, operates a for-profit jazz music label to help support its employment and training programs. Many other nonprofits have created for-profit subsidiaries to provide earned income. Other types of nonprofits including universities and cultural institutions generate substantial income from the sale of goods such as clothing and other gift items. Further, many nonprofits, especially longstanding agencies such as Catholic Charities, have evolved into complex multiservice organizations. Newer agencies with roots in the social entrepreneurship and community service movement such as City Year, YouthBuild, and Pioneer Human Services have grown large through close partnerships with government, supplemented with grants from foundations and individuals. This shift toward greater size and complexity reflects the changed funding and political environment of nonprofit agencies. Low government payment rates in programs such as Medicaid encourage nonprofits to grow because it helps them achieve greater efficiencies and cross-subsidize their administrative costs. Many foundations are increasingly interested in leveraging their funding and enhancing their impact, so they have often been pushing nonprofits with proven results to "go to scale" (Letts, Ryan and Grossman 1999). Two notable examples are the Harlem Children's Zone and YouthBuild which have received major support for expansion from foundations and government.

Despite the ongoing attention to earned-income possibilities and social enterprises, many community-based nonprofits (if not most) are not well positioned to generate substantial earned income from non-government sources. As noted, many community agencies are quite small and thus do not have the capital to launch a new market venture. The creation of a for-profit subsidiary requires extensive legal and accounting consultation and an investment in greater staff capacity. These initiatives simply cannot be attempted by grass-roots agencies that have a high dependence on volunteers and a small group of paid staff. Also, the clientele of many nonprofit social service and health care organizations are poor and disadvantaged and consequently are unable to pay substantial service fees. Many community nonprofits may also view new earned-income activities as contrary to their mission, since it might suggest a move away from free or subsidized services for local citizens. Smaller-scale earned-income ventures such as fees paid for parent trainings or the sale of technical assistance videos are less controversial, but typically generate very modest amounts of money.

Data on nonprofit revenues reported on Form 990, which nonprofits are required to submit to the Internal Revenue Service, suggest substantial fee income in the revenue base of nonprofit social service providers. However, these data are quite inaccurate and misleading. Much of this income actually comes from government programs such as Medicaid, which is recorded on these forms as "program service revenue" along with true private market purchases. Voucher payments and fees paid to residential programs from government income maintenance payments such as Supplemental Security Income (SSI) are also reported as program service revenue. For example, one large innovative multiservice agency in Seattle, Pioneer Human Services, which provides correctional, housing, and behavioral health services, had $2.3 million in revenue from the sales of goods and services and over $35 million in funding from government as part of its program fee revenue in 2008. (This agency is also regarded as highly innovative social enterprise.) As illustrated by this example, government can play an almost hidden role in supporting the work of nonprofits in ways that are barely visible to regulators and citizens.

Greater scale and market orientation combined with greater competition from for-profit and nonprofit organizations raise the specter of the commercialization of nonprofit agencies, which is typically regarded as a management focus on the market for organizational services rather than on the charitable mission of the agency. In this context, commercialization is evident in the greater dependence on user fees and earned income and the lesser reliance upon volunteers, private contributions, and government grants (Weisbrod 1998; Hansmann 1980; Eikenberry and Kluver 2004). Commercialization is also associated with straying from the original mission of the organization such as serving the poor and moving into services for paying customers with higher incomes. Yet the reality of the situation for many nonprofits is more complicated. To be sure, many nonprofit agencies have changed their mission in recent years or moved into new program areas. An agency originally founded as a mental health agency may decide to provide correctional services with different government contracts. Or a drug treatment agency, faced with cutbacks in its core funding, might elect to contract with the county government to provide education and training for offenders charged with impaired driving. If these new program opportunities do not exist for particular agencies, the most likely programmatic response to cutbacks in government funding or declines in charitable donations or foundation grants is to reduce services and staff and remain mission-based but serving fewer clients with a smaller staff. Thus, agency movement into new fields can therefore be seen as an effective adaptation to new funding realities rather than a surrender of core mission.

However, the shift to new markets and the overall competitive environment does encourage nonprofit organizations to be more "business-like" in their management practices. This change can include: hiring individuals with a business background as executive directors; restructuring the board to include more members with a corporate background; implementing new management systems; and placing a greater emphasis on earned income. In markets with for-profit competitors, nonprofits can even begin to look quite similar to their for-profit counterparts. The interest in more corporate styles of management – even if the clients of a nonprofit might remain disadvantaged – has also fueled the investments in nonprofit capacity building by public and private funders.

Many nonprofits are also trying to create new organizational structures or entities to better compete for public and private funding. This effort can include affiliated 501 (c) (3) fundraising organizations, new advisory committees, and support groups to raise revenue and develop deeper community support. As part of this effort, the reliance on various types of special-event community fundraising such as benefit auctions, breakfasts and dinners, and walk-a-thons has increased substantially.

In this new era of greater competition and revenue scarcity, nonprofits also face an incentive to cooperate, at least to reduce cost. Cooperation can be conceptualized along a continuum from lesser to greater integration: less intensive strategies might be sharing a staff person with another nonprofit or cooperating in support of an advocacy campaign; more intense cooperation might be sharing all back-office functions among several organizations and sharing information to develop a more integrated set of services. (Some agencies are also required to collaborate as a condition of getting their grants from a public or private funder.) Ultimately, some organizations may decide that they are better served through a complete merger, although this strategy is usually difficult and frequently contentious.

ADVOCACY AND CIVIC ENGAGEMENT

Nonprofit agencies are valued in part because of their potential for representing community interests in the policy process. Indeed, many nonprofit agencies started as advocacy organizations with community members organized to advocate for an urgent community need such as more services for at-risk youth, or to address a serious social problem such as drug abuse or the lack of affordable housing. So at least initially, the nonprofit agency was primarily engaged in changing local policies rather than providing a service. As advocacy organizations, these agencies were often engaged in mobilizing the community and generating community support for their priorities. Eventually, many of these advocacy groups evolved into direct service organizations with much less focus on community mobilization and advocacy.

Importantly, though, the current economic crisis and the increased competition for public and private funding encourage community organizations to develop broad-based community support. This puts them in a stronger position to land government contracts and private foundation grants, and to win policies favorable to agency goals and services. Unfortunately, many newer nonprofit organizations are not well positioned to mobilize community support. Many of these agencies were founded by social entrepreneurs with innovative ideas on changing polices or providing services to the citizenry. At their inception, these agencies usually had small boards and lacked broad-based community support. An infusion of government or private funds allowed growth, but the board did not typically expand and the agency was often oriented toward its funders, especially the government, rather than toward the community.

In the current fiscal and political climate, nonprofit agencies need to engage their communities more deeply. Importantly, agencies need to enlist their boards, staff, volunteers, and community members to support the organization in the political arena. Many nonprofit organizations are surprisingly inactive politically; many worry that advocacy will create legal and political problems in light of the restrictions on advocacy in federal law. Service providers may worry that advocacy will have a deleterious effect on their relationship with government, including future funding and regulatory decisions. Perhaps even more important, newer and smaller community organizations often lack the resources and expertise to be effective political advocates. Also, some social service agencies, such as emergency shelters or food banks, may not necessarily view political activity and civic engagement as activities that align with their mission and program goals (Pekkanen and Smith, forthcoming; Bass et al. 2007; Berry and Arons 2003; Salamon and Geller 2008).

Despite these obstacles and limitations, many social service organizations are striving to be more effective advocates and to develop broader community support. One strategy is through active participation in coalitions and associations, especially at the state level, in service fields such as home care, child welfare, and mental health, where state regulations and policy are especially important. These statewide or regional associations typically are membership organizations with limited budgets that strive to build long-term relationships with legislators and government contract administrators in support of the funding and regulatory priorities of their members. These associations usually do not engage in more generalized advocacy on public policy issues such as higher cash assistance payments but instead focus their policy agendas on organization-related issues such as more contract funding or client eligibility criteria (Smith and Lipsky 1993).

Many of the larger nonprofit agencies also have ongoing contact and relationships with state and local legislators and administrators. This contact can include direct lobbying and advocacy pertaining to agency programs and funding needs, as well as more broad-based public education in support of better funding. The staff and board may also be mobilized to protest funding cutbacks or argue for rate and funding increases. Also, many community agencies participate in an advocacy day at the state capitol to push for their legislative priorities and agenda. Increasingly, agencies with substantial government funding employ former public officials in key leadership positions in order to help promote their programmatic and policy goals.

Civic engagement and advocacy can also occur through the board of directors, although evidence from the Johns Hopkins Listening Post project suggests that most board members are not engaged in significant advocacy on behalf of the organization (Newhouse 2010). However, the economic crisis and increased competition are pushing agencies to revisit their prevailing governance structures in the interest of financial and programmatic sustainability and improved civic engagement. Several strategies are evident, although great variation exists on the application at the agency level. Many newer organizations have small boards, placing them at a disadvantage regarding civic engagement. In response, many community organizations providing social services are striving to attract larger, more diverse boards that include more community members, client representatives where appropriate, and civic leaders. Research shows that nonprofits are more likely to be effective in their advocacy when they have a committee or staff person responsible for advocacy and government relations. Hence some larger social service organizations have established public policy committees comprising board members and staff (Berry and Arons 2003).

CONCLUDING THOUGHTS

The relationship between government and nonprofit organizations is in the midst of an important transition period. The US has witnessed a sharp expansion in the number of charitable nonprofit organizations. The rise in direct and indirect government funding encouraged this growth. Yet now government at all levels faces fiscal austerity. Public and private funding has been reduced to many agencies, although the extent of cutbacks varies widely. Further, the economic crisis has exposed the vulnerabilities of nonprofit agencies in a devolved service system. Federal financing for social and health programs is higher, especially given the prominence of large programs such as Medicaid and Medicare. But decisions on eligibility and funding, especially given the prominence of Medicaid, are at the state level, leaving agencies extremely vulnerable to the economy and state finances in particular. The core problem is not a reliance on nonprofit agencies for service delivery. For instance, many European countries – the Netherlands and Germany are two – have relied on nonprofit organizations supported by government for decades. Evidence also suggests that government funding is associated with higher levels of effectiveness by nonprofit agencies (Grønbjerg 1993; Lynn 2002; Salamon 1987). The challenge facing nonprofit organizations in its relationship to government in the United States is a federalism problem: state and local government face constrained finances with uneven government regulation of program quality and services. This lack of government administrative and funding capacity in turn undermines the capacity of nonprofits and their ability to provide quality programming and adequate representation. The United Kingdom and Australia have addressed this problem by establishing "compacts" between government and the nonprofit sector that provide a structured avenue for government and representatives of the nonprofit sector to work on funding and regulatory issues of mutual concern (Plowden 2003; Casey 2011). Although the UK-style compact seems unlikely to be introduced in the United States, the lessons of cooperation between government and the nonprofit sector and the commitment of government to specific principles of good practice would seem to be adaptable to the US context, especially at the state level.

Overall, the future of nonprofit organizations is inextricably intertwined with the future of American public policy. In the United States, we have tried to marry the equity of government with the innovation and community roots of nonprofit organizations by means of extensive public funding through contracts, grants, vouchers, and tax credits, complemented with philanthropic support and, in some organizations, earned income. But the current mixed public-private arrangement lacks the transparency of the government. Further, the government may not receive appropriate credit for supporting nonprofit programs, since the public may be unaware of the extent of government financial support for nonprofit organizations (Smith 1993). Current cutbacks in public and private funding also threaten the sustainability of many important community organizations and programs. Greater transparency and more extensive civic engagement by nonprofit agencies and their supporters could help broaden the political support for these organizations and improve their capacity for effective program execution. However, government and, by extension, the citizenry need to recognize that nonprofit organizations are critical components of American public policy.

Despite this importance, the current presidential election has not featured extensive discussion of nonprofit organizations. Indeed, nonprofits have tended to be overlooked or discussed in context of other issues such as education reform. Regardless of the winner of the November election, certain trends are likely to continue including the emphasis on performance management and more business-like management practices. Further, federal funding of many nonprofit programs is also likely to decline. With less government funding and stagnant private philanthropic funds, a consolidation of the nonprofit sector is likely to occur, albeit slowly. This consolidation will also further facilitate the growing division within the sector between large agencies with diverse funding and substantial political and community support, and smaller community organizations with unstable funding and governance. Given the major funding and regulatory uncertainties due to the election, nonprofits and their stakeholders should be directly engaged in developing political and community support for their programs. The sustainability and viability of their programs could hinge on the success of these efforts.

REFERENCES

Allard, S.W. 2009. *Out of Reach: Place, Poverty, and the New American Welfare State.* New Haven: Yale University Press.

Alter, K.S. 2010 *Social Enterprise Typology.* Portland, Oregon: Virtue Ventures. At www.4lenses.org/setypology (accessed 20 May 2012).

Bass, G., D. Arons, K. Guinance, and M. Carter. 2007. *Seen But Not Heard: Strengthening Nonprofit Advocacy.* Washington, DC: Aspen Institute.

Berry, J. M. with D. Arons. 2003. *A Voice for Nonprofits.* Washington, DC: Brookings.

Casey, J. 2011. "A New Era of Collaborative Government-Nonprofit Relations in the U.S.?" *Nonprofit Policy Forum* 2.1. At http://works.bepress.com/johncasey/1 (accessed 20 May 2012).

Center for Medicare and Medicaid Services (CMS). 2010. *New Freedom Initiative.* At http://www.cms.gov/NewFreedomInitiative/ (accessed 20 May 2012).

Considine, M. 2003. "Governance and Competition: The Role of Non-profit Organisations in the Delivery of Public Services." *Australian Journal of Political Science* 38 (1): 63-77.

Considine, M. and J.M. Lewis. 2003. "Bureaucracy, Network, or Enterprise? Comparing Models of Governance in Australia, Britain, the Netherlands, and New Zealand." *Public Administration Review* 63 (2): 131-140.

Cordes, J.J. and C.E. Steuerle, eds. 2009. *Nonprofits and Business*. Washington: Urban Institute.

Courtney, M.E. 2000. "Managed Care and Child Welfare Services: What are the Issues?" *Children and Youth Services Review* 22 (2): 87-91.

Deakin, S. and J. Michie. 1997. "Contracts and Competition: An Introduction." *Cambridge Journal of Economics* 21: 121-125.

Dees, J.G. 1996. *The Social Enterprise Spectrum: Philanthropy to Commerce*. Harvard Business School Publishing.

Eikenbery, A.M. and J.D. Kluver. 2004. "The Marketization of the Nonprofit Sector: Civil Society at Risk?" *Public Administration Review*, 64 (2): 132-140.

Esping-Andersen, G. 1991. *The Three Worlds of Welfare Capitalism*. Princeton, NJ: Princeton University Press.

Frank, R.G., H.H. Goldman, and M. Hogan. 2003. "Medicaid and Mental Health: Be Careful What you Ask For." *Health Affairs* 22 (1): 101-113.

General Accounting Office (GAO). 2004. *Medicaid Managed Care: Access and Quality Requirements Specific to Low-Income and Other Special Needs Enrollees*. Washington, DC: GAO. At http://www.gao.gov/new.items/d0544r.pdf (accessed 20 May 2012).

Goodman, A. 2006. *The Story of David Olds and the Nurse Home Visiting Program*. Princeton, NJ: Robert Wood Johnson Foundation. At http://www.rwjf.org/files/publications/other/DavidOldsSpecialReport0606.pdf (accessed 20 May 2012).

Grønbjerg, K. 1993. *Understanding Nonprofit Funding*. San Francisco: Jossey-Bass.

Grossman, A. and D. Curran. 2004. *The Harlem Children's Zone: Driving performance with measurement and evaluation*. Boston, MA: Harvard Business School.

Hansmann, H.B. 1980. "The Role of Nonprofit Enterprise." *Yale Law Journal* 89: 835-901.

Heinrich, C.J. and Y. Choi. 2007. "Performance-Based Contracting in Social Welfare Programs." *American Review of Public Administration* 37 (4): 409-435.

Henriksen, L.S., S.R. Smith, and A. Zimmer. 2012. "On the Eve of Convergence? The Transformation of Social Service Provision in Denmark, Germany and the US." *Voluntas* 23 (2): 458-501.

Hood, C. 1991. "A Public Management for All Seasons." *Public Administration* 69: 3-19.

Hwang, H. and W.W. Powell. 2009. "The Rationalization of Charity: The Influences of Professionalism in the Nonprofit Sector." *Administrative Science Quarterly* 54 (2): 268-298.

Letts, C.W., W.P. Ryan, and A. Grossman. 1999. *High Performance Nonprofit Organizations: Managing Upstream for Greater Impact*. New York: John Wiley.

Lynn, L.E. Jr. 2002. "Social Services and the State: The Public Appropriation of Private Charity." *Social Service Review* 76 (1): 58-82.

Metz, A.J.R., K. Blasé, and L. Bowie. 2007. *Implementing Evidence-Based Practices: Six "Drivers" of Success*. Washington, DC: Child Trends. At http://www.

childtrends.org/Files/Child_Trends-2007_10_01_RB_6SuccessDrivers.pdf (accessed 20 May 2012).

National Center for Charitable Statistics (NCCS). 2011. *Government Funding of the Nonprofit Sector 2005/2006 Estimates (Draft)*. Washington, DC: Urban Institute. Personal communication. 18 March 2009.

—. 2012. US Nonprofit Sector. Washington, DC: Urban Institute. At http://nccs.urban.org/statistics/index.cfm (accessed 20 May 2012).

Newhouse, C. 2010. *Report on the Listening Post Project Roundtable on Nonprofit Advocacy and Lobbying*, Listening Post Project Communiqué No. 18. Johns Hopkins University, Center for Civil Society Studies.

Osborne, D. and T. Gaebler. 1992. *Reinventing Government*. New York: Plume.

Pekkanen, R. and S.R. Smith, eds. Forthcoming. *Nonprofits and Advocacy*. Baltimore: Johns Hopkins University Press.

Phillips, S. and S.R. Smith, eds. 2010. *Governance and Regulation in the Third Sector: International Perspectives*. London: Routledge.

Plowden, W. 2003. "The Compact: Attempts to Regulate Relationships between Government and the Voluntary Sector in England." *Nonprofit and Voluntary Sector Quarterly* 32 (3): 415-32.

Ring, P.S. and A.H. Van de Ven. 1992. "Structuring Cooperative Relationships between Organizations." *Strategic Management Journal* 13 (7): 483-498.

Salamon, L.M. 1987. "Partners in Public Service: The Scope and Theory of Government-Nonprofit Relations." In *The Nonprofit Sector: A Research Handbook*, ed. W.W. Powell, 99-117. New Haven: Yale University Press.

—, ed. 2002. *The Tools of Government*. New York: Oxford University Press.

Salamon, L. and S. L. Geller. 2008. "Nonprofit America: A Force for Democracy?" Communique No. 9 Listening Post Project. Baltimore, MD: Johns Hopkins University Center for Civil Society.

Smith, S.R. 1993. "The New Politics of Contracting: Citizenship and the Nonprofit Role." In *Public Policy for Democracy*, ed. H. Ingram and S.R. Smith, 198-221. Washington, DC: Brookings.

—. 2006. "Government Financing of Nonprofit Activity." In *Nonprofits and Government: Collaboration and Conflict*, 2nd ed., ed. E.T. Boris and C.E. Steuerle, 219-256. Washington, DC: Urban Institute.

—. 2010a. "Nonprofits and Public Administration: Reconciling Performance Management and Citizen Engagement." *American Review of Public Administration* 40 (March): 129-152.

—. 2010b. "Hybridization and Nonprofit Organizations: The Governance Challenge." *Policy and Society* 29 (3): 219-29.

—. Forthcoming. "Social Services." In *The State of Nonprofit America*, ed. L.M. Salamon. Washington, DC: Brookings.

Smith, S.R. and M. Lipsky. 1993. *Nonprofits for Hire: The Welfare State in the Age of Contracting*. Cambridge, MA: Harvard University Press.

Smith, S.R. and J. Smyth. 1996. "Contracting for Services in a Decentralized System." *Journal of Public Administration Research and Theory* 6, 2 (April): 277-276.

Tough, P. 2008. *Whatever it Takes: Geoffrey Canada's Quest to Change Harlem and America*. New York: Houghton Mifflin.

Tuckman, H.P. 2009. "The Strategic and Economic Value of Hybrid Nonprofit Structures," In *Nonprofits and Business*, ed. J.J. Cordes and C.E. Steurle, 129-53. Washington: Urban Institute Press.

Van Slyke, D.M. 2009. "Collaboration and Relational Contracting." In *The Collaborative Public Manager: New Ideas for the Twenty-First Century,* ed. R. O'Leary and L. Blomgren Bingham, 138-156. Washington, DC: Georgetown University Press.

Weisbrod, B.A. 1998. "The Nonprofit Mission and Its Financing." *Journal of Policy Analysis and Management* 17 (2): 165-174.

CHAPTER 4

IMPACT OF THE ECONOMIC CRISIS ON THE NONPROFIT SECTOR IN THE UNITED STATES

JOHN CASEY[1]

INTRODUCTION

The 2008 collapse of the financial markets and the subsequent global fiscal crisis have had a profound effect on nonprofit organizations in the United States. Given the wide ranging service delivery and advocacy role of non-profits – they represent almost 10 percent of GDP and full-time employment and play key roles in the delivery of health, education, social and cultural services – the new financial conditions have caused considerable organizational strain, while demand for services has increased.

Some nonprofits that were directly funded by now failed financial entities have simply closed shop. For example, the New York based Justice, Equality, Human Dignity, and Tolerance Foundation (known as JEHT) learned in late 2008 that its major sponsor, who had invested most of her wealth in Bernard Madoff's ponzi schemes, could no longer support the organization. Although JEHT had been disbursing some US$24 million in grants annually until 2007, in January 2009 it ceased all operations. In the year before its September 2008 bankruptcy, the financial services firm Lehman Brothers had distributed US$39 million to 200 nonprofit organizations through its own foundation. When Lehman folded, those funded organizations scrambled to close substantial holes in their budgets.

The general one line script for nonprofits in the US has been that they are now being asked to do a whole lot more with a whole lot less. But, not surprisingly, the picture is more complex. The impact of the fiscal

Government-Nonprofit Relations in Times of Recession, ed. Rachel Laforest. Montreal and Kingston: Queen's Policy Studies Series, McGill-Queen's University Press. © 2013 The School of Policy Studies, Queen's University at Kingston.

crisis has varied significantly between different states and locations in the US, between different subsectors, and between organizations within any subsector. Moreover, even during the depth of the recession, employment in the nonprofit sector continued to grow, in contrast to the decline in the for-profit sector (Salamon, Geller and Sokolowski 2012). This was driven partly by the Obama administration's economic stimulus package, the *American Reinvestment and Recovery Act*.

By early 2012, the general trends in macro-economic indicators appear to signal that the worst of the crisis is over in the United States. Looking back, we can speculatively break down the recession into three periods: the onset (late 2007–early 2009), the depth (early 2009–early 2010) and a long, slow recovery (early 2010 onward). The exact date spans of these periods are a matter of dispute. Even now, there are those who cast doubt on the viability of the recovery and how it will play out for the nonprofit sector, especially for those nonprofit organizations that depend on the shrinking fortunes of governments, particularly at state and local level.

This chapter summarizes the survey research conducted to study the impact of the crisis on nonprofits. It is important to note that the surveys quoted in the following sections generally have considerable sampling errors, as they most often use self-reporting through online or telephone questionnaires. By definition, this method gathers information only from those organizations that continue to exist, and from those that have the time, resources and interest in responding. Moreover, many organizations surveyed, as well as the organizations doing the surveys, may have an interest in misrepresenting the financial situation and organizational health of nonprofits in order to either elicit the sympathy of donors, or conversely to demonstrate how resilient they are. A definitive analysis of how the crisis has financially impacted nonprofits in the US will have to wait for future research based on more objective indicators. The chapter also examines the literature that emerged during this period to advise organizations how best to cope with the downturn conditions and explores the effects of the crisis on relations between nonprofits and governments. The impact of the crisis is illustrated through short case studies on government-nongovernment relations in New York City and on the strategies used by one nonprofit to thrive despite the adverse conditions.

TRENDS IN PRIVATE GIVING TO NONPROFITS

After years of steady growth in private giving to nonprofits throughout the 1990s and early 2000s, various surveys reported considerable declines in 2008 and 2009. According to the Center on Wealth and Philanthropy at Boston College, individual donations to the nonprofit sector in general decreased by an estimated 6 percent in 2008 and a further 4.9 percent in 2009 (Wallace 2010a). The *Chronicle of Philanthropy* reported an 18 percent decline in cash contributions to large charities in 2009 (Blum and Thompson 2010). A survey conducted by the Alliance of Arizona Nonprofits in February 2009 showed declines in revenue by "an average of 18 percent" with many Arizona nonprofits expecting further declines (Alliance of Arizona Nonprofits 2009).

However, more recent surveys appear to signal a turnaround. The *Chronicle of Philanthropy* reported that in the second quarter of 2010, cash giving to big charities grew by a median of 3.1 percent compared with 2009 (Wallace 2010b). This seems to be the general trend for larger nonprofits. For example, the Fidelity Charitable Gift Fund, a fund that focuses on large private donors, reported in August 2010 that it raised 67 percent more in the first six months of the year than it did in 2009 (Hall 2010). (Fidelity is a relatively new fund and part of the increase represents the success of their business model.) According to the Blackbaud Index of Charitable Giving, large organizations saw big increases in revenue in February 2010. However, this was largely attributed to a spike in donations in response to the January 2010 earthquake in Haiti (Blackbaud 2010). Other surveys indicated an upward trend in revenue throughout 2010 (although with fluctuations throughout the year), with a considerable increase in online giving, partly due to the growing acceptance of online, social media, and other electronic portals for donations (Wallace 2010b).

However, not all segments of the nonprofit sector appeared to be bene-fiting equally from the first periods of recovery in giving. The Blackbaud Index indicates that while large organizations saw significant increases in 2010, revenue for small organizations remained steadily positive but more modest, and medium-sized organizations still suffered from reduced revenue (Blackbaud 2010). By 2011 though, the trend towards increase in the Blackbaud Index was apparent for all organizations, with smaller organizations faring better than large ones (Blackbaud 2012).

Private giving trends can be broken down according to the following categories: individuals, corporations and foundations.

Giving by Individuals

A 2010 poll by Harris Interactive indicates that individuals gave to non-profits in smaller amounts and to fewer organizations. Further, the poll reported that the percentage of people who said they were not making any charitable donations at all increased throughout 2009, from 6 percent to 12 percent, though people were volunteering slightly more than they were in previous years (Harris Interactive 2010). In contrast, according to the Cygnus Donor Survey released in June 2010, the impact of the eco-nomic recession on philanthropy appears to be moderating with only 8 percent of typical donors planning to give less, compared to 2009 where 17.5 percent responded the same. A higher percentage of affluent donors (17 percent) indicated that they would give less this year, which may continue to pose a problem for many nonprofits that depend on donors who make large cash donations (Burk 2010). In early 2011, the percentage of donors planning to give less had dropped to 7 percent. However, in a supplemental survey in mid-2011, that number had bounced back up to 17 percent, reflecting the possible impact of a recovery that had not yet picked up pace (Burk 2011).

Giving by Corporations

While corporate giving is slowly bouncing back, a majority of big businesses signal it will be a while before they return to their pre-recession levels. In a 2010 survey of 162 of the country's largest companies, "54 percent of businesses say they gave less cash in 2010 than in 2009, 30 percent gave more, and 16 percent gave roughly the same." However, in-kind donations have increased as well as volunteering. Corporations have also indicated a narrower focus on organizations that "align with their business goals and expertise" and can provide measurable results (Barton and Preston 2010).

Giving by Foundations

Yearly trend studies conducted by the Foundation Center of the 75,500 grant making foundations in the United States indicate that awards increased from 2007 to 2008, but then fell 8.4 percent in 2009. (Specifically, independent and family foundations reduced their giving by 8.9 percent, corporate foundations by 3.3 percent, and community foundations by 9.6 percent.) The Foundation Center found that that grant levels remained flat in 2010 and estimated modest growth in 2011. For 2012, the Center noted that grant makers appeared to be fairly optimistic about their prospects and that, assuming no unexpected economic strife, foundation giving should show another modest gain (Foundation Center 2011).

In summary, although there are conflicting findings with current assessments ranging from optimistic to bleak, the majority of recent reports show that private giving has rebounded from the depths of 2009.

IMPACT OF THE ECONOMIC CRISIS ON PUBLIC FUNDING TO NONPROFITS

Survey work on the impact of the economic crisis on nonprofits has focused almost exclusively on private contributions or donations. Yet, government grants and other public sector payments are a considerably greater source of income for nonprofits. Sector-wide figures indicate that while private contributions represent 12 percent of nonprofit income, governments directly provide 29 percent of income to nonprofit organizations through grants and contracts (Sherlock and Gravelle 2009). Moreover, a significant proportion of private payments to nonprofits (i.e., fees for services), which represent 49 percent of total income, are also subsidized by government. Despite the importance of public funding, there appear to be no comprehensive surveys of the impact of the economic crisis on government funding to nonprofits in the US.

Anecdotal evidence indicates that the Obama administration's economic stimulus package eased the initial impact of the economic crisis for many organizations. However, as that stimulus package trails off, nonprofits stand to suffer directly from the severe shortfalls in public funding at federal, state, and local levels, resulting in steep budget cuts and delayed payments (Bridgespan Group 2012). The federal landscape is now dominated by the 2011 *Budget Control Act*, which mandates US$1.2 trillion in as yet unspecified spending cuts over ten years. Severe budget deficits in numerous states have resulted in cuts to government programs and services and funding for nonprofits, as well as to the imposition of new fees and taxes that are increasing organizational costs. Moreover, increasing delays in government payments and contract abuses have caused significant cash flow problems for many organizations (National Council of Nonprofits 2010).

While the fiscal conditions of states are improving along with the broader economy, the states are coming out of a very deep hole, leaving an air of uncertainty (McNichol, Olif and Johnson 2012). Furthermore, funding for services continues to be cut. No precise figures on cuts to government funding for nonprofit organizations appear to be available, but extrapolation from the numerous declarations of governors and mayors about impending budget cuts do not augur well for organizations that rely on these funds. As one commentator notes, "[f]ear and uncertainty have become mainstays for nonprofit groups that rely on government money" (Wallace 2011, 1). Human services organizations are particularly impacted as they receive a greater portion of their income from government sources. The danger is that these cuts have the most impact on organizations working in the areas of greatest social needs and may lead to the creation of "nonprofit deserts" with severely inadequate services. A survey on funding by a research collaborative including Blackbaud and the Urban Institute warned in late 2011 that a large numbers of nonprofit organizations, particularly the smaller entities, are struggling to secure funding for the vital services they provide in their communities (Nonprofit Research Collaborative 2011).

CONSEQUENCES FOR NONPROFIT ORGANIZATIONS

Throughout 2008–2009 there were numerous anecdotal reports of declining revenues and increased costs for nonprofits, limiting their ability to plan for the future. This has led some organizations to lay off workers, hold off on hiring new workers, and in the worst cases, cut services. In the period between September 2008 and March 2009, 80 percent of organizations surveyed by the Johns Hopkins University Listening Post Project reported some fiscal stress and 40 percent considered it to be either "severe" or "very severe" (Salamon, Geller and Spence 2010). Organizations reported significant losses in revenue resulting from the decline of individual contributions, corporate contributions and foundation support (Salamon, Geller and Spence 2010, 5). The Nonprofit Finance Fund (2010a) warned of the "precarious situation" of many nonprofits due to the loss of revenue, which served to highlight the risky financial situation of organizations that lacked financial reserves and worked with constrained cash flows.

Significant cuts and delays in many areas of government funding produced cash flow problems for organizations, especially for those highly dependent on state dollars. Even as private giving slowly returned to pre-recession levels, the losses incurred by funding cuts continued to hamper recovery (National Council of Nonprofits 2010). Human service organizations were particularly vulnerable to loss of income streams, since government funding accounts for over 65 percent of total revenue, with 60 percent of organizations indicating that it is their largest funding source (Boris et al. 2010). Though nonprofit–government contracting has always had its challenges, further cuts and delays in funding have exacerbated tensions. The National Council of Nonprofits (2010) noted that nonprofits that rely on government contracts to provide funding for their services have been forced to "involuntarily bankroll government services" by reducing costs and obtaining bridge loans with high levels of interest in order to meet contracted benchmarks. The Council also notes that there is a rising trend of government proposals to "squeeze money" from nonprofits through the elimination of tax exemptions and the imposition of new fees and other payments. Some city governments, knowing they cannot levy "taxes" on nonprofit education, health, and social services facilities, have begun to institute new "fees" for the delivery of city services, such as trash collection and street cleaning. These fees are designed specifically to collect revenue from large nonprofit landholders. City governments have also pressured these landholders to provide other so-called PILOTs (payments in lieu of taxes).

In addition to declining revenues, nonprofits have had to deal with the increasing costs of health benefits and wages. Larger organizations were more likely to experience increasing costs as they have larger staffs and accompanying escalating benefits (National Council of Nonprofits

2010). But, organizations of all sizes have cut back by reducing services, foregoing salary increases, implementing hiring freezes, and laying off staff, all in spite of the growing need for services (Wallace 2011; National Council of Nonprofits 2009).

Despite the dire challenges, more than two-thirds of the organizations in the 2009 Johns Hopkins Listening Post survey indicated that they have been "successful" or "very successful" in coping with the crisis (Salamon, Geller and Spence 2010). Well-managed organizations are instituting classic organizational strategies for risk management in hard times, including cost reductions and scenario planning. Some have found that they are in fact expanding as they take over contracts from other failed nonprofits and attract new funding through fiscal stimulus packages. Many in the sector have simply been "philosophical," pointing out that they have survived recessions in the past and that, although this is the end of the boom times, they are not worse off now than they were in past lean times. Nonprofits have been urged to see hard times as an opportunity for needed restructuring and repositioning. Probably the most overused expression of the last few years has been, "You never want a serious crisis to go to waste," a quote attributed to Rahm Emmanuel when he was President Obama's Chief of Staff (Seib 2008).

RESPONSE STRATEGIES OF NONPROFIT ORGANIZATIONS TO THE FISCAL CRISIS

The economic downturn has spawned a wide range of literature that documents how organizations are coping and advises on how best to manage organizations in times of crisis (see for example, Bridgespan Group 2010). While much of the advice simply follows the same managerial and governance recommendations that nonprofits have been receiving over the last two decades as the sector has grown and professionalized, there has also been a new focus on strategic management and survival in times of crisis. Organizations are being exhorted to restructure, explore mergers, cut costs, intensify fundraising, strengthen communication–and simply understand better how to do more with less.

Restructures and Mergers

The fiscal crisis has forced many organizations to restructure, consolidate, or worse, shut down entirely (Banjo and Kalita 2010). Mergers have provided a way for struggling organizations to continue their mission while they shore up finances to appear more attractive to funders (Cortez, Foster and Milway 2009). In the San Francisco Bay Area, a portion of the emergency funding set aside by the San Francisco Foundation for struggling organizations was used to create a Nonprofit Transition Fund. The fund gives financial assistance to pay for lawyers, planners, and facilities managers to organizations interested in pursuing mergers (Meridith 2009). Similarly, The Lodestar Foundation in Arizona put up a US$250,000 annual collaboration prize in 2008 as an incentive for organizations "to increase efficiency and eliminate duplication" (Banjo and Kalita 2010). As funders and donors become more discerning about which causes they choose to support, mergers have become an increasingly promising tool for organizations to survive the economic recession. They also provide a proactive approach for healthy organizations to "strengthen effectiveness, spread best practices and expand reach" (Cortez, Foster and Milway 2009).

Although mergers have helped many struggling organizations stay afloat, some experts caution that mergers can also be incredibly problematic, as missions do not always "match up" (Cohen 2009). As the recession continues, organizations that are acquired may find some of their programs being inevitably "shed" so the acquiring organization can survive. In order to protect themselves and ensure continuity of services, organizations looking to merge must be vigilant about finding ways to protect their programs by including provisions in contracts that can ensure a program's survival after an acquisition (Bridgespan Group 2008).

Cutting Costs and Contingency Planning

Because organizations are faced with difficult choices about where to focus their resources, they have had to find effective ways to cut costs without severely hindering their ability to carry out their mission. A survey conducted by The Bridgespan Group documented several cost-cutting measures organizations have used to tighten their operational budgets. For example, pay cuts and furloughs have been used as a means to cut costs without eliminating employee positions. Reassigning staff, such as shifting employees' roles towards fundraising, has also helped some organizations meet the growing demand for their services (Bridgespan Group 2008). The report also highlighted that organizations were renegotiating vendor contracts as a way to reduce overhead costs. In times of recession, organizations are finding that many vendors would rather adjust rates than lose business entirely. According to the *Nonprofit Quarterly*, organizations have also achieved economies of scale through collaboration, by exploring joint purchasing with neighboring organizations and job-sharing, as well as by hiring consultants instead of full-time staff. The surveys note the importance of employee participation in these measures, as they can potentially impact staff morale and hinder productivity (Nonprofit Quarterly 2008).

Another important measure highlighted by the surveys is program assessment. By analyzing which programs are critically needed, an organization can find more efficient and effective ways to achieve its mission. This can be accomplished by evaluating how well certain programs align with the community's needs and the organization's capacity to deliver services in a quality and cost-effective way (Nonprofit Quarterly 2008; Bridgespan Group 2008). Thorough program analysis and assessment can help organizations better understand the choices they must make to successfully navigate the financial crisis. The Bridgespan Group report also highlights the importance of "approaching cost-cutting within the context of long-term planning," also commonly referred to as contingency planning. By looking at several possible outcomes, leaders can plan for potential scenarios and be prepared for the impact they will have on their organizations.

Paul Light, a professor at New York University's Wagner School of Public Service, offered four possible scenarios the nonprofit sector and individual organizations would face in the tough economy: a "rescue fantasy" in the form of an unusual gift or infusion of money; a "withering winterland" in which the elimination of workers and services would prevent the organization from accomplishing its mission; an "arbitrary winnowing" in which many organizations, particularly mid-size organizations, closed due to fiscal stress leaving the sector with "fewer but bigger nonprofits and a lot of smaller nonprofits that already live hand to mouth"; or a positive "transformation" in which organizations use the faltering economy as an opportunity to reinvent themselves (Light 2008). While external conditions might largely determine how such scenarios play out, organizations have control of their own strategic choices and contingency planning tools. The Nonprofit Assistance Fund's scenario planning worksheet helps organizations prepare for such scenarios and "adapt to changing circumstances" as they arise (Nonproft Assistance Fund 2011). According to *The Chronicle of Philanthropy*, organizations that have implemented contingency plans are "faring better" in the recession, indicating that such tools are not only useful but also vital (Gose 2009).

Intensify Fundraising

The intensified competition for donations and contracts created by the financial crisis has highlighted the need for organizations to define their missions clearly, provide measurable results, and communicate effectively with stakeholders. Close to half of the respondents in the Listening Post Project report to having "improved or expanded" marketing (48 percent) and advocacy (45 percent) efforts in addition to cutting costs during the recession. Organizations have increased their efforts to strengthen relationships with key stakeholders, core funders and board members while also developing new marketing and communication strategies as a way to aid fundraising activity (Salamon, Geller and Spence 2010).

Having a diverse set of revenue streams is crucial, especially in times of deep budget cuts. According to a survey conducted in 2010 by the Nonprofit Finance Fund (2010b), a majority of organizations (61 percent) have less than three months of cash available while 12 percent have none. The Nonprofit Finance Fund suggests bringing together leaders, board members and advisors to review the organization's financial assets in three critical areas – cash deposits, investments, and revenue – to determine how diverse and safe their funding streams are. The economic crisis has coincided with the rise in online giving and many organizations have utilized the Internet to attract new donors and strengthen relationships with existing ones.

As organizations faced difficult choices about how to move forward, many became more adaptable. Contingency planning, comprehensive fiscal strategies, and collaboration with other organizations were key in determining whether an organization survived the recession. According to the Listening Post Project, the organizations that pursued only "fund-raising and belt-tightening strategies" were likely to achieve "on par or slightly below" outcomes, while those organizations that implemented more comprehensive "entrepreneurial" strategies were more likely to report financial success (Salamon, Geller and Spence 2010, 1).

Ensure Open and Frequent Communication

A number of surveys and advice documents have emphasized the need to strengthen institutional communications, both internal and external, in times of crisis. Staff, boards, and stakeholders should be fully aware of the challenges facing an organization and should receive that information through official channels and not through the rumor mill. According to the Bridgespan Group, "leaders who have weathered past downturns find such transparency is one of the best ways to keep teams engaged and enthusiastic – focused on the needs of the people they are serving and not on the organization's woes" (Bridgespan Group 2008).

Other Impacts of the Crisis

In addition to the impacts on individual organizations, the economic crisis is also altering other important aspects of the nonprofit sector in the United States. During the economic bubble, much of the energy of nonprofits was focused on private philanthropy, social enterprise, and business venturing. Now, however, there are major shifts in attitude. Organizations are rethinking their relations with the [former] benefactors on their board, and entrepreneurs seem to matter less. In the US, the effective activities of many boards had stopped being about stewardship of the organization and had instead focused almost exclusively on fundraising. To secure and maintain a place on the board, a person had to "give, get, or get off." When the crisis hit, relationships with board members changed dramatically, particularly if the board members were from the finance industry. One Executive Director of a prominent New York nonprofit with [former] blue-chip board membership commented at a workshop soon after the market collapsed that she now "hated" her board members. While that initial anger has largely receded, board members are being asked to take a more active part in shepherding organizations through difficult times.

Attitudes towards government are also shifting. The upheavals since 2008 appear to have heightened the sense that nonprofits should be paying more attention to their relationship with government. Before the crisis, the focus was on relations with the private sector. Now, more attention is being given to what government can provide and how government policies impact constituencies. After years of almost ignoring government as simply a steady contractor, nonprofits are again focusing on what government can provide through stimulus funds and how government policy can help avoid the next, perhaps worse, crash. The National Council on Nonprofits is urging nonprofits to again assert their "historic role as champions of the common good" by helping monitor government operations and ensuring accountability (National Council of Nonprofits 2009).

Unlike other countries, there has been little evidence in the US of the development of formal sector-to-sector partnership arrangements between governments and non-profits. These arrangements, such as the *Compact* in the UK, foster more horizontal governance (Casey 2011). Until recently, relations between nonprofits and governments in the US have tended to be based on more hierarchical, principal-agent market relations. Yet, there is now increasing evidence that new more horizontal partnership processes and entities are emerging. In January 2011, the Governor of Connecticut created the cabinet position of Nonprofit Liaison and Head of the Community Nonprofit Human Services Cabinet, one more in a string of new nonprofit liaison *tsars* that have recently been appointed at state and city levels around the US to foster more collaborative relations.

In February 2012, a committee of nonprofit sector and business leaders convened by the Attorney General of New York State issued a report, which also called for the creation of a cabinet-level liaison position in that state. The committee also proposed a new initiative, dubbed *Nonprofits 2020: A Blueprint for the Future*, which would work to reduce administrative burdens for nonprofits, particularly those contracting with the state, and to improve the governance of nonprofit organizations (Leadership Committee for Nonprofit Revitalization 2012). At one of the official presentations of the Committee's report, the head of a major New York City nonprofit sector umbrella group noted that it signaled the beginning of a new era of partnership.

The link between the evolution of these government-nonprofit relations in the US and the economic recession is open to interpretation. While the genesis of many of the new processes is in dynamics that began before the recession (Casey 2011), there is little doubt that the new realities have accelerated the sense that the relationship paradigms are ripe for change. The New York report expresses this sentiment in the following terms:

> New York's nonprofits face a period of genuine uncertainty. The lingering recession, resulting revenue declines, and precarious economic outlook present unprecedented financial, strategic, and governance challenges for nonprofits. Throughout the state, nonprofits are doing heroic work to continue their programs and services as demand increases and cash flow tightens. Amid these challenges, a historic opportunity exists for government and nonprofits to join forces to revitalize and strengthen New York's non-profit sector. Working together, government and nonprofits can ensure that the sector not only survives these precarious times, but thrives. (Leadership Committee for Nonprofit Revitalization 2012, 1)

Human resources concerns have also been impacted. The baby boomer activists who founded many organizations in the nonprofit sector are reaching retirement. Until 2008, the focus of much of the human resources discussions was generational change and leadership vacuums. The concern was that the sector could not successfully replace all the retiring leaders. Post-crisis, the new concern appears to be how to get the older generation to retire now that much of their equity has disappeared and their retirement has become unaffordable (Leadership Committee for Nonprofit Revitalization 2012). Also, some organizations have reported an increase in the number of highly skilled volunteers formerly employed in the private sector who want to use their unemployment time "doing good," or as a way of transitioning to the nonprofit sector.

Responding to the Fiscal Crisis in New York City

New York City is a good example of how the economic crisis is reshaping relations between the nonprofit sector and government. New York City has a population of 8 million, giving it the critical mass to create large-scale, city-level initiatives. There are 42,000 registered nonprofits in New York City, 2,500 of which contract with city government for the delivery of services. The decade before the economic crisis was a boom time for nonprofits in New York (notwithstanding the impact of the September 11, 2001 terrorist attacks). The complex capital-generating processes of Wall Street were increasingly being applied to nonprofits. The years 2005–2008 were punctuated by multiple meetings and seminars discussing how best to increase social venture capital that would allow more nonprofits to "go to scale." These sessions were usually led by socially conscious titans from Wall Street firms. Through their philanthropic activities, they had become the new heroes of the nonprofit sector, along with an emerging cadre of young social entrepreneurs who transitioned from business and law schools into poor neighborhoods to start social ventures, private and nonprofit, which leveraged their financial sector connections most often through their former classmates and other graduates of their alma maters. They claimed to apply new business models to solving social problems and eschewed many of the traditions of charity-based nonprofits, including low wages and mission-based community support. Instead, they sought to achieve social outcomes by operating with the financial discipline, innovation, and determination of private sector business. One of the signature mottos that emerged from that period is "you can do good, but still do well." But, that approach has now been tempered and New York nonprofits are adjusting to the new realities.

The New York City administration, led by Mayor Michael Bloomberg, instituted a number of programs in 2008–2009 to strengthen its relations with nonprofits, particularly those with city contracts. These programs, collectively referred to as the *Mayor's Nonprofit Initiative* (City of New York 2011), include:

- An online portal for assisting nonprofits.
- A Chief Services Officer to promote service to the community.
- A Nonprofit Contract Facilitator in the Mayor's Office of Contracts Services, who is charged with improving the timeliness of city contracting, and working with agencies to provide training and technical assistance through a Capacity Building and Oversight project.
- A Memorandum of Understanding with the nonprofit Human Services Council that guarantees Cost of Living Adjustments in city contracts.
- A Master Services Agreement to be used by key city agencies as a common contracting process.
- The Health and Human Services Accelerator, a new unit that will focus on increasing efficiency and transparency in the relationship between government and the 1,300 nonprofit providers that have contracts with 12 city human services agencies. This will include a "data vault" of the relevant documents required for contracting, such as boards of director lists, audits, signature approvals, insurance forms, and IRS reports.
- Bridge loans from the Mayor's Office of Contract Services and the Fund for the City of New York through the Returnable Grant Fund, so the City is not only the contractor but also in effect the guarantor during cash flow difficulties.
- Other city-sponsored fiscal programs to assist nonprofits in weathering the fiscal crisis through lines of credit and group purchasing.

These initiatives are coordinated through a series of working groups convened by the Office of the Deputy Mayor for Health and Human Services that include city agency and nonprofit representatives as well as academics, consultants, and representatives from private philanthropy. As a result of these meetings a number of new initiatives have been started, including a new fiscal manual. This manual, to be developed by the Health and Human Services Accelerator and Mayor's Office of Contract Services, would ultimately establish common indirect cost rates for the administration of human services programs. The City also intends to develop a uniform taxonomy to define the terms and elements of services across different programs, city departments, and provider agencies.

It should be noted that in New York City the relationship between city government and nonprofits is marked by the fact that the city has a track record of creating its own nonprofits and the Mayor himself is a major philanthropist. The Mayor's Fund to Advance New York City (formerly known as Public-Private Initiatives) is a city government sponsored nonprofit which facilitates innovative public-private partnerships. The Fund relies on private donors to support a wide range of social and cultural public programs. The Mayor is the city's richest man and its most generous philanthropist, giving over US$40 million annually in grants through the Bloomberg Family Foundation and many millions more through other charities and foundations. The complex nature of the interplay between the Mayor's roles as the city's chief executive and its chief philanthropist became even more evident in March 2010 when he appointed Patricia Harris, the First Deputy Mayor in the city administration, as the chief executive and chairwoman of the Bloomberg Family Foundation – positions she would hold in conjunction with her city responsibilities.

ORGANIZATION CASE STUDY: THE URBAN ARTS PARTNERSHIP
THRIVES IN THE MIDST OF THE RECESSION[2]

Urban Arts Partnership (UAP) is a New York City arts education organization dedicated to improving public education through the provision of interdisciplinary programs in filmmaking, music production, photography, visual arts, theatre, design, dance, and language arts. UAP's programs are both integrated into regular classrooms and provided through after-school programs, summer programs, arts festivals, and special projects.

Created in response to the 1991 race riots in the Crown Heights neighborhood, the organization, originally known as Working Playground, has grown considerably over the last 20 years. Though many nonprofit organizations are reporting fiscal stress during the current crisis, UAP is experiencing the opposite. At the end of 2007, the organization's annual budget was at US$1.2 million. By the end of fiscal year 2008, it had jumped to US$1.698 and by the end of 2010 it was US$4 million. The organization attributes their success to four factors:

1. Access to federal funding. Before the recession, the organization received most of its funding from government grants and program fees (including service payments from schools). The organization's continued success in obtaining government funding has spared it from the worst consequences of the fiscal crisis. UAP had grown, in part, because it obtained a new revenue stream through a successful application to a federal grant source, the 21st Century Community Learning Centers program, which supports academic enrichment in low-performing schools, and so far has been exempt from cuts to federal funding.

2. The ability and willingness to adapt to changing times. Even though the organization did not experience a drop in funding as a result of the recession, the directors understood the importance of adapting to the changing economic climate. They began scenario planning by looking at the current economic situation and figuring out how to change in order to respond to it. Recognizing that there would be more competition for funding, the organization asked itself two core questions that, in their view, would define whether they stayed in business or not: first, do our programs work? And second, how do we know they work? Discussion around these questions began an elaborate process of refining the organization's identity by building on programs that fit their core mission and achieved results while eliminating those that they were merely exploring.

3. Appointment of a Development Director. Prior to 2007, no one in the organization had the specific job of helping the organization grow. Creating the position of the Development Director prompted all units to come together and to define their mission and their roles within the larger context of the organization. By studying what foundations were looking for and how they made their decisions, the Development Director was able to set UAP apart from other arts organizations, and so make it a stronger competitor for foundation and corporate funding.

4. Increased focus on measurable outcomes. The organization attributes most of their growth to more clearly measured outcomes. They started using hard data, such as passing rates, attendance rates, and test scores, to measure academic performance and link their programs to outcomes that "a lot of foundations especially in the education world really hold on to." One of their new programs, Fresh Prep, is designed specifically to help raise student achievement on the Regents Exams through hip-hop music. While some have argued that "teaching to the test" is no longer arts education, Philip Courtney, the Executive Director of UAP has said that, "the idea of innovation

and accountability or statistics is inextricably linked" (Urban Arts Partnership). By showing a real commitment to measuring their success, UAP has seen growth in all areas.

In October 2009, UAP added the Robin Hood Foundation to their growing list of funders. When previous attempts to lure this distinguished foundation failed, UAP focused even harder on achieving their goal of linking programs with measurable outcomes. The strategy worked. With the Robin Hood grant, there was a 300 percent increase in foundation giving in 2009, and they project another 50 percent in 2010. Corporate giving, which was traditionally a small part of their revenue line, has also grown due to better marketing and communication strategies and an increase in volunteer initiatives. Likewise, individual giving, though also a small portion of revenue, is increasing as the organization has become more aggressive about board recruitment, constantly seeking new blood and new donations. The only area where the organization has not seen growth is in program fees, where a percentage of the program is paid partly by the schools themselves. This is due to the massive budget cuts that continue to hurt public schools every year.

Currently, UAP has 17 full-time staff with 65 teaching artists in 65 schools across the city. In order to expand, UAP is developing model curricula and training teachers to use them, rather than increasing direct service programs through hiring more teaching artists. By using model curricula, UAP can reach more schools and more students while keeping program levels manageable to maintain quality.

Although most surveys have shown that arts and education nonprofit organizations have seen significant declines in giving, surveys also point to funders favoring organizations that show clear and measurable outcomes. UAP understood the importance of proving the value of their work in something that can be measured. This enabled them to attract prominent funders like The Robin Hood Foundation, grow their overall foundation and corporate funding sources, and diversify their revenue streams. By employing these strategies, the organization has succeeded in overcoming many of the challenges the economic recession has imposed on the nonprofit sector.

CONCLUSION

In late 2008, New York University professor Paul Light predicted that 100,000 nonprofits in the United States would close as a result of the fiscal crisis (McCambridge 2010). It is impossible to confirm that his dire prediction was realized–particularly as the crisis happened to coincide with a push by the Internal Revenue Service to tighten registration requirements which led to some 275,000 organizations (16 percent of the total nonprofit sector) losing their tax-exempt status for failing to file a tax return for three consecutive years. However, there is no doubt that the fiscal crisis has had significant negative consequences on the nonprofit sector and some organizations may never recover. Trends in private giving are showing some improvement since the depth of the crisis, but government funding remains restricted. In some cases, government funding is likely to be further cut, even as so many organizations are still suffering from the steep revenue declines of the previous years. In early 2011, the *Chronicle of Philanthropy* described the coming year as potentially "perilous" (Wallace 2011) and early indications from 2012 suggest that the prediction was correct (Bridgespan Group 2012; McNichol, Olif and Johnson 2012). Various commentators have anticipated that it may take up to a decade for the nonprofit sector to fully recover (McCambridge 2010).

Overall, the impact of the economic crisis has been deep and organizations have had to adopt a number of coping strategies to survive. Many have been forced to cut costs amid the growing need for their services. Organizations that implement contingency plans and devise comprehensive strategies to deal with the fiscal crisis will most likely outlast those that employ only stop-gap measures such as cost-cutting and fundraising. According to the consultants of the Bridgespan Group, if leaders use the crisis as an opportunity to become "stronger," they may be able to come out of it even "healthier and more sustainable as a result" (Bridgespan Group 2012).

The crisis has also served to recalibrate the relations between government and nonprofits. A shift in attitude in response to the financial crisis has served to reinforce a range of initiatives that favor more collaborative relations with government. While there continue to be contradictory dynamics and there is pushback from those concerned about developing too close a relationship with government, the general tendency appears to favor the development of more interdependency between the sectors (Casey 2011).

Notes

1. An earlier version of this chapter was published as Casey, John. 2011. "Third Sector, Social Economy and Solidarity Economy in the U.S." In *El impacto de la crisis económica en la economía social y solidaria (The Impact of the Economic Crisis on the Solidarity Economy)*, ed. C. Parra and F. Porta. Barcelona: Bosch.
2. The case study is based on interviews with senior managers in the organization and a review of organizational documents.

References

Alliance of Arizona Nonprofits. 2009. *Alliance of Arizona Nonprofits – 2009 Economic Survey*. Alliance of Arizona Nonprofits. At http://www.arizonanonprofits. org/arizona-nonprofits/feb-09-az-nonprofit-economic-survey-results.aspx (accessed 29 March 2012).

Banjo, S. and S. Mitra Kalita. 2010. "Once-Robust Charity Sector Hit with Mergers, Closings." *Wall Street Journal (Online)*, 2 February. At http://online.wsj.com/article/SB10001424052748704586504574654404227641232.html (accessed 29 March 2012).

Barton, N. and C. Preston. 2010. "America's Biggest Businesses Set Flat Giving Budgets." *The Chronicle of Philanthropy*. At http://philanthropy.com/article/Big-Companies-Hold-Steady-in/123792 (accessed 29 March 2012).

Blackbaud. 2010. "The Blackbaud Index of Charitable Giving – Full View." At http://www.blackbaud.com/bb/index/bb-giving-index.aspx (accessed 9 July 2011).

—. 2012. "The Blackbaud Index of Charitable Giving – Full View." At http://www.blackbaud.com/bb/index/bb-giving-index.aspx (accessed 29 March 2012).

Blum, D.E. and C. Thompson. 2010. "In 2010's Second Quarter, Big Charities See Slow Giving Growth." *The Chronicle of Philanthropy*. At http://philanthropy.com/article/In-2010-s-Second-Quarter/124239/ (accessed 9 September 2011).

Boris, E.T., E. de Leon, K. Roeger, and M. Nikolova. 2010. *Nonprofits and Government Collaboration – Findings from the 2010 National Survey of Nonprofit Government Contracting and Grants*. Washington DC: Urban Institute.

Bridgespan Group. 2008. *Managing in a Tough Economy: 7 Steps*. Bridgespan Group. At http://www.bridgestar.org/Library/ManagingToughEconomy.aspx (accessed 3 June 2011).

—. 2010. "Tough Times: A Collection of Resources for Nonprofit Organizations Dealing with Financial Turmoil." At http://www.bridgespan.org/LearningCenter/?id=2786 (accessed 11 February 2011).

—. 2012. *The View from the Cliff: Government-Funded Nonprofits Are Looking Out on Steep Cuts and an Uncertain Future*. Bridgespan Group. At http://www.bridgespan.org/government-funded-nonprofits.aspx (accessed 29 March 2012).

Burk, P. 2010. *The Cygnus Donor Survey – Where Philanthropy Is Headed in 2010*. Cygnus Applied Research, Inc.

—. 2011. *The Cygnus Donor Survey – Where Philanthropy Is Headed in 2011*. Cygnus Applied Research, Inc. At http://www.cygresearch.com/publications/orderReport.php (accessed 21 April 2011).

Casey, J. 2011. "New Era of Collaborative Government-Nonprofit Relations in the U.S.?" *Nonprofit Policy Forum* 2 (1): 1-21.

City of New York. 2011. "Nonprofit Assistance Initiatives." At http://www.nyc.gov/html/nonprofit/html/initiatives/initiatives.shtml (accessed 29 March 2012).

Cohen, R. 2009. "Recession Will Change Nonprofits." *Philanthropy Journal*. At http://www.philanthropyjournal.org/news/recession-will-change-nonprofits (accessed 29 March 2012).

Cortez, A., W. Foster, and K. Smith Milway. 2009. *Nonprofit Mergers and Acquisitions: More Than a Tool for Tough Times*. Bridgespan Group. At http://www.bridgespan.org/Nonprofit-M-and-A.aspx (accessed 29 March 2012).

Foundation Center. 2011. "Foundation Growth and Giving Estimates 2011 Edition." At http://foundationcenter.org/gainknowledge/research/pdf/fgge11.pdf (accessed 9 September 2011).

Gose, B. 2009. "Worst-Case Scenarios." *Chronicle of Philanthropy*, 2 July. At http://philanthropy.com/article/Worst-Case-Scenarios/57034/ (accessed 29 March 2012).

Hall, H. 2010. "Nation's Third Largest Charity Sees Revival in Giving." *The Chronicle of Philanthropy*. At http://philanthropy.com/blogs/prospecting/nations-third-largest-charity-sees-revival-in-giving/26165 (accessed 29 March 2012).

Harris Interactive. 2010. "Substantial Numbers Still Willing to Donate Time and Money." *Harris Interactive*. At http://www.harrisinteractive.com/NewsRoom/HarrisPolls/tabid/447/mid/1508/articleId/611/ctl/ReadCustom%20Default/Default.aspx (accessed 29 March 2012).

Leadership Committee for Nonprofit Revitalization. 2012. *Revitalizing Nonprofits; Renewing New York. Report of Attorney General Eric T. Scneiderman.* New York State Attorney General's Leadership Committee for Nonprofit Revitalization. At http://www.ag.ny.gov/sites/default/files/press-releases/2012/NP%20Leadership%20Committee%20Report%20(2-16-12).pdf (accessed 29 March 2012).

Light, P. 2008. "Four Futures." *Nonprofit Quarterly (Online)*, 20 December. At http://www.nonprofitquarterly.org/index.php?option=com_content&view=article&id=1039:four-futures&catid=148:editors-notes&Itemid=996 (accessed 29 March 2012).

McCambridge, R. 2010. "Back to the Future: Paul Light's Recession Predictions Revisited." *Nonprofit Quarterly (Online)*, 15 December. At http://www.nonprofitquarterly.org/index.php?option=com_content&view=article&id=8071:back-to-the-future-paul-lights-recession-predictions-revisited&catid=153:features&Itemid=336 (accessed 29 March 2012).

McNichol, E., P. Olif, and N. Johnson. 2012. *States Continue to Feel Recession's Impact – Center on Budget and Policy Priorities.* Center on Budget and Policy Priorities. At http://www.cbpp.org/cms/index.cfm?fa=view&id=711 (accessed 29 March 2012).

Meridith, M. 2009. "Bay Area Charities Unite, Share Aid to Survive." *San Francisco Chronicle (Online)*, 29 April. At http://www.sfgate.com/cgi-bin/article.cgi?f=/c/a/2009/04/29/BASA17AOE9.DTL (accessed 2 September 2010).

National Council of Nonprofits. 2009. *Stimulus Grant Tips and Thoughts.* Economic Stimulus & Recovery. National Council of Nonprofits.

—. 2010. *State Budget Crises: Ripping the Safety Net Held by Nonprofits.* Special Report. National Council of Nonprofits.

Nonprofit Assistance Fund. 2011. *Scenario Planning.* At http://www.nonprofitsassistancefund.org/index.php?src=gendocs&ref=scenario_planning&category=Healthy%20Financial%20Practices (accessed 29 March 2012).

Nonprofit Finance Fund. 2010a. *2009 State of the Sector Survey.* Nonprofit Finance Fund. At http://nonprofitfinancefund.org/state-of-the-sector-surveys (accessed 29 March 2012).

—. 2010b. *A Guide to Navigating Changing Times.* Nonprofit Finance Fund. At http://nonprofitfinancefund.org/nonprofit-consulting/navigating-financial-crisis (accessed 29 March 2012).

Nonprofit Quarterly. 2008. *The Nonprofit Quarterly, It May Be Hard Times: How to Navigate a Financial Downturn*. Nonprofit Quarterly. At http://store.nonprofitquarterly.org/itmaybehati.html (accessed 29 March 2012).

Nonprofit Research Collaborative. 2011. *Late Fall 2011 Nonprofit Fundraising Study*. Urban Institute. At http://www.urban.org/publications/412466.html (accessed 29 March 2012).

Salamon, L.M., S.L. Geller, and S. Wojciech Sokolowski. 2012. *Holding the Fort: Nonprofit Employment During a Decade of Turmoil*. Nonprofit Economic Data Bulletin. Baltimore, MD: John Hopkins University. At http://ccss.jhu.edu/publications-findings?did=369 (accessed 29 March 2012).

Salamon, L.M., S.L. Geller, and K.L. Spence. 2010. *Impact of the 2007-09 Economic Recession on Nonprofit Organizations*. The Listening Post Project. Baltimore, MD: John Hopkins University.

Seib, G.F. 2008. "In Crisis, Opportunity for Barack Obama." *Wall St Journal (Online)*, 21 November. At http://online.wsj.com/article/SB122721278056345271.html (accessed 29 March 2012).

Sherlock, M.F. and J.G. Gravelle. 2009. *Congressional Research Service, an Overview of the Nonprofit and Charitable Sector*. Washington DC: Congressional Research Service. At www.fas.org/sgp/crs/misc/R40919.pdf (accessed 29 March 2012).

Urban Arts Partnership. "Executive Director Philip Courtney at TEDxDUMBO." *Urban Arts Partnership News*. At http://www.urbanarts.org/news/view/30 (accessed 29 March 2012).

Wallace, N. 2010a. "Giving Dropped 4.9% in 2009, Researchers Estimate." *The Chronicle of Philanthropy*. At http://philanthropy.com/blogs/prospecting/giving-dropped-49-in-2009-researchers-estimate/24346 (accessed 29 March 2012).

—. 2010b. "New Index Finds Charitable Giving Is Up Compared With Last Year." *The Chronicle of Philanthropy*. At http://philanthropy.com/blogs/prospecting/new-index-finds-charitable-giving-is-up-compared-with-last-year/24793 (accessed 29 March 2012).

—. 2011. "Nonprofits Strategize to Help Them Cope With a Perilous 2011." *Chronicle of Philanthropy*, 9 January. At http://philanthropy.com/article/Nonprofits-Seek-Ways-to-Cope/125838/ (accessed 29 March 2012).

CHAPTER 5

NOT MEETING THE CHALLENGE OF CHANGE: GOVERNMENT, THE VOLUNTARY AND COMMUNITY SECTOR, RECESSION AND THE COMPACT IN ENGLAND, 1997–2012

META ZIMMECK AND COLIN ROCHESTER

INTRODUCTION

Voluntary and community organizations in England are, like their counterparts in other countries, feeling the chill wind of the recession. The austerity program of the Conservative-Liberal Democrat Coalition that came to power in May 2010 has meant substantial reductions in public spending, including funding of the voluntary and community sector. Further, "the cuts" come at a time when demand for the sector's services has increased because of the changing economic and political situation. Over and above the impact on individual organizations, moreover, the recession has stimulated an administration whose radical policies aimed at shrinking the state and privatizing public services have led to a profound change in the relationship between government and the sector as a whole. Like New Labour (in power from May 1997 to May 2010), the Coalition expects the sector to play an important role in meeting social need. Unlike its predecessors, it does not believe that this can best be achieved by a close working relationship or partnership between government and the

Government-Nonprofit Relations in Times of Recession, ed. Rachel Laforest. Montreal and Kingston: Queen's Policy Studies Series, McGill-Queen's University Press. © 2013 The School of Policy Studies, Queen's University at Kingston. All rights reserved.

sector. Instead, it aims to create a bigger space for voluntary action by reducing the scale and scope of publicly-provided services.

This chapter will examine this important shift in policy and the relationship between government and the sector in England. It begins by outlining the impact of the recession on the sector. It then maps the rise and fall of the Compact from the beginning of a period of national prosperity in 1998 to its failure to protect voluntary organizations from the full consequences of the recession. Finally it asks questions about what next.

IMPACT OF THE RECESSION

The recession has justified and accelerated the application of the Coalition's policies aimed at shrinking the state and cutting the state's spending. Given the dearth of high-quality data and the evolving nature of the changes, it is difficult to quantify precisely the current and future impact of the recession and the cuts on the voluntary and community sector, other than to observe that it is likely to be significant, what some have likened to a "perfect storm" (PwC et al. 2012). It is clear that the cuts have involved a reduction in the sector's total funding from government, as well as a reduction in income from other sources such as charitable trusts and donations. Further, the cuts have been applied disproportionately – above and beyond the average – to the sector. And finally, the cuts have been distributed unevenly among organizations operating in different places, providing different services, and working with different client groups. All of this is happening at a time when demand for the sector's services is increasing rapidly.

First, there has been a reduction in the sector's total funding from government. On the basis of its analysis of civil society organizations that applied for funding from the Transition Fund, the Association of Chief Executives of Voluntary Organizations (ACEVO) estimated that charities in the UK faced cuts of between £970 million (7.6 percent, best case scenario) and £5.6 billion (43.4 percent, worst case scenario) in 2011/12 (ACEVO 2012, 2-3, 24-27). On the basis of a series of annual surveys, the London Voluntary Services Council (LVSC) estimated that organizations in London faced cuts of between £300 million and £800 million in 2011/12 (van der Feen 2011, 17). Taking a longer view, the National Council for Voluntary Organizations (NCVO) estimated that over the years between 2010/11 and 2015/16 the sector in the UK will lose at least £2.8 billion in real terms, which represents cumulative cuts of 7.7 percent in funding provided by central government and local authorities jointly; 6.2 percent, by central government; and 8.9 percent, by local authorities (Kane and Allen 2011, 5, 33).

Second, there has been a reduction in the sector's funding which is greater than the government's headline cuts. In other words, the cuts are "not being applied consistently, proportionately or strategically" (Kane and Allen 2011, 6), despite assurances of fair treatment. LVSC found that local authorities in London passed on cuts to organizations greater than the cuts imposed on them by central government in their funding settlements. It calculated that between 2010/11 and 2011/12, 19 of 33 local authorities for which information was available received cuts of between 5.2 percent (± 2.6 percent) but passed on cuts of 11.5 percent (± 12.0 percent) to local organizations (van der Feen 2011, 21-27). NCVO found that over half of local authorities were making disproportionate cuts and documented over five hundred cases on its crowd-sourced database, voluntarysectorcuts.org.uk (Kane and Allen 2011, 5).

Finally, there has been an uneven distribution of this reduction in the sector's funding from government. NCVO found that organizations funded by particular government departments (Department for Culture, Media and Sport; Home Office; Department for Business, Innovation and Skills; Department for Communities and Local Government; and Department for Education) were affected to a greater extent than those funded by others (Kane and Allen 2011, 12-13). ACEVO found that applicants to the Transition Fund working in the 25 percent most deprived areas received 66.4 percent of the total cuts reported, while those working in the 25 percent least deprived areas received only 7.5 percent (ACEVO 2012, 2, 12-13). LVSC noted that organizations providing advice and health services and those working with children and young people experienced disproportionate cuts. Voluntary Organizations' Network North East (VONNE), operating in a region hard-hit by the recession, noted that organizations working with children and young people, mental health service users, asylum seekers, refugees, and homeless people experienced disproportionate cuts (van der Feen 2011, 4-7, 47-56; VONNE 2011, 8).

For the sector these cuts came at a time of rising demand for its services and took the form of a "big squeeze," a ratcheting-up of pressure on resources and a ratcheting-down of capacity. In May 2009, 47 percent of respondents to VONNE's survey reported that demand for their services had increased, while 56 percent reported that their funding had decreased. Two years later in June 2011, 59 percent reported increased demand; and 73 percent, decreased funding. In May 2009, 25 percent reported that they had lost staff; and 15 percent, that they were using reserves. In June 2011, 40 percent reported that they had lost staff; and 64 percent, that they were using reserves. In addition, 48 percent reported that they might have to close a service in the next year; and 23 percent, that they might go out of business in the next year (VONNE 2011, 5).

Eighty-two percent of respondents to LVSC's survey reported in April and May 2011 that demand for their services had increased in the past year as a result of economic or policy changes. Further, while 86 percent said they anticipated increased demand in the next year, only 23 percent were confident that they could meet this demand. Ninety-four percent reported that they had taken action to help them survive. Of these, 56 percent had taken on volunteers, 54 percent had made staff redundant, and 51 percent were working in collaboration with other organizations (van der Feen 2011, 31-34).

Sixty-three percent of respondents to a survey carried out by PricewaterhouseCoopers, Charity Finance Group and Institute of Fundraising in October and December 2011 reported that government's spending policies were having a negative impact. Sixty-nine percent of those delivering services reported that they had experienced an increase in demand for their services over the last year; and 70 percent, that they anticipated an increase in the next year. They also detailed a number of coping mechanisms. Forty-seven percent indicated that they planned to use reserves in the next year; 36 percent, to freeze staff pay; 28 percent, to make staff redundant; 21 percent, to reduce staff hours; 7 percent, to sell assets; and 1 percent, to wind up the organization. Forty-three percent reported that they had considered or were actively considering collaborating; 23 percent, outsourcing; and 20 percent, merger (PwC et al. 2012, 3, 6-9, 13-15, 18).

WHY THE COMPACT FAILED

The impact of the recession and of the Coalition's response to the recession on large parts of the voluntary and community sector has been, as indicated above, substantial and destructive, a push-me-pull-you of reduced and unevenly allocated resources and increased demand for (and pressure to provide) services. The sector had at least one mechanism for shoring up its position and attempting to mitigate the effects of the cuts. This was the Compact, "a new approach to partnership ... based on shared values and mutual respect" (Home Office 1998, Foreword). Agreed in 1998, "refreshed" in 2009 (Compact Voice et al. 2009) and "revised" in 2010 (Cabinet Office 2010a), it is still on the books. The Compact was intended to work in all weathers, in sunny times of prosperity as well as in the "perfect storm" of economic meltdown, but it has failed to do so.

In the remainder of this chapter we explore the reasons why such an initiative, which embodied hopes of a brave new way of partnership working, failed to deliver. We believe that these reasons are many, some structural and some contextual, including the unprecedented scope and complexity of the Compact's remit (relationships up, down and across all government bodies and all voluntary and community sector/third sector/civil society organizations); the fragility of partnership based on goodwill and unequal power; the evolution of political agendas; the weaknesses of the "architecture of implementation"; the legacy of pre-existing cross-sectoral relationships; and, last but not least, the recession. Instead of demonstrating that the Compact, created in "the best of times," was fit for the "worst of times," the recession has done the reverse. Instead of demonstrating that the Compact was a powerful way of "meeting the challenge of change" (Commission on the Future of the Voluntary Sector and NCVO 1996), the recession has done the opposite. It is now clear that the Compact is dead in the water and that government and the sector must now look towards a post-Compact future (Zimmeck, Rochester and Rushbrooke 2011).

THE COMPACT UNDER NEW LABOUR

High Hopes: The Origins of the Compact

The signing of the Compact in November 1998 was the high point of belief in and commitment to partnership between government and the voluntary and community sector. The Compact began with a statement of "shared vision" that "the scope and nature of activity by voluntary and community organizations is such that whenever Government legislates or regulates it can have an impact on their work, positive or negative. The Compact will help to make that impact positive." It then set out "shared principles" of which the most salient were: "Voluntary action is an essential component of democratic society; "An independent and diverse voluntary and community sector is fundamental to the well-being of society"; and "In the development and delivery of public policy and services the Government and the voluntary and community sector have distinct but complementary roles." Although it was not "legally binding," it drew its authority "from its endorsement by Government and by the voluntary and community sector itself through its consultation process." It was "deliberately not exhaustive" but was intended to be "an enabling mechanism to enhance the relationship between Government and the sector" (Home Office 1998, paras.1, 2, 7, 8.1-8.3).

The circumstances in which the Compact was negotiated were uniquely favourable for such an idealistic venture. The Compact was launched in the heady early days of New Labour, which announced that it was (and seemed to be) ushering in a new age of optimism and progress – variously labelled the "Giving Age" and the "Third Way." While in opposition, New Labour had conducted an extensive consultation with the sector and had made a commitment to establishing a compact "as a simple statement of the broad principles" that would lead to "building strong, creative relationships, rather than a bureaucratic approach" (Labour Party 1997, 3).

The Context of Implementation

Although the Compact has been seen as the first instance of "mainstreaming" the voluntary and community sector into government's policy agenda and "a major break from the past" (Kendall 2000, 542), its initial iconic status among New Labour's projects was gradually eroded by the practical difficulties of implementation and changes in government's views about the nature and proper role of the sector.

Rolling out the Compact was a daunting task, and there were formidable obstacles to success. One obstacle was the document itself, which, together with its five Codes of Good Practice, ran to 140 pages of text and 273 undertakings – hardly a user-friendly basis for action. By the time the Codes were finally in place in 2005, it was already seen to be in need of modernization.

A second obstacle was the sheer amount of effort required for implementation. Unlike other "vertical" initiatives that were hosted by a single government body or covered a single service area or group of users, the Compact was a national "horizontal" initiative (Kendall 2003). It required change and adaptation across the whole of government – central government departments and their agencies and non-departmental public bodies, government offices of the regions and regional development agencies, local authorities, the National Health Service, police forces, and fire services. The changes were to impact the whole of the sector – from the largest national organizations to the smallest community groups. It required change and adaptation in principle and in detail, since success (or failure) was determined at every point of contact between government and the sector. It required adaptation on a sustained basis – through changes in political leadership, programs, administrative structures, methods of operation and staff.

A third obstacle was the nature of pre-existing relationships between government and the sector. An early study (Craig et al. 2005) found that there was a kind of paradox at the heart of the implementation of the Compact: it succeeded where it was least needed, where relationships were productive, and failed where it would have been most beneficial, where relationships were fraught. If relationships were poor and there was no joint will to change them, then signing up to local compacts, as all local authorities and other local government bodies were urged to do, was just a paper exercise and had little, if any, impact. Perhaps only a third of local compacts currently on the books are "live," as evidenced by updated texts, well-used websites, dedicated staff, regular meetings to review progress and "buy-in" from both sides (Zimmeck and Rochester 2011).

New Labour was "hyper-active" in its generation of policies, programs and initiatives (Kendall 2005), and over its thirteen years in power it changed its priorities in ways that also changed the environment in which the Compact operated. First of all, government moved away from general support for the sector in all its multifarious activities towards particular support for those parts and activities of the sector that contributed to the delivery of public services. This meant that the Compact, which was about the sector as a whole and its relationships with government as a whole, lost traction with policies aimed at marketization and privatization of public services. Secondly, central government took an increasingly prescriptive approach to local authorities, with which sector organizations were most likely to have relationships. Instead, government put in place new fora for cross-sectoral relationships (local strategic partnerships), controls over spending, stringent targets for performance and detailed monitoring arrangements. This meant that the Compact and local compacts were in many cases "crowded out" by newer initiatives for which documented compliance was mandatory. Finally government ascribed a new identity to the sector – that of the "third sector" – and prioritized social enterprises as the way to square the circle of greater involvement in the delivery of public services without greater public funding. This meant that the Compact was less relevant to the emerging project of reformatting the sector as "governable terrain" capable of competing with the private sector to deliver public services and using methods and performance management systems imported from the private sector (Carmel and Harlock 2008). Thus over time New Labour defined the sector more broadly but cast it in a narrower role. This meant, inevitably, reducing the scope and perceived value of the Compact.

New Labour made three attempts to regain momentum in the implementation of the Compact. The first of these, in 2005, was the proposed bolt-on program, Compact Plus, a sort of business-class Compact which aimed to create "a more mature partnership" for organizations that opted in – that is, "voluntary organizations bidding for public contracts" – through capacity-building, enhanced support and individualized trouble-shooting (Home Office 2005, Foreword, 2; and Charles Clarke, Home Secretary, quoted by Cook 2005). Compact Plus never got beyond the planning stage.

The second attempt was the appointment of a commissioner for the Compact in 2006 and the establishment of his administrative home, the Commission for the Compact, in 2007. In its comparatively short existence the Commission worked hard to raise the profile and credibility of the Compact, carried out an extensive program of research to establish a much-needed evidence base, and provided guidance and face-to-face support for government bodies and sector organizations aiming to apply Compact principles to their work and relationships.

The third attempt was the "refreshed" Compact in December 2009. This new version was a shortened and refocused unitary document (no codes). It set out shared principles (under the headings of respect, honesty, independence, diversity, equality, citizen empowerment, and volunteering) and focused on three areas considered to be of the greatest importance – allocating resources, involvement in policy development and advancing equality (Compact Voice et al. 2009, 5 et passim).

Despite these efforts the Compact was not implemented comprehensively, consistently or sustainably. Long after the project should have bedded in, progress was slow and halting. For example, in 2004/05, six years after the Compact was signed, 89 percent of organizations that were members of the State of the Sector Panel stated that they were aware of the national Compact; but of these only 33 percent, that they had actually used it. Further, 47 percent stated that they were aware of local compacts; but of these only 21 percent, that they had actually used them (Green 2009, 13-16, 24-25). In 2009, eleven years after the Compact was signed, 91 percent of civil servants responsible for relations with the sector reported that they were aware of the national Compact; but only 28 percent, that they had implemented it (nfpSynergy and Digital Public 2010, 51, 54). This suggests that the "Compact way of working" had made little headway.

The Architecture of Implementation

The implementation of any policy initiative is in the end about focus and effort – leadership, resources, management and co-ordination. Even at a time when the Compact was at its zenith in the policy firmament, the architecture of its implementation was exceedingly rickety. Over time it got more rickety – to the point of collapse. There were a number of weaknesses.

- **Leadership by ministers:** Ten ministers were responsible for the voluntary and community sector and the Compact between 1997 and 2010. These varied in status, closeness to the levers of power, knowledge of the sector, commitment to partnership working, and energy/opportunity (among other responsibilities) to promote the Compact. While the first two ministers provided energetic leadership, their successors on the whole did not. While rapid turnover of ministers was the norm under New Labour, in the case of the Compact this had a greater-than-average negative effect, simply because the Compact, as a new and cross-cutting initiative, needed heroic or at least better-than-average leadership to make it work.
- **Resourcing and commitment of government's responsible unit:** Between 1996 and May 2010, the responsible unit for the sector and later the Compact was hosted by three central government departments, all of which had high levels of staff turnover and multiple reorganizations. Its resources were clearly insufficient to manage a national program of implementing the Compact, even without the distractions of machinery of government changes, churn of knowledgeable and experienced staff, and "inconsistency (even ambivalence)

about the strategic importance of the Compact" (Carrington 2002, 26).

- **Resourcing and representativeness of the sector's lead body:** The lead body for the sector was the Working Group on Government Relations / Compact Working Group / Compact Voice, initially funded by NCVO and then by the Home Office / Cabinet Office. Its resources were modest and allowed for one member of staff at the beginning and five in 2010 – also insufficient to carry out the immense task of promoting the Compact, supporting sector organizations, particularly those that were having problems, and documenting progress. By 2006, it had discontinued its series of surveys of progress and failed to maintain the register of local compacts. More damaging was its claim to representativeness as "the voice of the sector on the Compact," which early on had been based on assiduous consultation and outreach but then relaxed into assertion. It had no constitutional arrangements for the open election of members to its board, no mechanism for organizations to sign up individually to the Compact, and no demonstrable independence from its host, NCVO.
- **Powers and status of the Commission:** The Commission saw its role as that of an "honest broker" between government and the sector, but it had to manage the contradictions between its expectations of independence and government's ultimate political control. As Richard Corden, its chief executive, put it, "We're independent because we've been instructed to be by the government" (quoted by Little 2008). The Commission campaigned hard to establish itself as a "permanent, independent, statutory body" (H.C. Deb. 2009) and to acquire powers to investigate breaches, demand papers and make reports to Parliament. However, when push came to shove, it faced the hostility of both the Cabinet Office and Compact Voice. It was first overridden on the drafting of the refreshed Compact in 2009, then excluded from the consultation / preparation of the revised Compact in 2010, and finally terminated at the end of March 2011.
- **Mechanisms for liaison and accountability:** Because the Compact was a cross-cutting initiative, it needed strong mechanisms for liaison and accountability. However, those put in place were too late and too weak to do the job. Although within central government the Home Office / Cabinet Office housed the responsible minister and the responsible unit, lines of flow on policies affecting the sector and the Compact were not always clear, and from time to time the Prime Minister's Office (No. 10), H.M. Treasury and Communities and Local Government (and its predecessors) disputed or attempted to override the leadership of the Home Office / Cabinet Office. This was particularly the case with regard to funding and the civil renewal / local government agendas.

THE COMPACT UNDER THE COALITION

The New Context of Implementation

Like New Labour, the Coalition began with a bang by announcing a new social ideal, not the "Giving Age" or the "Third Way" but the "Big Society." This, it stated, could only be achieved by a radical transfer of the responsibilities of the state to society and to individuals: "We are not going to solve our problems with bigger government. We are going to solve our problems with a stronger society. Stronger families. Stronger communities. A stronger country. All by building responsibility" (Cameron 2009). Its program of action has three elements: empowering communities through decentralization and localism, encouraging social action through the giving of time (volunteering) and money (charitable giving), and transferring the delivery of public services from the public sector to the private sector and the voluntary and community sector. All of these have had an impact on government's relationship with the sector and the salience of the Compact.

First, this program of action has justified dismantling the state's own mechanisms for leadership and liaison. Second, it has undermined the relevance and position of the very infrastructure organizations that represented the sector and led on the implementation of the Compact. Finally, it has indicated a unilateral abandonment of partnership as the proper basis for a working relationship between government and the sector. The recession did not so much create an obstacle to the Coalition's implementation of its policies for the sector as a golden opportunity to go harder and faster.

The Coalition's program for empowering communities, enshrined in the Localism Act 2011, is intended to facilitate the transfer of powers of decision-making and service-providing from the centre downwards to local communities in what was advertised as "the biggest, most dramatic redistribution of power from elites in Whitehall to the man and woman on the street" (Cameron 2010b). Key to the program are the "community right to challenge," which enables local organizations, parish councils, and others to express an interest in and bid to provide local authorities' services; and the right to bid to buy "assets of community value" listed by local authorities such as community centres, playing fields, and libraries. Although these new rights in principle provide opportunities for local organizations, in practice they have delivered less than expected. On the one hand the community right to challenge has also opened up the local market for the provision of public services to the private sector. Winning bidders tend to be private-sector firms and in-migrating large national charities rather than local organizations. On the other hand the right to acquire community assets is not generally accompanied by funding for acquisition and maintenance of those assets, and these opportunities tend to be unobtainable or unsustainable for local organizations. The localism program, then, reduces the scope, accountability and resources of local authorities, marketizes relationships between local authorities and local organizations, and thus diminishes the relevance and use of the Compact.

The Coalition's program for encouraging social action, the giving of time and money, is based on behaviouralist or "nudge" theory for creating pro-social norms: people should "get involved, support each other and create the change they want to see" (Cabinet Office 2011, 8). The aim is to plug volunteers (and charitable giving) into the gaps created by the withdrawal of the state at all levels, particularly the local level, and to provide services at the least cost – not only because social action is a "good thing" but because in its absence there may be no provision at all. While the Coalition has followed New Labour in creating flagship volunteering programs for young people – National Citizen Service in place of Millennium Volunteers and 'v' – it has given much greater prominence to informal volunteering than New Labour ever did: "Social action is about much more than formal volunteering opportunities – helping those around you, such as checking in on an elderly neighbour is every bit as valuable as giving time to an organized activity" (H.M. Government 2010, 5). It has also focused its volunteering programs – National Citizen Service, Community Organizers, Near Neighbours – at the grassroots, through the recruitment, preparation/training and activation of volunteers from local communities who will, even if hosted by organizations, ideally operate independently of them. Finally, it has opened up the delivery of (in the first instance) National Citizen Service to private sector providers. Given the recent declaration by Francis Maude, Cabinet Office Minister, that businesses "are a fundamental part of our expansion plans," this diversification is likely to increase (Maude 2012). The social action program, then, reinforces the Coalition's privatization of public services and embodies its optimistic belief that volunteers will spring forth and serve without the support of infrastructure organizations or indeed volunteer-involving organizations. The Church Urban Fund played a winning hand when it suggested that one of the advantages of Near Neighbours was its "ability to work from embedded local contexts without creating new structures or multiple layers of administration" (Church Urban Fund 2010) – that is, beyond local government, beyond the local sector, and beyond the local compact.

The Coalition's program of privatization of public services has both an ideological aim, reducing the role of the state, and an operational aim, reducing costs. While New Labour envisaged a substantial role for the sector on the basis of its track record of providing high-quality services to hard-to-reach client groups and the "added value" of these services, the Coalition plans to let the market decide, generally in favour of the private sector. It has done so by espousing the concept of the "level playing field," which in effect, discounts the sector's added value and "local experience, local focus or degree of 'embedded-ness' within local communities" (Adur Voluntary Action and NCIA 2010, para.3.35) when these are not available at the lowest price. It also does so by scaling up to the greatest extent possible opportunities for these cross-sectoral transfers.

When New Labour came to power in 1997 its main method of funding the sector was grants, which were flexible and proactive. Grants enabled the sector to identify the needs and wishes of clients, propose a means of addressing them, and then secure funding. New Labour began to put greater emphasis on funding through contracts, which gave government greater control over ways and means. Contracts were based on clearer and more detailed specifications of the scale and scope of the services to be provided but retained an element of negotiation about how needs should be addressed. Finally New Labour embraced commissioning, which gave government even greater control over ways and means and price. Commissioning enabled government to decide – often unilaterally – what kind of services it wanted, how much it was prepared to pay, what outcomes it expected and, increasingly, how it required the services to be delivered. Between 2000/01 and 2009/10 the proportion of government funding of the sector from contracts/commissioning increased from 50 percent to 73 percent (Clark et al. 2010, 47). Given the Coalition's determination to maximize its use of commissioning, albeit with a more attractive cast of characters such as "mutuals, co-operatives, charities and social enterprises" Cabinet Office 2011, 5), this is likely to increase and increasingly to advantage those organizations prepared and able to operate in the marketplace.

The Revised Compact and the Collapsing Architecture of Implementation

Immediately after the election in May 2010, David Cameron announced that "one of the early bits of work … is to refresh and renew the Compact" (Cameron 2010a), even though the ink was barely dry on the previous version. The Coalition carried out this task with haste and without subtlety. It bypassed the Commission, used Compact Voice to carry out a non-Compact-compliant consultation of the voluntary and community sector, largely ignored the sector's views and, in effect, dictated the text. While both the original and refreshed versions were couched in terms of apolitical values and generic partners, the revised version was political and specific. It was the Coalition's Compact, and its purpose was to promote the Big Society:

> The role of the Government is to enable this cultural change by shifting power away from the centre, increasing transparency and building capability. It

believes that strong and independent CSOs [civil society organizations] are central to this vision through their role in encouraging social action and campaigning for social change, through playing a bigger part in designing and delivering public services and through driving community empowerment.

Instead of "shared vision" there was the Coalition's vision, and instead of "shared principles" there were five business-like "outcomes," mainly about the design and delivery of public services (Cabinet Office 2010a, 6 et passim). It is worth noting that at the point when the Coalition was embarking on the revision it felt that the most pressing practical use for the Compact was as an element to be considered "as decisions on in-year budgetary savings and efficiencies [that is, the cuts] are taken" (H.C. Deb. 2010).

Given the Coalition's declaration of ownership and intent, it is somewhat surprising that renewal seems to have been somewhat ephemeral. Its leadership, resourcing, and co-ordination of implementation have been weaker than New Labour's in its last days. Nick Hurd, Minister for Civil Society, has shown little interest in the Compact and in the wider non-public-service-delivering sector and more interest in creating new sources of non-government funding such as the Big Society Bank. According to the long-awaited evaluation by the National Audit Office (NAO), the role of the Office for Civil Society with regard to the Compact is "unclear." Indeed, the Cabinet Office's position seems to be that responsibility for the Compact has devolved to individual government bodies, which must implement it, monitor it and account for their own implementation (OCS 2011).

Once the Coalition was prepared to abandon the Compact as an ideal, an initiative, and a remit, then it was easy for it to abandon the rest: the Commission (sacrificed to the bonfire of the quangos); the notion that Compact Voice was a genuine partner rather than a client; support, via the Big Lottery, of the Compact Advocacy Programme, which investigated non-compliance (funding ended November 2011); organized cross-departmental liaison (liaison officers and senior champions meetings last held in early 2011); annual meetings and annual reports (last held/submitted February 2010). The only measure of co-ordination that remained, the inclusion of statements on the implementation of the Compact in departments' business plans in 2012/13, as required by the Accountability and Transparency Guide to the revised Compact (Cabinet Office 2010b), seems to have been generally overlooked (departments were "not in a position" to perform) and, following publication of the NAO's report, were subject to catch-up measures (NAO 2012, 6, 11, 14, 21, 25; Plummer 2012).

After the beginning of the economic crisis in 2008 and, more particularly, after the Coalition's austerity measures began to bite in 2010, what was left in the Compact's armoury to help the sector?

The answer is "not much," as can be seen by the lack of take-up of the only remaining option, complaint. Despite the revised Compact's Transparency and Accountability Guide, which gave detailed advice on making complaints, NCVO's collection of horror stories, and detailed reporting of breaches in the third-sector press, there were very few official complaints. That said, there were a number of successful public law actions not linked to Compact principles or procedures. Between 2006 and October 2011 the Compact Advocacy Programme recorded 130 allegations of non-compliance, including 22 in 2010 and only 7 in 2011 (to October). There were no complaints recorded by other routes. The absence of complaints, NAO dryly notes, "should not, on its own, be seen as an indicator of successful implementation" (NAO 2012, 5, 22-25). It should be seen as the end of hope. When Trafford Metropolitan Council was criticized for its plan to make efficiency savings to its library service by replacing librarians with volunteers, it clearly viewed the Compact as a fair-weather friend: "Asked whether he thought the proposals ran contrary to the spirit, if not the letter of the Compact, the spokesman said: 'It is open to that interpretation, yes. But the Compact was agreed before the scale of spending cuts hit home'" (Wiggins 2012).

Conclusion: What Next?

Thus the Coalition, energized by the recession, has brought the Compact's long goodbye to an end: it has simply stopped pretending about the voluntary and community sector and about partnership. Since 1998 government has taken an increasingly narrow and instrumental view of the nature of the sector and its proper role in society. Although it has widened the definition of the sector to the "third sector" and then to "civil society," it has done so in order to incorporate those parts of the sector (social enterprises, community interest companies, mutuals, etc.) most able to facilitate its progress in shrinking the state and privatizing its functions in the most business-like and cost-effective way. It is not interested in the weird and wonderful parts of the sector that are not likely to help it in this task. It is not interested in capacity building and the sector's infrastructure bodies, national and local, that were its "strategic partners" and the vanguard of the sector for Compact purposes. It is not even interested in service-providing or potentially service-providing organizations if they are too small to contract on the epic scale now thought appropriate, or unwilling to undertake the necessary mergers and restructurings to do so.

If the Compact and the model of partnership it represents are dead, what, if anything, can be put in their place and what, if anything, can stand up to the demands of hard times? Thinking out of the box is not easy. For example, Simon Blake, Chair of Compact Voice, took the line that there was, in effect, no alternative: "If we didn't have the Compact we would need something that did a similar job" (Plummer 2011). Joe Saxton, Head of nfpSynergy, suggested repeating the Deakin Commission for "post-Compact life" (Cook 2012). Emma-Jane Cross, Chief Executive of Beatbullying, suggested downshifting the Compact to the sector between large and small organizations ("itwillnotbecalledtheCompact") in order to foster the ethical fraternal conduct that is so clearly lacking (Mason 2011).

We conclude by offering alternative approaches which are likely to appeal to different parts of the sector. The first approach is based on acceptance of the role in which government has cast the sector and making the best of it. In this approach, organizations have a great deal to offer as contractors and providers of public services, and they and their representative bodies should vigorously promote inclusion in the market and obtaining the largest possible market share. The second approach is based on the rejection of the view that the interests of the sector and government are in many instances the same. Here, organizations exist to serve the interests of the people who use their services and the communities they serve, while government, with its duty to taxpayers and voters, has to balance a range of competing interests, meet the demands of equity and fairness across the board and balance the books.

Instead of a Compact, the first approach requires only a set of rules and procedures to ensure that there is a fair playing field on which organizations can compete with the private sector. The second approach also implies a set of rules which, unlike the Compact, would be based on the fundamental assumption that the interests of the two parties could be significantly different and that the relationship is as likely to be adversarial as consensual. What would then be needed would be a set of procedures, rules and expected behaviours that would enable the two parties to contribute to the development of better and more responsive services. The goal would be a critical dialogue that had a chance of generating light rather than heat.

What is certain, however, is that the government and the sector that emerge from the recession and the implementation of the Coalition's agenda and have to choose between these two approaches will be different. Government is likely to be "a very different sort of animal" with a role "confined to setting the level and terms of financing and determining the format for contracting it" – smaller, leaner, more detached (Nicholas Deakin, quoted in Zimmeck et al. 2011, 135). The sector is also likely to be different, with a large majority of local, volunteer-led organizations to which government is (thankfully) irrelevant; a small body of large, business-like service-providing organizations able to achieve success on the level playing field of commercial contractual relations; a reduced middle of medium-sized organizations; and a decimated local infrastructure.

REFERENCES

Adur Voluntary Action and National Coalition for Independent Action. 2010. *The local state and voluntary action in West Sussex: The results of exploratory qualitative research.* Lancing, West Sussex and London: Adur Voluntary Action and National Coalition for Independent Action.

Association of Chief Executives of Voluntary Organisations. 2012. *Cuts to the Third Sector: What can we learn from Transition Fund applications?* London: ACEVO.

Cabinet Office. 2010a. *The Compact: The Coalition Government and civil society organizations working effectively in partnership for the benefit of communities and citizens in England: Created in partnership with Compact Voice, representing civil society organizations on Compact Matters.* London: Cabinet Office.

—. 2010b. *The Compact – Accountability and Transparency Guide: Helping to build stronger partnerships between the Coalition Government and civil society organizations: Created in partnership with Compact Voice, representing civil society organizations on Compact Matters.* London: Cabinet Office.

—. 2011. *Modernising Commissioning: Increasing the role of charities, social enterprises, mutuals and cooperatives in public service delivery* [Commissioning Green Paper]. London: Cabinet Office.

Cameron, D. 2009. "David Cameron: Putting Britain back on her feet." Speech, 8 October. At http://www.conservatives.com/News/Speeches/2009/10/David_Cameron_Putting_Britain_back_on_her_feet.aspx (accessed 1 May 2012).

—. 2010a. "PM and Deputy PM's speeches at Big Society launch, Tuesday, 19 May 2010." At http://www.number10.gov.uk/news/pm-and-deputy-pms-speeches-at-big-society-launch (accessed 1 May 2012).

—. 2010b. "Big Society Speech: Transcript of a speech by the Prime Minister on the Big Society, 19 July 2010." At http://www.number10.gov.uk/news/big-society-speech/ (accessed 1 May 2012).

Carmel, E. and J. Harlock. 2008. "Instituting the 'third sector' as a governable terrain: partnership, procurement and performance in the UK." *Policy & Politics* 36 (2): 155-71.

Carrington, D. 2002. *The Compact – the Challenge of Implementation.* London: Active Community Unit, Home Office.

Church Urban Fund. 2010. *Near Neighbours by faithful interaction: Draft proposals, 15 October 2010.* London: Church Urban Fund and Church of England.

Clark, J., D. Kane, K. Wilding, and J. Wilton. 2010. *The UK Civil Society Almanac 2010.* London: NCVO.

Commission on the Future of the Voluntary Sector and NCVO. 1996. *Meeting the challenge of change: voluntary action into the 21st century: The Report of the Commission on the Future of the Voluntary Sector.* London: Commission on the Future of the Voluntary Sector and NCVO.

Compact Voice, Cabinet Office, Commission for the Compact and Local Government Association. 2009. *The Compact on relations between Government and the Third Sector in England.* London and Birmingham: Compact Voice, Cabinet Office, Commission for the Compact and Local Government Association.

Cook, S. 2005. "Government amends two flagship policies." *Third Sector Online,* 23 March.

—. 2012. "New Deakin-style inquiry might be needed, argues Joe Saxton." *Third Sector Online*, 10 January.

Craig, G., M. Taylor, N. Carlton, R. Garbutt, R. Kimberlee, E. Lepine, and A. Syed. 2005. *The paradox of Compacts: monitoring the impact of Compacts.* Home Office Online Report 02/05. London: Home Office.

Green, H. 2009. *State of the Sector Panel Survey: Report 3: Contacts with Public Sector Bodies.* London: Cabinet Office.

H.C. Deb. 2009. Text of Commission for the Compact Bill 2009, vol. 510, col. 1346, 19 May.

H.C. Deb. 2010. Nick Hurd, Minister for Civil Society, statement, vol. 513, col. 937, 14 July.

H.M. Government. 2010. *Giving Green Paper.* London: Cabinet Office.

Home Office. 1998. *Compact on Relations between Government and the Voluntary and Community Sector in England: Presented to Parliament by the Secretary of State for the Home Department by Command of Her Majesty* (Cm4100). London: Home Office.

—. 2005. *Strengthening Partnerships: Next Steps for Compact: The Relationship between Government and the Voluntary and Community Sector: A consultation document.* London: Home Office.

Kane, D. and J. Allen. 2011. *Counting the Cuts: The impact of spending cuts on the UK voluntary and community sector.* London: NCVO.

Kendall, J. 2000. "The mainstreaming of the third sector into public policy in England in the late 1990s: whys and wherefores." *Policy & Politics* 28 (4): 541-62.

—. 2003. *The Voluntary Sector: Comparative perspectives in the UK.* London: Routledge.

—. 2005. *The third sector and the policy process in the UK: ingredients in a hyper-active horizontal policy environment.* Third Sector European Policy Working Papers, No. 5. London: Centre for Civil Society and Personal Social Services Research Unit, London School of Economics.

Labour Party. 1997. *Building the future together: Labour's policies for partnership between Government and the Voluntary Sector.* London: Labour Party.

Little, M. 2008. "Little at Large: Charity spring challenge by MSP who ate all the pies." *Third Sector Online*, 17 September.

Mason, T. 2011. "New sector code aims to improve partnerships between charities." *Civil Society Online*, 6 January.

Maude, F. 2012. "Francis Maude speech – The Big Society and the City." Speech given at Institute of Directors' Big Society and the City" social event, 20 February. At www.cabinetoffice.gov.uk/news/francis-maude-speech-big-society-and-city (1 May 2012).

National Audit Office. 2012 *Central government's implementation of the national Compact.* London: National Audit Office.

NfpSynergy and Digital Public. 2010. *Compact Baseline Survey 2009/10: A study of the levels of awareness, knowledge, understanding and use of the Compact among Government and Non Departmental Public Bodies.* Birmingham: Commission for the Compact.

Office for Civil Society. 2011. E-mail from civil servant [name redacted], Office for Civil Society, to civil servant [name redacted], National Audit Office, 13 December 2011. Document released to Third Sector under Freedom of Information Act.

Plummer, J. 2011. "Interview: Simon Blake." *Third Sector Online*, 5 September.

—. 2012. "All departments must include Compact in their plans, says Cameron." *Third Sector Online*, 15 February.

PricewaterhouseCoopers, Charity Finance Group and Institute of Fundraising. 2012. *Managing charities in the new normal – A perfect storm? The latest instalment in the series of "Managing in a Downturn" Surveys.* London: PricewaterhouseCoopers, Charity Finance Group and Institute of Fundraising.

van der Feen, S. 2011. *The Big Squeeze: the Squeeze tightens: The economic climate, Londoners and the voluntary and community groups that serve them.* London: London Voluntary Services Council.

Voluntary Organisations' Network Northeast. 2011. *Surviving or Thriving: Tracking the impact of spending cuts on the North East's third sector.* Newcastle-upon-Tyne: Voluntary Organisations' Network Northeast.

Wiggins, K. 2012. "Trafford Council plans to run two libraries entirely with volunteers." *Third Sector Online*, 6 February.

Zimmeck, M. and C. Rochester. 2011. "Going Local: The Impact of the Compact in England on Relationships between the Voluntary Sector and the Local State." Paper presented at the 40th Annual Conference of ARNOVA, Toronto, Canada, 17-19 November 2011.

Zimmeck, M., C. Rochester, and B. Rushbrooke. 2011. *Use it or Lose it: a summative evaluation of the Compact.* Birmingham: Commission for the Compact.

CHAPTER 6

ENGLAND'S BIG SOCIETY: CAN THE VOLUNTARY SECTOR MANAGE WITHOUT THE STATE?

MARILYN TAYLOR

INTRODUCTION

When the global recession hit in 2008, the voluntary and community sector (VCS) in England had been enjoying a period of healthy income growth for a number of years, including year-on-year increases in government funding (Clark et al. 2009). This led a commentator from the National Council for Voluntary Organisations in England to suggest that the sector might be well-placed to ride out the recession (Wilding 2009). In the succeeding years, as the economy has continued to struggle, this increase in government funding has come to an end, as might have been expected. However, particularly significant in the unfolding picture has been the coming to power of a right-of-centre coalition government, with an ideological commitment to reducing the role of the state in welfare overall. In this new Big Society, citizens are expected to become less dependent on government to meet their needs.

This chapter focuses on the impact of the recession on government funding for the voluntary and community sector, especially since the election in 2010 of the Conservative-Liberal Democrat Coalition government. It then considers the implications of policies associated with the Big Society for the sector's future health. The chapter concludes by suggesting some of the critical challenges for the future if voluntary and community organizations (VCOs) are to make a full contribution to meeting the challenges of recession.

Government-Nonprofit Relations in Times of Recession, ed. Rachel Laforest. Montreal and Kingston: Queen's Policy Studies Series, McGill-Queen's University Press. © 2013 The School of Policy Studies, Queen's University at Kingston. All rights reserved.

The Changing Fortunes of the VCS in England

The Position Prior to the Recession

Prior to the recession, the English voluntary and community sector enjoyed a high profile. The New Labour government elected in 1997 saw an important role for the VCS in addressing major policy priorities: reforming public service delivery; reducing the democratic deficit; and promoting active communities. To support this role, the New Labour government introduced a comprehensive range of policies (Kendall 2000), including new funding programs for the sector, a major reform of Charity Law and a commitment to partnership and community empowerment. These policies were underpinned by the early and high profile agreement of the *Compact* between government and the voluntary and community sector, an agreement which has since achieved international renown (Home Office 1998; Zimmeck and Rochester, this volume).

Government funding has always been a significant source of funding for the English VCS (Kendall 2000, 544-6). Under New Labour, between 2000 and 2007, it accounted for just over a third of the sector's total income (Clark et al. 2009), a proportion that has remained fairly constant over recent years. A national survey in England in 2008, meanwhile, suggested that a third of VCOs were receiving some form of government funding (Clifford, Geyne Rajme and Mohan 2010), with half of this funding coming from local government.

Over the years, the nature of government funding to the sector has shifted from grants to contracts. This is a trend that began under the previous Conservative government and continued under New Labour, as part of a set of policies that sought to give the VCS a greater role in public service delivery. However, to support this, New Labour also made a significant investment in the VCS infrastructure. It provided core funding for 42 national VCS bodies as "strategic partners" and set up three funds at arm's length from government to build the sector's capacity. Capacitybuilders was designed to strengthen and streamline the infrastructure; Futurebuilders was designed to provide investment, primarily through loans for individual organizations seeking to enter the public service market; and Communitybuilders, another loan fund, was added later to support community enterprise.

New Labour also invested in the community sector. A comprehensive National Strategy for Neighbourhood Renewal (NSNR) put substantial funding into programs to address the needs of the most disadvantaged neighbourhoods in England (Communities and Local Government 2010), with an emphasis on community-led regeneration. A similar major program, Sure Start, was set up to address the needs of families with children under age four (NESS 2010). These programs were mediated through local cross-sector partnerships, which required significant community representation and supported many community and voluntary sector led projects. As part of its commitment to community empowerment, New Labour also set up small grants programs. These included programs to support community learning (Mayo and Annette 2010) and, through the Single Community Programme, to support VCS representation on local cross-sector partnerships (CLG 2005).

Government's Response to the Recession

All this was to change with the global economic downturn and, hot on its heels, the coming to power of a Conservative-Liberal Democrat coalition government in May 2010. The response of the new government to the recession was to make unprecedented cuts in public expenditure. The cuts were planned over a four-year period, but front-loaded in order to signal to the financial markets the government's determination to deal with the national debt. One estimate suggested, for example, that cuts in central government's block grant to local government for 2010–11 amounted to 11.6 percent on average (Community Care 2011). Another estimate calculated a 40 percent reduction in grants to local government over the four years of the 2010 Comprehensive Spending Review. These cuts mean a reduction of 25 percent in local government spending power (Hastings et al. 2012), with the most disadvantaged localities being hardest hit. Given the significance of local government as a VCS funder, these cuts were bound to have an impact on the sector.

An inquiry into the Big Society by the Public Administration Select Committee of the House of Commons (PASC 2011) found it difficult to calculate precisely the impact that public expenditure cuts were having on the VCS. But the National Council for Voluntary Organisations (NCVO) estimated that VCOs would experience cuts of 8 percent a year in government funding between 2011 and 2015 (Kane and Allen 2011).

The impact of these cuts will vary. The government has, somewhat disingenuously, urged local authorities not to pass on their cuts to the VCS. Nevertheless, early mapping showed that many felt they had no option but to do so, although the extent of the cuts varies considerably from authority to authority (False Economy 2011). As Zimmeck and Rochester point out elsewhere in this volume, size also matters. Prior to the recession, Clark et al. (2009) reported that statutory income was most likely to be received by the largest organizations in their sample (those with an income of £1 million or more). But medium-sized organizations were more dependent on government funding, which represented 40 percent of their total income, making them more vulnerable to cuts. An early study of social care charities found that smaller charities were hardest hit, with 39 percent experiencing cuts compared with just 3 percent of the larger charities (Community Care 2011).

The impact of these cuts is also affected by legal form, beneficiary, purpose, and role (Clifford, Geyne Rajme and Mohan 2010). In terms of beneficiaries, for example, a Children England survey of organizations in their field found that three out of five of respondents expected to have gone under by 2015 (Gill, La Valle and Brady 2011), while the Community Care survey cited above reported that children's charities were 16 times more likely than adult charities to experience cuts of more than 10 percent. Newspaper reports have highlighted other particularly vulnerable sectors. The UK Border Agency is reported to have cut state funding of asylum services by 60 percent in April 2011 and while 70 percent of these organizations have reduced their workforce, 60 percent report that demand has increased (Ramrayka 2012). Meanwhile, despite public and political concern following widespread riots, looting and arson by youth in major cities in August 2011, youth services in both the public and not-profit sector are reported to have been savagely cut. One organization reports that:

> One in four of England's youth services face catastrophic cuts of between 21-30 percent – three times higher than the general level of council cuts. Many authorities intend to get rid of their youth services completely, while 80 percent of voluntary organizations providing services for young people have said programs will be cut. (Jenkins 2011)

Meanwhile dedicated funding to the national voluntary sector infrastructure, to which beleaguered VCOs might turn, has also been severely cut. The government has reduced the number of national infrastructure organizations supported by its Strategic Partners Programme from the 42 supported by the New Labour government to 17 (in nine consortia). This funding will disappear completely by 2014. In its culling of the quangoes (quasi-autonomous public bodies), government has abolished a number of non-departmental public bodies set up to support the sector – among them the bodies administering Capacitybuilders and Futurebuilders, along with the funding that they disbursed.

VCOs are not only affected by cuts to their own funding. They operate in a wider local ecology, and if this is impoverished by the loss of the agencies and staff they work with, then those who survive are left without the networks on which they depend. Meanwhile cuts to local authorities and central government departments, as well as the subsequent restructuring, are leading to considerable turnover within government. This puts at risk the knowledge, support, and institutional memory that will be essential for informed commissioning and for the maintenance of constructive and supportive relationships with the wider sector.

All this is happening at a time when the impact of cuts on services and household budgets means that demand is increasing. Public expenditure cuts are widely predicted to hit the poorest in society hardest

(Browne 2010; nef 2010a; Hastings et al. 2012). The fear is that cuts will also "undermine the very networks and groups that are most needed as life gets tougher for those who are already disadvantaged" (nef 2010a, 3).

Whatever its political persuasion, any incoming government in 2010 would have had to make cuts. That much is clear from the international picture painted by this book. And, however sensitively implemented, any cuts strategy would have had an impact on the VCS, probably drawing sharp criticism from those involved.

However, as I have argued elsewhere (Taylor 2012), there are two key features of current policy that distinguish the Coalition from its main opposition, the Labour Party. The first is the pace and scale of the cuts, which have been frontloaded over the four years covered by the new government's Comprehensive Spending Review. This has opened up a "funding gap" (PASC 2011), since there is likely to be a delay before new sources of funding, however well conceived, kick in. Whatever happens in the long-term, the VCS sector has entered a period of great uncertainty with inevitable loss of expertise and capacity.

The second distinguishing feature is the ideological underpinning of the cuts and current policy. It is impossible to consider the impact of the recession on the sector without understanding the determination of this government to reduce the sector's dependency on the state and it is to this that I now turn.

INTRODUCING THE BIG SOCIETY

One of the major policy themes introduced by the Coalition government has been that of the Big Society. The Big Society seeks to open up public services to new providers, increase social action, and devolve power to local communities (PASC 2011, 3). While some have seen the Big Society as a device for filling the gap left by the cuts, the Prime Minister is adamant that this is not the case (Cameron 2011). As the foreword to the Coalition government agreement states, the intention is to "completely recast the relationship between people and the state: citizens empowered; individual opportunity extended; communities coming together to make lives better" (HM Government 2010, 8). This government seeks to introduce fundamental and irreversible behavioural and cultural change.

To understand the significance of the Big Society for the VCS, it is necessary to understand its roots in Conservative thinking. One strong stream of thought informing the Big Society can be traced back to Edmund Burke's opposition to the French Revolution, and his celebration of the "small platoons" at the heart of society and their role in holding society together. This combines with more recent concerns to encourage family and social responsibility but also with a longstanding and deep suspicion of the Leviathan of the state. In the late twentieth century, opposition to state intervention, boosted by the fall of Communism, found expression in the free market policies associated with the neo-liberal right wing of the party. But, as the agreement signed between the Conservative and Liberal Democrat Coalition partners claims, it also built on the classical liberal tradition of defending civil liberties and stopping "the relentless incursion of the state into the life of individuals" (HM Government 2010, 8).

The recasting of the relationship with the state is illustrated by the fact that the Coalition has rejected the "third sector" terminology adopted by New Labour and replaced it by "civil society." It has abandoned the partnership discourse. It has renegotiated the *Compact* into a much narrower and more instrumental agreement (Zimmeck and Rochester, this volume). It has distanced itself from the generic policies put in place by New Labour. The funding available to the Office for Civil Society, the central government unit responsible for relations with the VCS, is due to be cut by 61 percent by 2014.

But there is another stream of thinking with an equally lengthy tradition that challenges this neo-liberal ethos and argues for a more compassionate Conservatism. This has its roots in the One Nation Toryism of the Victorian era, championed by Benjamin Disraeli amongst others, but also in the concern expressed by the "father of capitalism," Adam Smith, about the impact of the narrow self-interest inherent in this system on social ties and concern for the welfare of others (Cnaan, Milofsky and Hunter 2007, 9). More recently it has been evident in the arguments being advanced by the self-professed "Red Tories" (Blond 2010). The extent to which this stream of thinking can be reconciled with the neo-liberal tradition or if not, which will win out, remains to be seen.

WHAT WILL THIS MEAN FOR THE SECTOR?

On paper, the introduction of the Big Society is a boost to VCOs struggling to cope with the cuts outlined earlier in this paper. But in the press and media, key figures in the VCS have argued that these cuts are killing the golden goose that can deliver the Big Society. In response, government has introduced some short-term measures to fill the funding gap. But in the long-term, it has put its faith in a series of new policies and programs designed to:

- encourage volunteering and philanthropy, mutuals and co-operatives;
- open up key public services, such as health and education, to non-statutory providers;
- transfer powers to local government and beyond, and give new powers to communities, including a right to challenge existing public service provision and if necessary take it over;
- mobilize communities through training 5,000 community organizers; and

- release new resources for social investment, for example, through setting up a Big Society Bank (Big Society Capital) drawing on funds from dormant bank accounts as well as commitments won from major high street banks.

Despite the rebranding represented by the Big Society, there are a number of continuities with earlier New Labour policies. Proposals to devolve powers, to introduce new community rights, to expand social investment, and to expand the market were all present during the New Labour era. However, some have been taken considerably further, while others – like the Big Society Bank – are ideas which were never put into practice. The commitment to community organizers, however, is quite new (although it has since been taken up across the political spectrum). And it is clear that the long-term aim is to make the sector, its members, and its beneficiaries far less dependent on government funding. These measures are now considered in turn.

Short-term Measures

The Transition Fund was an early response by government to vigorous representations from the VCS about the likely impact of funding cuts on their work. The Fund provided £100 million to give front-line organizations affected by cuts some breathing space to adapt to new form of funding. The Fund was, however, criticized by many in the sector as being insufficient and ill-timed. The turnaround time for bids was short, phased over the Christmas holiday period and, incidentally, not Compact-compliant.

In times of trouble, many local VCOs look to the local VCS infrastructure – councils for voluntary service and similar bodies – for advice and support. Fears for the survival of these support services have been met by the introduction of a new Transforming Local Infrastructure Fund, designed to encourage the diversity of local infrastructure organizations to rationalize their operations. This is an aspiration that New Labour's Capacitybuilders program shared but failed to achieve. Again, the turnaround for bids was criticized as being too short – seven and a half weeks for disparate organizations to collaborate on producing a coherent bid. It is too early to report on its impact, but it remains a one-off injection of funds. There is as yet no plan to support the national infrastructure, once Strategic Partners' funding tails off in 2014.

Giving and Volunteering

A basic tenet of the Big Society is that the state should be a resource of last resort. In the Big Society, communities and citizens will be set free to take responsibility for themselves. One assumption appears to be that there is an untapped pool of volunteers who, once the state retreats, will be able to rush into the vacuum. But the evidence suggests that there are very few people who do not participate at all. One recent study, for example, experienced great difficulty in identifying any "non-participants" – although it defined participation very widely (Brodie et al. 2011). The study also pointed out that there are many personal factors that affect people's capacity to participate and which are not open to influence by policy. Another study confirmed that the majority of people, 85 percent, are engaged in volunteering, civic participation or giving at some level (Mohan and Bulloch 2012). However, it did show that the bulk of these activities are dependent on a "civic core" of just over a third of the population. The study also demonstrated that engagement is higher in more affluent areas and among middle-class, professional and highly educated people than among people with lower levels of income and education (see also NCVO 2011a). These studies suggest that government needs to recognize how much some people are already doing and be realistic in its expectations. But they also suggest that reliance on giving and volunteering is likely to produce an uneven outcome.

As part of its Big Society policy, the Coalition government is looking at a range of ways to boost giving (Cabinet Office 2011). Individual giving accounts for over one-third of the income of UK charities. Not surprisingly, this has been affected by the recession. While the proportion of the population giving has remained more or less constant, the amount given fell by 11 percent between 2007–8 and 2008–9 (NCVO/CAF 2009). It is now recovering slightly but not yet to 2007–8 levels (NCVO/CAF 2011) let alone to a level that could compensate for losses elsewhere. Statistics also suggest that the burden of giving falls disproportionately on the poor insofar as the poor give a higher proportion of their income than the rich (Lumley et al. 2011).

Government has recognized some of these concerns with the announcement in the Giving White Paper (Cabinet Office 2011) of new funds to encourage and reward innovation in volunteering and giving, as well as a National Citizens Service for young people. But while the incentives offered by such funds are welcome, they do not represent a long-term sustainable strategy. Indeed, some feel they are a drop in the ocean in the face of funding that is being lost (NCVO 2011b).

Taking on Public Service Provision

A more sustainable option for VCOs wishing to secure their future may be to respond to government's drive to transfer public services to non-statutory providers, private and not-for-profit. This chapter has already referred to the new community rights to challenge and take over local public services. Government is encouraging local authorities to put their services out to tender on a much greater scale than previously. However, the extent to which VCOs, especially smaller organizations, will benefit remains to be seen. The tendency of the market is to go to scale. This is evident in the private sector in the UK, where supermarkets and large retail chains are often blamed for the demise of smaller "high street" shops (nef 2002). It has also been evident in the housing sector. Here, voluntary housing associations, given the opportunity since the 1980s to take over the provision of social housing, have grown and merged over the years, with the risk that they will become more and more like their private sector counterparts. Thus, while Conservative Party rhetoric celebrates the "small platoons," it may well be the corporate battalions who benefit most from opening up the public service market. This was a major concern of a recent Parliamentary report on the Big Society (PASC 2011). Procurement patterns are likely to favour large contracts as being easier to administer and smaller charities are unlikely to have the capacity to tender for these. There is the danger, too, that rigidly defined procurement policy will deliver a "scorched earth" policy with the bottom line trumping all other considerations. If this happens, the existing experience, trust, and valued relationships on which a Big Society depends may well be lost.

There is of course scope for consortium bids, with larger organizations, private or not-for-profit, subcontracting to smaller organizations. However, the experience of these so far has not been promising. A recent example is the Work Programme put out for tender by government in 2011 to tackle unemployment. Only two of the 18 contracts went to a voluntary organization. Many of the smaller VCOs mentioned in the bids as potential subcontractors found they were not offered work at all. On the contrary, they felt that they had simply been used as "bid candy." Meanwhile, those that were offered work argued that they were expected to carry a disproportionate amount of the risks and costs of delivery. It remains to be seen whether the checks and balances built into government's agreements with the prime contractors will be used or whether these contractors will be deemed too big to fail. The danger is that, through this process, government is outsourcing commissioning itself, thus creating a firewall between itself and any responsibility or accountability for the service.

More broadly, the Public Administration Select Committee report (PASC 2011) points out that a preference for payment by results, while it has much to recommend it, risks further excluding smaller providers who do not have the working capital to carry the inevitable delays between doing the work and receiving payment. The Committee also expressed concern about the likely mismatch between departmental commissioning, especially at central government level, and the holistic services that voluntary organizations tend to provide.

The guiding principle of the market is competition. The logic of procurement processes discourages sharing of ideas and information. Will reliance on competitive tendering breed mistrust within the sector? A number of policies consciously try to combat this tendency. The Local Infrastructure Fund requires infrastructure bodies to work together across local authorities while a number of community programs that have been introduced, rely on local panels to ensure coherence in developing local solutions. But a danger remains that the Big Society could be a more fragmented society.

Mobilizing and Devolving Power to Communities

Government has ambitious plans to mobilize and devolve powers to local communities. The Localism Act, tabled in 2011, introduces new community rights to challenge existing service provision and to buy threatened community assets. Government has also introduced new programs to build community resources, of which the three most significant are: Community First, the Community Organisers Programme, and Business Connectors. This package of programs is founded on government's firm belief that previous community empowerment programs have been compromised by excessive government control and professionalization – they have been top-down rather than bottom-up.

The first two programs in particular seek to develop an asset-based approach to community engagement, which builds on community strengths rather than focusing on problems and supports communities in identifying their own priorities. Community First will match local time, expertise, and goods with its own resources to stimulate community action, as well as work with community foundations and other philanthropic resources to build a national endowment fund. The Community Organisers Programme seeks to develop an army of 5,000 community organizers across the country. It arises out of government interest in the citizens organizing movement in the UK. The Programme is inspired by Alinsky's power-based approach in the US (Alinsky 1971), but also incorporates the ideas of Paolo Freire on popular education and political literacy (1969) and of Santo de Morais (Carmen and Chaves 2000) on income generation for the poor. The third program, Business Connectors, will draw in the resources of business to help local communities to address local needs.

Government's commitment to devolve power to communities and to build sustainable resources must be welcome. However, the new funds are unlikely to match the resources that have been lost to communities. The community grants program that the £80 million Community First replaced, for example, was worth £130 million. Further, the Community Organisers Programme is only committed to funding 500 senior community organizers for one year, a short time in which to build effective community action. How the resources of this Programme compare with previous provision is impossible to say as yet, since there is no estimate how many community workers have been lost as a result of the cuts. But in the Big Society, the plan is that future funding will come from new forms of social investment rather than government. The Community First Programme aims to build a local endowment fund, while another £200 million endowment-based fund has been introduced by the Big Lottery Foundation, at arm's length from government.

Regardless of the prospects for overall funding, these programs pose a number of challenges (Taylor 2011a, 2012). Some of these relate to the equality and scale issues discussed earlier in this chapter. As the New Economics Foundation has reminded us (nef 2010b), the energy, time, resources, and political know-how to take up the new community rights – for example, to run services – are not equally distributed in society. Heavy cuts in local services as well as welfare benefit reform will only put more pressure on already disadvantaged communities. It remains to be seen whether the resources in these programs can redress that balance.

Meanwhile, where services are put out to tender, community organizations will find it difficult to enter the procurement process. And whether as providers or consumers, communities are likely to find large private sector providers difficult to influence and hold accountable. The Big Society may thus turn out to be both unequal and unaccountable.

Devolving power to local communities begs the question: who exactly is "the community"? The neighbourhoods and villages to which this term is applied may contain many different communities. And dominant communities may be intentionally or unintentionally exclusive (Taylor 2011b). Even within community groups, Brodie et al. (2011) found in their study of participation that a major cause of people disengaging was because of conflicts or clashing personalities in their group. Sherry Arnstein's famous ladder of participation (1969) has often been used as a template for thinking about power in citizen participation processes. It moves from non-participation through degrees of tokenism to degrees of citizen power, with community control right at the top. But whole communities do not run services and community leaders may need to be tested against Arnstein's criteria before it can be assumed that their services are more empowering than those provided by external agencies.

Finally, there is always the risk that, if communities do not perform as expected – or if government interests move to new pastures – the programs introduced with enthusiasm at the beginning of their term will lose support. The New Labour government's commitment to closing the gap between the most disadvantaged neighbourhoods and the rest of society, for example, was dropped towards the end of its years in power. Further, New Labour's financial support for VCS engagement in local cross-sector partnerships through the Single Community Programme was devolved to the local level where the funds were often diverted elsewhere. Its commitment to community empowerment, too, ebbed and flowed as Ministers changed. Since the introduction of the Big Society, media commentators have questioned how long commitment to this theme will last. Commentators still find it too vague to be convincing (PASC 2011). The Community Organisers Programme may be particularly vulnerable in this respect. As I have argued elsewhere (Taylor 2011a, 2012), the Coalition government's commitment to a mode of organizing associated with Saul Alinsky's radical power-based approach was surprising and intriguing. Its continued commitment to hands-off support of bottom-up action is impressive. But whether this commitment will survive the kind of creative disruption implied by an Alinskyite approach, particularly if it attracts media interest, remains to be seen.

In pointing out the pitfalls of relying on the mobilization of community resources, it is important not to deny the considerable achievements made by local community action over the years, nor the ways in which community anchor organizations, like settlements and development trusts, have evolved to meet community needs. Community initiatives have brought tremendous energy to the task of tackling complex and long-term problems, and will continue to do so. But their survival may depend heavily on the prospects for social investment as a major and dependable source of funding. Relying too heavily on the resources of some of the most vulnerable communities is unlikely to be a long-term and sustainable solution.

Social Investment

The coalition government's community programs are putting their faith in social investment and local entrepreneurial innovation as the alternative to state funding. The Community Organisers Programme is drawing on innovative models from the global South as a way of addressing the economic challenges in the most disadvantaged communities (Carmen and Chaves 2000). If new and sustainable resources can be developed through these means, it can only be good news. But as yet, they are an unknown quantity. The Public Administration Select Committee examined the idea of social impact bonds, which are one much discussed option, for example (PASC 2011), but concluded that the metrics involved would rule out a number of the complex social issues that VCOs tend to address. And, as was the case with payment by results, the returns were likely to be long-term. The coalition's Big Society Bank – Big Society Capital – drawing on funds from dormant bank accounts and a commitment from high street banks may offer a more promising alternative, although this again is a long-term project. The Public Administration Select Committee report concluded that the time involved in building up social investment options meant that this approach to funding the Big Society would not solve the immediate funding gap. It also pointed out that the risks involved in a loan from social investment sources might not suit smaller charities.

THE WAY FORWARD

It is not possible to assess the impact of the recession on the VCS in England without reference to the ideological shift involved in the coalition government's Big Society policy and the determination, by no means confined to England, to reduce the role of the state in welfare. Whatever the outcome of current austerity measures, the pressure on state funding – which represents a significant resource for many VCOs – is likely to continue. Whether philanthropy, mutuality and new forms of social investment can fill the gap remains to be seen.

The discussion in this chapter so far has suggested that there are potential contradictions in the philosophies that inform the Big Society: seeking to celebrate the "small platoon" as the basis for social order, seeking to restore the social ties that are eroded by capitalism, while at the same time relying increasingly on the market. The risk, it has argued, is that the Big Society, freed from the state, could be a more unequal, unaccountable, fragmented, and unsustainable society.

There is a tendency in much of the current rhetoric about "community" and civil society to see voluntary and community action as an alternative to the state, moreover as a force that needs to be set free from the state's malign influence. But many civil society scholars are skeptical about the likely outcome of such a course. Civil society is a forum for the expression of diverse voices and identities. This is a source of its strength, but it also means that it can be a place of conflict and tension as much as of resolution (Taylor 2011b, 77). "Community" defines outsiders as well as insiders. Wolfe (1992, 113) called the communitarian perspective "a recipe for parochialism and privilege." Cornwall and Coelho (2004, 6) question the assumptions that are commonly made about the inherently democratizing potential of civil society. Indeed, John Keane (1988) argues that civil society and the state are the condition for each others' democratization. He blames the increasing marginalization and pauperization that he sees in society on the retreat of the state.

Evers (2009) prefers to explore the concept of civility, which he defines as the capacity to rise above personal self-interest. This, he argues, can be found in all sectors. Certainly, the problems of recession and continuing economic instability need the resources of all parts of society – public, private and community – if they are to be addressed. But what is the role of the VCS in maintaining civility as a defining feature of future forms of welfare? And how can VCOs move forward against a background of continued economic restraint?

The VCS is not a homogenous entity and the answer to these questions is likely to differ for the different organizations within it. I conclude with three challenges that need to be addressed in the future if VCOs are to fulfill their diverse potential.

The first relates to the role of the VCS in public service provision. How can procurement processes create a diverse and responsive market, which encourages the release of new energies and ideas? Experience so far suggests that this will require new skills, new cultures, and new mindsets among commissioners, which allow for risk, innovation, diversity, and new kinds of relationship between commissioners and providers. The creation of a diverse and responsive market is not solely the responsibility of the commissioners. It also requires the winners in the market to take responsibility for supporting potential partners and to build their capacity for partnering and subcontracting on fair terms. There are precedents for this and they need to become much more widespread. Procurement processes will need to be designed to place a premium on such relationships. Meanwhile, if the sector is not to become increasingly fragmented and polarized, there is an urgent need to find and share ways of building new kinds of consortia, building on collaboration and solidarity rather than competitiveness.

Second, although there are many in the voluntary and community sector who welcome new opportunities in the public service market, there are many others who will want to take a different route. In the New Labour years, some argue that the VCS became too dependent on government funding and were co-opted by partnership arrangements into agendas that were not their own (Zimmeck and Rochester, this volume; Taylor 2012). During the partnership years, partnership risked becoming the "only game in town," with alternative voices silenced (Taylor, Howard and Lever 2010). From this perspective, the current austerity measures are an opportunity for the sector to rediscover its soul. Cuts in public spending have brought out opposing voices and led to the creation of new spaces for change outside the state. New technology, too, has played its part in challenging the accepted hegemony, with the growth internationally of new kinds of campaigning organizations, such as *38 degrees* and *avaaz*. In England, citizens' organizing has captured political attention on the right and left.

The reality is that different VCOs will take different routes. As always, there will be those who choose to be in the tent and those who choose to stay outside (Craig, Taylor and Parkes 2004). But, either way, the sector's role in framing public debate will be greatly needed. Recession creates divisions and hardens social attitudes. To take just a few examples: while all the evidence suggests that the cuts are hitting the poor and the most disadvantaged areas hardest, a recent survey in Britain found that the majority of the population support benefit cuts and more stringent conditions for benefit claimants (Wells 2011). While youth employment is soaring, youth provision is being drastically cut. While reform of the National Health Service and education has been prioritized, often in the face of considerable opposition, much needed reform of social care – surely a major concern for VCOs – has been repeatedly put on the back burner. And this, despite the challenges of an ageing population (Dartington 2010). A concerted voice for those at the sharp end of the cuts is sorely needed if the temptation to blame the most vulnerable is to be avoided.

The third challenge, as we watch the pendulum swing back and forth over the decades between market, state, and civil society as the solution to society's problems, is to escape from ideological certainties about the primacy of any one sector and seek to combine the virtues and values of each. The last time the Conservative Party came to power, in 1979, alliances were created between local government, the unions, and local communities to challenge what was seen as an attack on the public sector. Nothing similar has happened this time around, despite the fact that the attack appears to be far more severe. Public sector cultures may need to change significantly to address the failures of the past. But the unpopular case needs to be made for the long-term efficiency of public spending and public intervention in meeting social needs.

REFERENCES

Alinsky, S. 1971. *Rules for Radicals.* New York: Random House.
Arnstein, S. 1969. "A Ladder of Participation in the USA." *Journal of the American Institute of Planners* 35 (4): 216-24.
Blond, P. 2010. *Red Tory: How Left and Right Have Broken Britain and How We Can Fix It.* London: Faber.
Brodie, E., T. Hughes, V. Jochum, S. Miller, N. Ockenden, and D. Warburton. 2011. *Pathways through Participation: What Creates and Sustains Active Citizenship?* London: National Council for Voluntary Organisations, Institute for Volunteering Research and Involve.
Browne, J. 2010. *Distributional Analysis of Tax and Benefit Changes.* London: Institute for Fiscal Studies.
Cabinet Office. 2011. *Giving White Paper.* London: HM Government.
Cameron, D. 2011. Speech to Conservative Party conference, October.
Carmen, R. and M. Chaves. 2000. *A Future for the Excluded: Job Creation and Income Generation for the Poor.* London: Zed.
Clark, J., J. Dobbs, D. Kane, and K. Wilding. 2009. *The State and the Voluntary Sector: Recent Trends in Government Funding and Public Service Delivery.* London: National Council for Voluntary Organisations.
Clifford, D., F. Geyne Rajme, and J. Mohan. 2010. How Dependent is the Third Sector on Public Funding? TSRC Working Paper 45. Birmingham: Third Sector Research Centre.
CLG (Communities and Local Government). 2005. *Making Connections: An Evaluation of the Community Participation Programmes.* London: CLG.
—. 2010. *Evaluation of the National Strategy for Neighbourhood Renewal.* London: CLG.
Cnaan, R., C. Milofsky, and A. Hunter. 2007. "Creating a Frame for Understanding Local Organizations." In *Handbook of Community Movements and Local Organizations,* ed. R. Cnaan, C. Milofsky, and A. Hunter, 1-19. New York: Springer.

Community Care. 2011. "Voluntary Sector Cuts Threaten Big Society Vision." Community Care 13 January. At www.communitycare.co.uk/Articles/13/01/11 (accessed January 2012).

Cornwall, A. and V. Coelho. 2004. *Spaces for Change? The Politics of Democratic Participation in New Democratic Arenas*. London: Zed Books.

Craig, G., M. Taylor, and T. Parkes. 2004. "Protest or Partnership? The Voluntary and Community Sectors in the Policy Process." *Social Policy and Administration* 38 (3): 221-39.

Dartington, T. 2010. *Managing Vulnerability, the Underlying Dynamics of Systems of Care*. London: Karnac Books.

Evers, A. 2009. "Civicness and Civility: Their Meanings for Social Services." *Voluntas* 20 (3): 239-59.

False Economy. 2011. At http://falseeconomy.org.uk/.

Freire, P. 1969. *Education for Critical Consciousness*. New York: Continuum.

Gill, C., I. La Valle, and L.M. Brady. 2011. *The Ripple Effect: The Nature and Impact of the Children and Young People's Voluntary Sector*. London: National Children's Bureau.

Hastings, A., G. Bramley, N. Bailey, and D. Watkins. 2012. *Serving Deprived Communities in a Recession*. York: Joseph Rowntree Foundation.

HM Government. 2010. *The Coalition: Our Programme for Government*. London: HM Government.

Home Office. 1998. *The Compact: Getting it Right Together*. London: The Stationery Office.

House of Commons Public Administration Select Committee (PASC). 2011. *The Big Society*. Seventeenth Report of Session 2010–2012, HC 902-1. London: The Stationery Office.

Jenkins, K. 2011. Youth Services are Being Savaged by Government Cuts. At http://falseeconomy.org.uk//blog/youth-services-in-crisis (accessed 12 March 2012).

Kane, D. and Allen, J. 2011. *Counting the Cuts: The Impact of Spending Cuts on the UK Voluntary and Community Sector*. London: NCVO.

Keane, J. 1988. *Democracy and Civil Society*. London: Verso.

Kendall, J. 2000. "The Mainstreaming of the Third Sector into Public Policy in England: Whys and Wherefores." *Policy and Politics* 28 (4): 541–62.

Lumley, T., M. Brookes, R. Macdougall, and P. Lomax, P. 2011. *Ten Ways to Boost Giving*. London: New Philanthropy Capital.

Mayo, M. and J. Annette. 2010. *Taking Part: Active Learning for Active Citizenship and Beyond*. Leicester: National Institute of Adult and Continuing Education.

Mohan, J. and S. Bulloch. 2012. The Idea of a "Civic Core": What are the Overlaps between Charitable Giving, Volunteering, and Civic Participation in England and Wales? TSRC Working Paper No. 73. Birmingham: Third Sector Research Centre.

National Council for Voluntary Organisations (NCVO). 2011a. *Participation: Trends, Facts and Figures: An NCVO Almanac*. London: NCVO.

—. 2011b. NCVO Policy Analysis: Giving White Paper. London: NCVO.

The National Evaluation of Sure Start Research Team (NESS). 2010. *The Impact of Sure Start Local Programmes on Five Year Olds and their Families*. London: Department of Families and Education.

NCVO/CAF. 2009. *The Impact of the Recession on Charitable Giving in the UK*. London: NCVO and West Malling, CAF.

—. 2011. *UK Giving 2011*. London: NCVO and West Malling, Charities Aid Foundation.

New Economics Foundation (nef). 2002. *Ghost Town Britain: The Threat from Economic Globalisation to Livelihoods, Liberty and Local Economic Freedom*. London: New Economics Foundation.

—. 2010a. *Cutting It: The Big Society and the New Austerity*. London: New Economics Foundation.

—. 2010b. *Ten Questions About the Big Society*. London: New Economics Foundation.

Ramrayka, L. 2012. Can Refugee Charities Ride Out the Cuts Storm? *The Guardian*, 17 January.

Taylor, M. 2011a. "Community Organising and the Big Society: Is Saul Alinsky Turning in his Grave." *Voluntary Sector Review* 2 (2): 259-66.

—. 2011b. *Public Policy in the Community*, 2nd ed. Basingstoke: Palgrave Macmillan.

—. 2012. "The Changing Fortunes of Community." *Voluntary Sector Review* 3 (1): 15-35.

Taylor, M., J. Howard, and J. Lever. 2010. "Citizen Participation and Civic Activism in Comparative Perspective." *Journal of Civil Society* 6 (2): 45-64.

Wells, A. 2011. Strong Public Support for Benefit Cuts. At http://labs.yougov. co.uk/news/2011/05/16/strong-public-support-benefit-cuts/ (accessed 9 March 2012).

Wilding, K., 2009. How Important is the Voluntary Sector in Public Service Delivery? At http://www.ncvo-vol.org.uk/networking-discussions/ blogs/209/09/10/02/how-important-voluntary-sector-public-service-delivery (accessed 17 February 2012).

Wolfe, A. 1992. "Democracy vs. Sociology: Boundaries and their Sociological Consequences." In *Cultivating Differences: Symbolic Boundaries and the Making of Inequality*, ed. M. Lamont and M. Fournier. Chicago: University of Chicago Press.

Chapter 7

Post-Partnership Ireland: Organizational Survival and Social Change Strategies in an Era of Economic Restraint

Gemma Donnelly-Cox and John A. Healy

Introduction

This chapter examines the impact of recession on government-nonprofit relations in Ireland and draws out the implications for civil society, nonprofit organizations, and social change. Analyses of the Irish economy – and Irish society – post-2008 detail the many ways in which so much has fallen apart. Economic collapse, the abandonment of National Partnership, political disruption, and the establishment of external control of the economy are all manifestations of the systemic failures. So far, policy responses have been focused on resuscitating the economy, with very limited attention paid to state-nonprofit relations. Against this background, our chapter addresses the ramifications for civil society and its role in bringing social change as well as the survival of nonprofit organizations in a very difficult environment.

We also reflect on the role of civil society itself in a time of crisis. The nonprofit sector in Ireland is both dependent on the state and also the forum for formulating and advocating for alternative practices. In some ways the Irish nonprofit sector is an extreme example of the situation in other countries where the sector has become increasingly reliant on the state (Salamon 1993). Yet, the sector finds itself, as a result of the fiscal retrenchment, faced with a choice between advocating and resisting, or

Government-Nonprofit Relations in Times of Recession, ed. Rachel Laforest. Montreal and Kingston: Queen's Policy Studies Series, McGill-Queen's University Press. © 2013 The School of Policy Studies, Queen's University at Kingston. All rights reserved.

attempting to service the increased need and securing organizational survival. According to researchers who have explored the impact of state funding dominance on nonprofit organizations, this reliance on a single source can result in nonprofit organizations adopting the bureaucratic processes and similar institutional logics as the state (e.g., Smith and Lipsky 1993). Others have found evidence of resilience amongst nonprofits in terms of retaining their own identity and capacity to challenge even when faced with reliance on state funding (e.g., Binder 2007). This paper highlights the potential for civil society to instigate debates about changing social institutions, even in the midst of economic crisis. At a time when trust in the state is so low (Edelman Trust Barometer 2011, 2012), and the traditionally close relationship between nonprofit organizations and the state has been disrupted, how is the role of civil society affected? What ought civil society to do?

In a "state-dominant" sector such as Ireland, the relationship with the state has played an important part in the resource mix of nonprofit organizations. In this context, the role of private funders and civil society itself may receive less attention in analysis. We attempt to address the possible omission of private funders by considering their role in the current scenario facing Ireland. We explore the self-perceptions of funders, and the ways in which those self-perceptions may influence the relationships that private funders form with the state. We also discuss that in a time of crisis, when norms and practices that are usually taken for granted come to be considered in a more conscious way (Swidler 1986), private funding can play a crucial role in helping the sector to present and progress a vision of alternative social arrangements (Healy and Clark 2006) that would not normally be considered.

Setting the Context

The rapid demise of formal government-nonprofit relations in Ireland is most clearly illustrated by the collapse of Social Partnership in 2009. From 1987 to 2009, agreements were developed every three years between government and the three "pillars" of employers, trade unions, and farmers. These agreements addressed wage growth, industrial relations, taxation policy, and social welfare. From 1997, some actors within the nonprofit sector were invited by the state to participate in the process (O'Donnell and Thomas 2006). They joined as the "Community and Voluntary Pillar," the fourth pillar in the negotiations.[1] When Social Partnership ended in 2009, with it went the only national-level forum for negotiation of nonprofit sector-state relations. Its termination interrupted the existing policy framework underlying state-nonprofit relations. Regarded by Pillar participants as "the only game in town," without it the complete absence of other frameworks for nonprofit sector representation became obvious.

The two strongest cross-sectoral membership organizations, the Wheel and the Irish Charities Tax Reform Group, do not have a mandate (or, so far, a formal objective) to serve as the representative forum for the non-profit sector. However, the seventeen organizations that were invited by government "to provide voice and representation for vulnerable people and communities in developing Ireland's social and economic policies" (Community and Voluntary Pillar [CVP] 2011) remained together as the Community and Voluntary Pillar after the collapse of Social Partnership. These organizations occasionally issue briefing papers with recommendations for government (CVP 2011; The Wheel 2011).

The end of Partnership reflects the conditions of precipitous economic collapse and political turmoil afflicting Ireland. The problems facing the country are easier to comprehend when expressed in financial terms. The scale of the financial challenges facing the country following the "double whammy" of economic downturn and an Irish banking crisis is clearly indicated by the change in the growth rate of GDP over the decade 2000 to 2009. In 2000, the annual real growth rate of GDP was nearly 10 percent per annum. It remained at greater than 5 percent per annum through 2007. However, in 2008 it slumped to –5.2 percent and, in 2009, to –10.8 percent (Central Statistics Office [CSO] 2011a, 3). The unemployment rate jumped from 4.5 percent in 2007 to 17.3 percent in the first quarter of 2011 (CSO 2011b, 10). The exchequer deficit grew from 25 percent of GDP in 2007 to 66 percent of GDP in 2010 (OECD 2010; Lau 2011).

The economic challenges facing the state are made even clearer if the focus is shifted to the structure of government expenditure. In 2008, after more than a decade of record-breaking economic growth, 31.1 percent of government spending, equivalent to 9.9 percent of GDP, was on social protection (Department of Social Protection 2011). By 2010, in spite of strong pressure to limit state expenditure, 33.3 percent of government spending was on social protection, by then equivalent to 13.8 percent of GDP (Lau 2011). This increase in the proportion of spending on social protection was due to an increase in demand for social protection payments, especially to the newly unemployed. The state therefore faces the twin challenges of rising unemployment and rising national debt against a backdrop of constrained fiscal resources (Kearney 2012).

The Irish government has seen no choice but to respond to the precipitate fall in tax revenue with "austerity budgets," slashing public spending and in particular seeking ways to reduce expenditure on social protection. In November 2010, Ireland signed a borrowing agreement known as the IMF-EU Programme. The so-called "Troika" of the International Monetary Fund (IMF), the Commission of the European Communities (CEC) and the European Central Bank (ECB) monitor the Irish government's implementation of the program, which has required year-on-year budget cuts and taxation increases (IMF/EU 2011). The scope for economic manoeuvre outside the IMF-EU Programme is, at the current time, very limited.

These developments have disrupted and devalued the network of relationships, informal understandings, and formal agreements that have characterized state-nonprofit relations in Ireland for decades. The IMF-EU program is, in effect, external control of the Irish economy. Under these conditions, the nature of government-nonprofit relations is fundamentally altered. Even without the extra barriers to engagement with the state that the IMF-EU Programme has created, the political upheaval of 2010–2011 has uprooted the political relationships carefully nurtured by nonprofit organizations. In the 2011 general election, there was a fundamental shift away from Fianna Fáil, the party that had most often held office since the establishment of the state. Fianna Fáil experienced an unprecedented collapse in support (Kirby 2011), disrupting the influence networks of many nonprofits. Through 2011 and into 2012, the political decision-making context in Ireland has remained tumultuous and uncertain (Moran 2011). Certainly, there has been no indication given – nor, indeed, no real scope even if there was appetite – of an interest within the state to return to social partnership.

The Irish nonprofit sector is described in the international comparative context as "state dominant," reflecting a long history of sector-led delivery of public services, in particular in education and health (Donoghue et al. 2006). For example, more than 90 percent of the state's primary schools are voluntary organizations funded by the state. The intertwining of voluntary organizing and public service delivery has resulted in a high degree of dependency on the state. Public service-delivering nonprofit organizations are quasi-public bodies, obliged to operate to the standards and conditions of state enterprises but often without the state infrastructure to support all functions. More than 60 percent of the sector's income comes from state sources (Donoghue et al. 2006, 47).

Outside of the relationship with the state, voluntary organizations are no more likely to find financial security in private sources of funding. Recent annual fundraising surveys document annual double-digit declines in fundraising revenue (Kelleher and O'Connor 2010, 2011). Organized philanthropy, including the foundation sector, is small and shrinking; the two major foundations – both large and private – are spend-down foundations that will cease to operate in Ireland by 2017. While philanthropy is important, it too is in the throes of significant change and is similarly affected by the economic crisis (Donnelly-Cox and McGee 2011). In the fifth section of this paper, we turn our attention to the changing role of philanthropy and the part it may play in this context.

Under the current conditions, nonprofit organizations have been placed in an extraordinary position in managing their relationship with the state. Does it even make sense to consider nonprofit organizations in relation to the state, when the state is unable to play its traditional role in that relationship (Donnelly-Cox et al., forthcoming)? We argue that it is necessary to shift the focus away from sector-state relations in order to fully appreciate the issues facing nonprofit organizations in the context of the recession and beyond. We therefore turn our attention now to considering what is actually happening to nonprofit organizations at the present time, and to the role of civil society more broadly. What is it and what *should* it be doing in extraordinary times?

WHAT IS HAPPENING TO NONPROFIT ORGANIZATIONS?

The ways in which nonprofit organizations are responding to current conditions has been addressed in detail elsewhere (Donnelly-Cox and Cannon 2010). Irish nonprofit organizations are responding to the sudden, very dramatic changes largely brought about by the financial crisis and the state's austerity response to its fiscal problems. These major changes in the organizational environment are driving organizational transformations. They are however also affected by continual, gradual changes that have slowly reshaped their roles and relationships.

Another factor that poses both spike-like crises as well as ongoing problems within the sector is the legacy of sexual abuse of children within the Roman Catholic Church. This disturbing history was not addressed adequately by church authorities, despite their knowledge of the details of some of the worst cases, until very recently and in response to external pressure. Whilst the church has introduced child protection policies that are regarded as current best practice, the utter failure to deal fully and effectively with previous cases of abuse casts a long shadow over the church and the many church-affiliated institutions within the nonprofit sector.

Nonprofit organizations are not entirely passive in a hostile environment. In various ways they are responding to and also influencing their operating environments, bringing about changes that in turn affect the range of options available. Whilst the collapse of National Partnership has limited the opportunities for direct influence on and changes within the policy environment, the scope for individual organizations to cope with change and act as social change agents still exists. We consider here the range of ways in which organizations are both responding to and impacting on their environment.

The most obvious response is *economizing* (Donnelly-Cox and Cannon 2010). Driven by the financial reality of decline in income and (often) increase in demand, nonprofit organizations are becoming skilled at doing more with less. Organizations are prioritizing efficiency, communicating their effectiveness in stretching donations / dues / contract funds further, and generally seeking to convince their stakeholders that they can create a positive social return on their operating funds. Membership organizations such as the Wheel are supporting their organizational members to manage their limited resources as effectively as possible. Whether the economizing response serves as a further driver for more managerialist approaches to organizing (Maier and Meyer 2011) still remains to be determined.

Another approach taken by nonprofit organizations – both those who have worked closely with the state and those that have remained independent of state support – is to *harmonize* their core activities with underserved national priorities (Donnelly-Cox and Cannon 2010). For example, health sector nonprofit organizations are targeting their resources to what they see as key health programs that are unlikely to secure state funding. Local community groups are focusing on local economic regeneration and job creation in the local economy.

Even organizations that are focusing their program activities using harmonizing strategies are willing to *diversify* when it comes to finding new ways to widen their funding base and bring in resources (Donnelly-Cox and Cannon 2010). Organizations may also diversify by opening up their core services to new groups. Further, organizations are operating in new geographic areas. For example, Irish peace organizations – affected heavily by both the acute current financial crisis and also by the perception that following the peace process in Northern Ireland, peace organizations are less necessary – are seeking to use their expertise in other parts of the world where communities are in conflict.

Finally, we may expect to see some nonprofits seeking to *monopolize,* expanding their activities to gain control of organizational fields (Donnelly-Cox and Cannon 2010). There is support, both from private funders and from the state, for mergers within nonprofit fields so as to reduce the complexity of exchanges and to concentrate resources in a single service provider. For example, there have been recent mergers in the fields of refugee and asylum seeker services, and in the development and coordination of volunteering centres.

These responses are driven by organizations seeking to achieve their mission under difficult conditions, but also purely by the drive to survive.

Indeed, the very survival of nonprofits is a major concern within the field. Over the last decade, many organizations have scaled up and invested in infrastructure and skills to offer more professional services. However, many have considerable overheads and limited flexibility to economize on an ongoing basis. In an operating environment where legitimacy and efficiency is equated with leaner operations oriented towards continued growth and development, nonprofit organizational survival may be more closely tied to the ability to scale back, scale down, and generally reduce the scope and range of organizational operations to a sustainable level. The struggle to survive may push organizations to become increasingly mission-driven, concentrating all available resources on core purposes. Or, it may direct resources to preservation of the entity, with stakeholders arguing that unless the organization is preserved, the long-term service of its mission will be lost.

We now move on to considering the role of civil society. We explore the potential for the nonprofit sector to serve the needs of the increased group of people who require social assistance and/or to influence the narrative of the crisis and present compelling alternative visions for the type of society which citizens wish to see emerge from the crisis. We argue that these dual roles (Frumkin 2002) also require organizations to examine their own collective identities (Young 2001) and consider how they can intentionally influence the institutionalized discourse in society (Suddaby and Greenwood 2005; Zilber 2009). Looking across the nonprofit sector and the broader civil society space in Ireland, what can and should it do in the current context?

WHAT IS THE ROLE OF CIVIL SOCIETY?

The role of civil society in the context of economic collapse, political reconfiguration, and societal upheaval is curiously (largely) absent from public debate. This may reflect the reality that the conversation about the economic crisis has been focused on its financial dimensions. It may reflect the perspective that the Irish nonprofit sector, being so close to the state in its service delivery role, is difficult to distinguish from the state itself. It may also reflect the fact that without a coherent system of representative structures, the nonprofit sector is not sufficiently organized to take up a vociferous role in public debate. From an institutionalist perspective, the lack of an alternative narrative in the public policy debate reflects the institutionalization of the discourse around the fiscal crisis. That is, the constraints of the fiscal situation are "taken for granted" and have become cognitively accepted (Jepperson 1991).

Drawing on our knowledge of what nonprofit organizations are actually doing, and also on the needs that have arisen from the fallout from the economic crisis, we identify two elements that can be seen as key roles of Irish civil society today. They are:

- *To address the inequalities directly.* Many Irish citizens are suffering extreme personal economic consequences as a result of the economic collapse. Retirees whose pensions are resting on property values or bank shares, families with large mortgages who have become unemployed, and those who were already on the periphery of society in boom times are now struggling to hold on to the basics for daily life. The collapse of the means for so many to make a living has contributed to an increasingly unequal society in economic and social terms. A key role of nonprofit organizations is to challenge societal inequalities and to address them directly. This draws on the more instrumental role of nonprofit organizations as set out by Frumkin (2002) and would be consistent with a service delivery collective identity. In the current context, directly addressing inequalities requires nonprofit organizations to both challenge the societal system in which they emerge, and to work with those who are negatively affected by that system.

- *To inform and question policy change and to help define the narrative.*
  The post-2009 period in Ireland has been defined almost exclusively
  in economic terms, with the strongest, clearest commentary voices
  being those of economists. As economic necessity has driven government policy change, the narrative has been largely concerned with
  the management of the budget deficit and, more recently, the ways
  in which growth may be achieved in the battered economy. It could
  be argued that the important roles of civil society within this period
  include informing the policy debate, questioning policy changes and
  their implications, and, where possible, defining the narrative that
  accompanies the changes. This latter role is consistent with Frumkin's
  (2002) expressive role of nonprofit organizations and more of an
  activist collective identity. Given that many of the important decisions that are made arise from the external control of the economy,
  the voice of civil society must reach external stakeholders as well as
  Irish policymakers. An important analytical task for civil society is
  to identify what scope for manoeuvre there is within the IMF-EU
  program and, indeed, what functions lie outside its remit.

NONPROFIT ORGANIZATIONS AND SOCIAL CHANGE

Against the background of the potential roles for civil society, what is the
evidence of the actual impact of nonprofit organizations, individually
and collectively?

Individually, the impact of nonprofit organizations to effect social
change greatly reflects their power to mobilize a support base, to communicate effectively, and to influence the narrative on the status quo. If
nonprofits are to have any impact on the direction of economic and social
policy, they must be able to convince other stakeholders that they have the
capability to make sense of the crisis – and offer up options that have a
positive impact. However, nonprofit organizations are constrained by the
limits of the state. Proposals made to government need to be at worst cost-
neutral within the constraints of the existing institutionalized discourse.

Any assessment of the impact of the Irish nonprofit sector will conclude
that groupings or campaigns of nonprofit organizations across different
fields are not as robust as one might expect. This may reflect difficulties
that organizations have in reaching compromise, agreeing on common
positions, or making tough choices. Where they do manage to offer up
collective positions, such as has been attempted by the 17 organizations
of the former fourth pillar of Partnership, they are sometimes dismissed
by policy-makers as offering "unrealistic" solutions. And, individually or
collectively, if nonprofit organizations are to make an impact, they have to
be able to reach beyond the state and influence the external players who
are in effect controlling government decisions. Credible academics are

beginning to highlight that Europe had phases of far more indebtedness from which it emerged with enhanced social protection (Fahey 2012). However, the prevailing narrative, albeit socially constructed, is a very real constraint on these organizations. There is a very real danger that organizations which choose to advocate for ambitious social change will be dismissed as deluded. Therefore organizations need to intentionally consider how they can best influence or disrupt the existing institutionalized ways of interpreting the problem (Hargrave and Van de Ven 2006; Marti and Mair 2009).

Though civil society and most individual nonprofit organizations have not been known for flying a collective banner, one organization has stood out consistently since 2009. Social Justice Ireland (SJI) has taken the position that a role of civil society is to dispel the idea that the IMF-EU Programme equals "No Choices." Instead, it has challenged the state's response to the crisis and its treatment of the most vulnerable in society. In a note to the "Troika" in July 2011, Social Justice Ireland stated:

> In precarious times such as these a country, a government, a society or an international institution defines itself by: the cuts it makes; the people it protects; its effectiveness on economic growth/jobs; its actions on public services; the values underpinning its choices. In making decisions on these areas nothing is inevitable. Choices are always being made. (Social Justice Ireland [SJI] 2011, 3)

SJI may be seen as an isolated example that underscores the general inability within civil society to organize for social impact and social change. However, it is also an example of how a nonprofit organization may have significant influence. SJI demonstrates that even a very small organization is able to offer an interpretation of what the key issues are and challenge the current thinking on how they should be addressed. It is thus an important example of the role of civil society in the current Irish context to intentionally influence institutionalized beliefs about what is possible in terms of choices within a deep recession. As Kraatz (2009) highlights, a key role of leadership in these situations is to interpret and frame what is possible. Hargrave and Van de Ven (2009) drawing on Alinsky's *Reveille for Radicals: A Practical Primer for Realistic Radicals* (1969), argue that using contradictions skillfully and creatively is critical for activists seeking to bring about change to social institutions. The challenge of "institutional work" is to intentionally bring about changes to norms and practices (Lawrence and Suddaby 2006; Lawrence, Suddaby and Leca 2010) and ways of interpreting the crisis which have become part of the socially constructed reality. Activists have the capacity to influence this discourse by skillfully exploiting opportunities to present opportunities for reform (Hargrave and Van De Ven 2009). Crises provide greater opportunities for reforming institutions but this requires actors with the social skills and power to interpret the opportunities and bring about a change in how people think (Fligstein 1997; Marti and Mair 2009). By drawing on and combining the espoused logic of the state, actors can advocate for more efficient and effective social services under the rubric of reform. As the Irish SJI example highlights, this requires flexibility and the combining of multiple institutionalized logics to disrupt the prevailing discourse and institutionalize a new way of interpreting the problems (Marti and Mair 2009).

WHAT ARE THE OPTIONS FOR PRIVATE FUNDERS?

We now turn our attention to private funders in the current context and their options. How should private funders, specifically private nonprofit foundations with a mandate to support organizing within civil society, focus their efforts in an economic crisis? This question may not seem the most obvious one to ask in a context in which organized private funding has not been regarded as a key source of support for nonprofit organizing. Within Ireland, historically the foundation sector has been small both in numbers of organizations and total funds committed (Donoghue 2004). However, in the past two decades the profile of this sector has been raised, in the main by the engagement of the Atlantic Philanthropies. Currently, there is a membership body for private funders, Philanthropy Ireland, and a philanthropy-state deliberation body, the Forum on Philanthropy. These entities contribute to a nascent framework for organizing philanthropic action and for developing policy on the interface between private funding and the state. The two largest foundations operating in Ireland, the One Foundation and the Atlantic Philanthropies, are both spend-down foundations which, by 2013 and 2017 respectively, will have allocated all of their resources and exited the field (Proscio 2010). Currently, there is no indication that there will be any successors of comparable size or influence (Proscio 2010).

The ways in which foundations can engage under the current conditions are important considerations for private funders, and for the Atlantic Philanthropies and the One Foundation in particular. Both foundations have focused on capacity building within the sector and have been acutely aware of the importance of the sector-state relationship. They have also been involved in several co-funding projects with the state. When they have supported nonprofit organizations to develop significant voice and service delivery capacity, there has been the explicit expectation that substantial state funding as well as private funding will underpin future organizational operations. However, both funders are departing the field at a time when the capacity of the state is severely compromised.

Setting aside the context of economic crisis, there are several important factors that will influence the position a funder takes on how it will focus its resources. These include its value set, core logic of action, and capacity to act. These will all influence the way it addresses the identified need. The timeframe is also of importance. Spend down foundations are by definition working to shorter timeframes and are seeking to make a significant difference in the areas in which a need has been identified.

The need that is identified by the funder will reflect their self-perception. *Traditionalist* foundations tend to target their resources to social and medical innovations. *Venture philanthropic* foundations employ business logics and look to support causes for which revenue-generating models can be identified that will hopefully sustain the entity after their investment has ended. *Social justice* focused foundations focus on identifying areas of social division and support organizations and causes that can facilitate the poor to realize their power in society.

The self-perception of the foundation/private funder also has implications for their relationship, if any, with the state. For example, where possible, traditionalist foundations seek partnership with the state, on the assumption that the state will continue to support these organizations or activity domains after the departure of the funder. By contrast, venture funders tend to by-pass the state, looking instead for self-sustaining funding flows that keep the organizations they support independent of the state. Almost inevitably, social justice oriented funders tend to end up in conflict with the state, as in the course of addressing their identified need, they end up confronting and challenging the position of the state. The longer-term support of the causes or organizations that social justice foundations support deserve a well thought through exit strategy, given the difficulty of replacing the funder's support. And finally, some funders may be regarded as pragmatists, with their activities reflecting a hybrid of all three approaches.

Given the various influencing factors on how funders focus their resources, what options exist for funders in the current context in Ireland? We have seen that within the Irish economic crisis, the efforts of nonprofit organizations within civil society have been directed both to organizational preservation (both survival of the entity and survival of the mission focus) and, to some limited extent, to addressing the way the state is managing the context in which their survival has become so difficult. We see the same choices facing private funders. They may be concerned with the way in which the state is managing the economic crisis, or they may be focused on enabling nonprofit organizations to operate within the existing context. To the extent that funders are committed to supporting social change, both domains are important.

Funders who seek to question the way in which the state is coping with the crisis can take a long-term view, studying the longer-term implications of the neo-liberal economic orthodoxy that is guiding the government response under the direction of the Troika. In addition to the longer-term analysis, foundation funders may also engage in short-term questioning of the effectiveness and the equity of specific policies. For example, they may identify the short-term problems that may arise for marginalized people who can't cope effectively and question the wisdom of the policy decisions that exacerbate their situation.

Funders are centrally concerned with organizational outcomes and with securing the best social return for the investment they have made in nonprofit organizations (Brest and Harvey 2008; Kibbe et al. 2004). The reality is that the major philanthropic funders are leaving the field, the state has very limited resources, and there are to date no major new sources of funding on the horizon. As a result, foundations that have invested heavily in nonprofits are now working to assist them in moving forward without that foundation support. Foundations are likely to adopt a realist position vis-à-vis organizational support. How should limited resources be best allocated for maximum impact? The analysis that funders make of state policy, and both its long and short term implications, is likely to influence the decisions that they make about provision of support to nonprofit organizations. For example, funders who have invested in improving the effectiveness of nonprofit services and who have evaluated the outcomes produced by those organizations may see one of their options as helping the government to target resources at "proven" programs. Alternatively, funders' analysis of the current environment may lead them to the conclusion that the best option now is to assist sector organizations to rationalize in the face of further funding cuts. Thus, foundations may support merger talks within an organizational field with a view to preserving organizational capacity while lowering overheads. Finally, funders may adopt a hybrid approach in which they are concerned both with the policy context and nonprofit organizing. It would appear that in Ireland, despite the severe constraints that exist, funders are attempting to take a hybrid approach and have an eye to both influencing the policy context and to supporting nonprofit organizing.

Now that we have outlined the context, the changing sector-state relationship, the ways in which civil society is responding, and the impact of private funding, we return to the big picture. What are the critical choices facing the country and civil society, and what is the potential role of nonprofit organizations?

Conclusion: Critical Choices and Key Dimensions of Change

At time of writing, the Irish drama is playing out in the larger context of chaos in Greece, impending crisis in the Spanish banking system, uncertainly in Italy, and ongoing attempts by French and German leaders to provide direction. Within Ireland, the social context that remains paramount is that a third of our national budget continues to be spent on social protection. The state is struggling to respond adequately to social need while meeting the conditions of economic bailout. Immediate social need is painfully clear, quite apart from the aspirations for bringing about positive social change.

In this context, nonprofit organizations have a crucial role to play in influencing the narrative and the Irish political and social cultures that emerge. But, as we have seen so far, that crucial role is a potential one only. Thus far, Irish civil society has played only a very limited role. As outlined above, it is important that nonprofit leaders consider the ways they can influence and institutionalize new ways of analyzing and addressing the social problems which emerge during this period of fiscal and social crisis. History is replete with the design of ambitious social change initiatives during periods of crises. The Beveridge model of the welfare state was designed at the height of the second world war in 1941 as London was being bombed during the blitz and during a period when debt to GDP ratios were rising to unprecedented levels (Fahey 2012). The research on changing social institutions would suggest that if Irish nonprofit sector organizations can play a catalytic role in this civic space, it will require leadership which intentionally presents a vision whilst combining and adapting elements of the prevailing discourse on public sector reform (Hargrave and Van de Ven 2006; Marti and Mair 2009).

If Irish nonprofit organizations are to play a more central role, there are several critical choices facing them, individually and collectively. First, there is the issue of where to position and how to relate to the state. The status quo of relationships has dissolved; now is the time to establish and forge new relationships. It remains to be seen what new relationships will be established, and how nonprofit organizations will work to broker these.

Second, there is the question of how Irish nonprofits will develop effective relationship with other nonprofits. Outside the state-mandated and now defunct system of National Partnership, the sector has heretofore not seen value in seeking out other potential policy allies – or competitors – in order to develop working relationships.

There is also the internal, organizational concern of funding. The challenges of securing sufficient core funding to sustain organizational activities, and sufficient project funding to stay mission-focused, are consuming vast quantities of organizational capacity. The operating reality of Irish nonprofits is that they are in an ongoing state of managing sudden and profound organizational change. There is a need for private funders to understand the opportunity which exists for civil society to play a role in reshaping social institutions, and for nonprofits to seize that opportunity.

Irish nonprofits must balance their immediate need for funds against their desire to maintain independence in the use of those funds. They must grapple with the need to regulate themselves – with no resources to do so – in the absence of the full implementation of charities legislation. They must navigate the political sphere, lobby for recognition with those who are really controlling the policy process, and make the case for their own engagement in that process. Perhaps the greatest challenge for both funders and nonprofit organizations will be to dis-embed themselves from the cognitive patterns of thinking which have become institutionalized within the sector. Then, the sector must recognize the need to present alternative visions of the future that are compelling and realistic, and which offer hope.

For decades, mutual dependence has characterized state-nonprofit relations in Ireland. The system has been underpinned by functioning government-nonprofit relations. Now that the system is undermined, and the relationships are in turmoil, there is an opportunity for Irish nonprofits to play a critical role in influencing the narrative of society, and the political and social cultures which emerge. Perhaps now, despite the desperately difficult social and organizational conditions, there is an opportunity to redraft the rule book.

NOTE

1. A fifth pillar, the Environmental Pillar, was also engaged in social partnership negotiations in 2009.

REFERENCES

Alinsky, S.D. 1969. *Reveille for Radicals*. New York: Vintage Books.
Binder, A. 2007. "For Love and Money: Organizations' creative responses to multiple environmental logics." *Theory and Society* 36 (6): 547-71.
Brest, P. and H. Harvey. 2008. *A Strategic Plan for Smart Philanthropy*. New York: Bloomberg Press.
Central Statistics Office (CSO). 2011a. *National Income and Expenditure Annual Results for 2011*. At http://www.cso.ie/en/media/csoie/releasespublications/documents/economy/current/nie.pdf (accessed 25 June 2011).
—. 2011b. *Quarterly National Household Survey Q1 2011 Results*. At http://www.cso.ie/en/newsandevents/pressreleases/2011pressreleases/quarterlynationalhouseholdsurveyquarter12011 (accessed 25 June 2011).
Community and Voluntary Pillar (CVP). 2011. "Securing a Viable Future in Precarious Times: Briefing Paper on the Decisions Government Should Make." Dublin: Community and Voluntary Pillar, January.
Department of Social Protection. 2011. *Statistical Information on Social Welfare Services 2010*. Dublin: Government Publications Office.
Donnelly-Cox, G. and S.M. Cannon. 2010. "Responses of Non-Profit Organisations to Altered Conditions of Support: The Shifting Irish Landscape." *Voluntary Sector Review* 1 (3): 335-53.
Donnelly-Cox, G. and S. McGee. 2011. "Between Relational Governance and Regulation of the Third Sector: The Irish Case." In *Governance and Regulation in the Third Sector: International Perspectives*, ed. S. Phillips and S.R. Smith, 99-114. New York: Routledge.

Donnelly-Cox, G., C. Reid, C. Begley, J. Finn, and D. Harmon. Forthcoming. "Nonprofit-State Relations in Ireland: Contexts, Issues and Alternatives." *Nonprofit Policy Forum.*

Donoghue, F. 2004. *Foundations in Ireland.* Dublin: Centre for Nonprofit Management.

Donoghue, F., G. Prizeman, A. O'Regan, and V. Noel. 2006. *The Hidden Landscape: First Forays into Mapping Nonprofit Organisations in Ireland.* Trinity College Dublin: Centre for Nonprofit Management.

Edelman Trust Barometer. 2011. *Annual Global Study.* Available at http://trust.edelman.com/ (accessed 25 June 2011).

—. 2012. *Annual Global Study.* Available at http://trust.edelman.com/ (accessed 25 June 2011).

Fahey, T. 2012. "Welfare and Debt: Lessons from Beveridge and his Times." In *Does the European Social Model have a Future?*, ed. S. Healy and B. Reynolds, 18-29. Dublin: Social Justice Ireland.

Fligstein, N. 1997. "Social Skill and Institutional Theory." *American Behavioral Scientist* 40 (4): 397-405.

Frumkin, P. 2002. *On Being Nonprofit: A Conceptual and Policy Primer.* Cambridge: Massachusetts: Harvard University Press.

Hargrave, T.J. and A.H. Van de Ven. 2006. "A Collective Action Model of Institutional Innovation." *Academy of Management Review* 31 (4): 864-88.

—. 2009. "Institutional Work as the Creative Embrace of Contradiction." In *Institutional Work Actors and Agency in Institutional Studies of Organizations,* ed. T.B. Lawrence, R. Suddaby, and B. Leca, 120-140. Cambridge: Cambridge University Press.

Healy, J.A. and C.M.A. Clark. 2006. "The Economics of Altruism in a Time of Affluence." In *Social Policy in Ireland: Principles, Practices and Problems,* ed. S. Healy and B. Reynolds, 453-68. Dublin: Liffey Press.

International Monetary Fund/European Union (IMF/EU). 2011. *Memorandum of Understanding between the IMF, EU and the Government of Ireland.*

Jepperson, R.L. 1991. "Institutions, Institutional Effects, and Institutionalism." In *The New Institutionalism in Organizational Analysis,* ed. W.W. Powell and P.J. DiMaggio, 164-82. Chicago: University of Chicago Press.

Kearney, I. 2012. "Economic Challenges." In *Does the European Social Model have a Future?*, ed. S. Healy and B. Reynolds, 1-17. Social Justice Ireland.

Kelleher, S. and D. O'Connor. 2010. *Fundraising Performance: The First Annual Report on Fundraising in Ireland.* Dublin: 2into3.

—. 2011. *Fundraising Performance: The Second Annual Report on Fundraising in Ireland.* Dublin: 2into3.

Kibbe, B., K. Enright, J. Lee, A. Culwell, L. Sonsini, S. Speirn, and M. Tuan. 2004. *Funding Effectiveness: Lessons in building nonprofit capacity.* Washington: Grantmakers for Effective Organizations/Jossey-Bass.

Kirby, P. 2011. *Briefing Paper on the Irish Elections 2011.* At www.ul.ie/peadarkirby/kirbypublications_files/FEB.pdf (accessed 23 June 2011).

Kraatz, M.S. 2009. "Leadership as Institutional Work: a bridge to the other side." In *Institutional Work Actors and Agency in Institutional Studies of Organizations,* ed. T.B. Lawrence, R. Suddaby, and B. Leca, 59-91. Cambridge: Cambridge University Press.

Lau, E. 2011. The Recommendations of the OECD Public Management Review – Ireland 2008 – still valid? A paper to the Wheel's conference, Putting People at the Heart of Public Services. OECD.

Lawrence, T.B. and R. Suddaby. 2006. "Institutions and Institutional Work." In *Handbook of Organization Studies* , ed. S. Clegg, C. Hardy, T.B. Lawrence, and W.R. Nord, 215-254. London: Sage Publications.

Lawrence, T., R. Suddaby, and B. Leca. 2010. "Institutional Work: Refocusing Institutional Studies of Organization." *Journal of Management Inquiry* 20 (1): 52-58.

Maier, F. and M. Meyer. 2011. "Managerialism and Beyond: Discourses of Civil Society Organization and Their Governance Implications." *Voluntas: International Journal of Voluntary and Nonprofit Organizations* 22 (4): 1-26.

Marti, I. and J. Mair. 2009. "Bringing Change into the Lives of the Poor: Entrepreneurship outside traditional boundaries." In *Institutional Work Actors and Agency in Institutional Studies of Organizations,* ed. T.B. Lawrence, R. Suddaby, and B. Leca, 92-119. Cambridge: Cambridge University Press.

Moran, D. 2011. *LSE Blog.* At eprints.lse.ac.uk/33441/1/blogs.lse.ac.uk-The_spectacular_fall_from_grace_of_Ireland%E2%80%99s_Fianna_Fail_should_serve_as_a_warning_to_the_UK_and_othe.pdf (accessed 23 June 2011).

O'Donnell, R. and D. Thomas. 2006. "Social Partnership and the Policy Process." In *Social Policy in Ireland: Principles, Practices and Problems,* ed. S. Healy and B. Reynolds, 109-32. Dublin: Liffey Press.

OECD. 2010. *OECD Economic Outlook.* Vol. 2010/2. Paris: OECD Publishing.

Phillips, N. and N. Malhotra. 2008. "Taking Social Construction Seriously: Extending the Discursive Approach in Institutional Theory." In *Handbook of Organizational Institutional Theory,* eds. R. Greenwood, C. Oliver, K. Sahlin, and R. Suddaby, 702-20. London: Sage

Proscio, T. 2010. "When Aims & Objectives Rhyme: How Two of Ireland's Largest Foundations Found Common Ground." At http://www.atlantic philanthropies.org/learning/case-study-when-aims-objectives-rhyme-how-two-ireland%E2%80%99s-largest-foundations-found-common-gr (accessed 23 June 2011).

Salamon, L.M. 1993. "The Marketization of Welfare: Changing nonprofit and for-profit roles in the American welfare state." *Social Service Review* 67 (1): 16-39.

Smith, S.R. and M. Lipsky. 1993. "Nonprofits for Hire: The welfare state in the age of contracting." *Social Service Review* 69: 310.

Social Justice Ireland (SJI). 2011. "Note for: IMF/ECB/EC From: Social Justice Ireland Re: current Bailout Agreement in Ireland, Meeting on Monday, July 11, 2011." Dublin: Social Justice Ireland.

Suddaby, R. and R. Greenwood. 2005. "Rhetorical Strategies of Legitimacy." *Administrative Science Quarterly* 50 (2): 35-67.

Swidler, A. 1986. "Culture in Action: Symbols and strategies." *American Sociological Review* 51 (2): 273-286.

The Wheel. 2011. "Structured Dialogue with the Community and Voluntary Pillar: Submission to Government Consultation." Dublin: The Wheel, 11 March.

Young, D.R. 2001. "Organizational Identity in Nonprofit Organizations: Strategic and structural implications." *Nonprofit Management and Leadership* 12 (2): 139-157.

Zilber, T.B. 2009. "Institutional Maintenance as Narrative Acts." In *Institutional Work Actors and Agency in Institutional Studies of Organizations,* ed. T.B. Lawrence, R. Suddaby, and B. Leca, 205-235. Cambridge: Cambridge University Press.

Chapter 8

Citizen Advocacy or Death from a Thousand Cuts: What Determines the Fate of Third Sector Organizations in Welfare States after the Economic Crisis? A View from Ireland's Two Jurisdictions

Nicholas Acheson

Introduction

This chapter adopts a comparative approach to throw light on dynamics that shape the responses of third sector organizations to the current global financial crisis. Both the nature of the crisis and the extent of retrenchment in welfare budgets vary greatly between different countries (Farnsworth and Irving 2011; Kuhner 2012). Despite well documented trends towards greater integration of the third sector into the governance of welfare cross-nationally (Gidron and Bar 2009; Kendall 2010a; Bode 2006), there remains considerable variation in the ways that this has been done in line with broad welfare regime types.

This paper draws on the experience of the third sectors in each of Ireland's two jurisdictions. I argue that the continuum of responses depends not just on the unfolding context, but also on the narratives that third sector organizations draw on to understand their options. These narratives are formed within specific institutional histories of relationships

Government-Nonprofit Relations in Times of Recession, ed. Rachel Laforest. Montreal and Kingston: Queen's Policy Studies Series, McGill-Queen's University Press. © 2013 The School of Policy Studies, Queen's University at Kingston. All rights reserved.

within individual jurisdictions. The cases of Northern Ireland and Ireland exhibit contrasting responses at different ends of this continuum and their consideration can help uncover some of the ways these factors interlink. The economic contexts of Northern Ireland and Ireland are of course unique and their respective exposure to the economic downturn has different elements. As part of the UK, Northern Ireland remains outside the eurozone. As a result, the onset of recession in the local economy was for a time masked by public expenditure, which only began to contract in 2010. In Ireland, on the other hand, the banking collapse in 2008 had an immediate impact as it threatened to turn the years of a booming economy into an existential threat to the future of the country as an independent state. Membership of the eurozone and the terms of the international bailout from the International Monetary Fund and the European Central Bank in 2010 have severely squeezed budgets. They also forced a re-examination of the methods of public administration that had previously been extolled as an important factor in the economic success of the country in the years leading up to the collapse.

These differences are important for understanding the role of third sector organizations in governance arrangements in each jurisdiction since 2008. However, it is argued here that to understand the choices that third sector organizations actually make in response to the crisis, what matters more is the way they interpret their roles, the extent to which there is a guiding narrative about the role of the third sector as a single policy actor, and the extent to which they have access to narratives that continue to ground them in constituencies of identity and interest. These narratives are themselves a function of the manner in which third sector organizations have become more or less integrated into the structures of welfare states. In that sense, the fate of the sector is a chapter in a larger story about national adjustments to the forms of delivery and scope of welfare entitlement in the face of recession and collapsing budgets.

In Northern Ireland relations between the local state and the third sector have been guided by a variation of the "hyperactive" development of relations in the UK as a whole (Kendall 2010b). Northern Ireland has its own compact (recently renewed as a "concordat"), a commitment to a narrative of partnership, and a history of significant investment in third sector infrastructure to mediate the relationship. The effects of budget restrictions began to be felt in 2009 to 2010. The response of the local administration has been to adapt the existing structures to exert much more direct control over how these reducing budgets are being spent in a state-led strategy informed by neo-liberal values of efficiency and the need to bolster private sector economic performance. The argument will be that the historical context of the Northern Irish conflict and a strong sectoral identity has left the sector over-committed to partnership with little room for manoeuvre. The political structures have been hostile to the emergence of identity or interest-based movements that would otherwise be a source of renewal.

In contrast, in Ireland, the nature of the welfare state has made interest group representation a relatively more important function of the third sector. Coherent national policies towards the third sector as a single policy actor have never developed (Donoghue and Larragy 2009). Rather, the system has been marked by a pragmatic invitation to leading interest groups within the sector to join a community and voluntary pillar in national partnership structures otherwise comprising trades unions, employers, farming interests, and government. The main business of the partnership was wage negotiation, but its focus broadened to achieving national consensus on broad social and economic policy.

After the banking crisis in September 2008, the Irish government abandoned the partnership commitments entered into only the previous year and collapsed the partnership structures. Members of the community and voluntary pillar were forced to refocus from long-term strategies to achieve social and economic gains for their constituencies to firefighting cuts. A dramatic campaign against restrictions in access to free health care for older people in 2008 has subsequently been a template for action for these groups as they return to their interest group representation origins.

FROM SECURING THE PEACE TO SECURING A PLACE IN PUBLIC
SERVICE MODERNIZATION: THE FATE OF NORTHERN IRELAND'S
THIRD SECTOR

Structuring the Relationship with Government

Northern Ireland remains a post-conflict transitional society in which many of the underlying dynamics and legacies of the conflict are yet to be resolved. Relations between the two main ethno-religious communities in Northern Ireland remain wary (Devine, Kelly and Robinson 2011) and across many measures, the evidence suggests that significant risks to long-term stability remain (Nolan 2012). This underlying task of transition (variously conceived) provided a framing narrative for voluntary and community sector engagement with government and it continues to inform the context of relations between the local state and civil society.

The 1998 political settlement produced a compulsory coalition between two nationalist party blocs representing each of the Irish and British national identities within Northern Ireland and now, the cross-community Alliance Party. As in previous elections, the most recent Assembly election in 2011 had almost no transfers of votes between the two main ethnoreligious blocs (Nolan 2012). As a result, the two main parties are not in competition with each other for votes and consequently, ideologically based policy directions are never decided at the ballot box. This has tended to result in government by the "lowest common denominator" (Gray and Birrell 2012) with political differences over policy, when they arise, never being resolved and a distinct risk-averse and extremely path dependent style of public administration. "Northern Ireland is a policy-light zone, almost a policy free zone.... It's because the inter-communal divide and constitutional issues take up so much precedence and all the policy issues are seen through the prism of the position of the respective communities" (Trench cited in Nolan 2012, 121).

The conflict in Northern Ireland over national identity lasted over 30 years and has had a devastating long-term effect on society and the economy (Horgan 2006). The conflict continues to impact the policy challenges faced by government in dealing with that legacy. This political context has also shaped the development of the voluntary sector as a policy player. Three distinct aspects of this context can be helpfully identified.

The first concerns the weakness of interest group representation in a context where politics has generally been constructed as a zero sum game between competing ethno-religious blocks (Acheson and Milofsky 2008). Organizations built around identities and interests that cut across ethno-religious divisions have no political space to articulate these identities and interests in ways that challenge ethno-religious divisions and they have generally found it prudent to avoid doing so (Acheson 2010).

Second, however, voluntary and community organizations have exploited their perceived capacity to cross the ethno-religious divide and set about constructing a distinctive role in Northern Irish society around peace-building and transition from conflict. In the early years of the peace process in the 1990s, third sector organizations sold themselves, and came to be seen, as important building blocks in establishing and then sustaining the community-based elements that underpinned the paramilitary ceasefires (Acheson et al. 2004; Acheson and Milofsky 2008). By 1993, the then direct rule administration run by a Conservative government at Westminster acknowledged that the state had a responsibility to support and nurture community development in a policy shift that also had a clear, albeit distinct focus on community relations (Morrow 2012). As a result, third sector organizations came to believe themselves to be and were seen as an essential element in the core task of government, "the alpha and omega of public life" (Morrow 2012, 45), which was the transition from conflict. This re-imagining of interest group and identity representation rather than providing a secure base for maintaining a critical distance from government, put the voluntary and community sector on the same side as government in a shared task, locking them into partnership.

The third element concerns the way that partnership continues to be understood in Northern Ireland, making it quite distinctive to recent policy developments in England, especially (Taylor 2012). There is little enthusiasm among the governing political parties for viewing the voluntary and community sector as an alternative to the state. Unlike in England, the 1998 compact has been renewed as a "concordat" on very similar terms to the first document. The political settlement that gave the two ethno-religious blocks in Northern Ireland an equal status in its government, has guaranteed the state and its institutions as the main source of stability and social advance. Partnership with the third sector thus continues to make sense in this context. The current Programme for Government makes this clear by calling for partnership with both the private and voluntary sectors to underpin the social and economic advance for which government is clearly seen as having a primary responsibility (Northern Ireland Executive 2011).

The Trap Closes

The formal structures, built around a compact and a joint government voluntary sector forum, were similar to elsewhere in the UK. They were initially based on a distinct agenda built around a shared understanding between the sector and government that this transition process was a joint enterprise with a guaranteed and important role for community-based organizations in particular (Knox 2003; Acheson 2010).

This was never an easy relationship. The members of the Assembly elected in 1998 felt that the sector was playing too big a role; it was time for it to "stand aside" (McCall and Williamson 2002). There was a lack of political commitment to the Civic Forum, a participative advisory body to government, a third of whose members were reserved for nominees from voluntary and community organizations. But nevertheless the joint government voluntary sector forum has continued to meet. In practice, the accountability mechanisms proved to be weak, but the principle of partnership between government and the sector was never formally abandoned. That principle provided a platform for the sector to continue to press the case that it had a right to be at the table.

These structures might have provided a leading role to the sector in shaping the emergence of a more distinctive set of Northern Ireland policies had the Assembly elected in 1998 survived and been able to develop its nascent and distinctive welfare regime (Horgan 2006). However, the suspension of the devolved institutions between 2002 and 2007 meant that the direct rule New Labour administration based in London introduced a series of reforms that closely followed English precedent, most notably a speeding up of the outsourcing of public services. In effect, the modernizing transitional society narrative to which the voluntary and community sector elites were committed was captured by a narrative about modernizing public services through extending competition and choice that had become central to Labour's third term of government (Acheson 2010; Lister 2010).

At the centre of this dynamic was the imbalance between funding for peace building and funding for delivering public services. Funds for peace building were enormous at the end of the 1990s and the beginning of the 2000s. But almost all this money came from the European Union, the International Fund for Ireland, and private philanthropy, bodies with no responsibility for public policy in Northern Ireland. Between 1994 and 2006, for example, the European Union alone had contributed over €1.6 billion to the Peace Programme, almost €1.billion of which was channeled through the voluntary and community sector (Special European Union Programmes Body 2008). In contrast, government funding for the sector was always focused on public service delivery. As the European Union programs wound down after 2006 and became more closely focused on achieving reconciliation outcomes, funding for public service delivery continued to grow.

Another underpinning factor was the extent to which the Northern Ireland third sector was dependent on government funding. Alcock (2012) notes that the proportion of funding from statutory sources is 61 percent in Northern Ireland compared to a UK average of 36 percent. This relatively high level of dependency coupled with an immediate need to replace lost incomes from the variety of peace building related programs had the understandable consequence of many organizations repositioning themselves as essential public service modernizers. Because this crucial narrative shift took place within a continuing partnership discourse, the significance of what was going was hidden. By the time the devolved institutions were re-established in 2007, the Northern Ireland voluntary sector was as reliant on contracts to deliver services on behalf of government for their income as their counterparts in England (Acheson 2010). The most recent evidence suggests that 58 percent of all third sector income in 2009/10 was earned from the provision of goods and services, higher than the UK average of 54.7 percent (Northern Ireland Council for Voluntary Action 2012; National Council for Voluntary Organisations 2012).

Despite the switch in focus to public service delivery, the direct rule administration that governed Northern Ireland between 2002 and 2007 also continued to view the third sector as having a central role in the transition from conflict in its 2005 policy, *A Shared Future* (Office of First Minister and Deputy First Minister 2005). The policy extolled the ability of the sector to generate bridging social capital and offered it the promise of access to funding streams that would facilitate this contribution. But there was no time to integrate this policy initiative into the development of joint structures before the devolved administration was re-established in 2007.

One of the first acts of the new administration was to shelve this policy and in the five years since, it has been unable to agree a replacement. It is one of a number of critical policy issues that are blocked because compromise between the two party blocks in the Northern Ireland Assembly has proved impossible to reach, in this case because each is committed to a diametrically opposed interpretation of the basis of the Northern Ireland conflict. As a consequence, there has been no policy space for the sector to argue for an updated version of its 1990s position on its role in conflict transition. In this context, there has been little room for alternative strategies based on a return to interest group representation. In effect, the third sector policy field was left open to be wholly populated by concerns over public service modernization. The trap was effectively shut.

Consequences

Evidence from England on the ability of third sector organizations to maintain a degree of ambiguity despite close involvement in public service delivery (Cairns et al. 2010; Buckingham 2012) suggests that the situation in Northern Ireland may be more nuanced and complex than this overview may suggest. Nevertheless the pattern is quite clear and the potential consequences as government budgets are squeezed are clearly identifiable in the light of emerging evidence.

While there is evidence that budget reductions are affecting a wide variety of policy areas and programs, this section will focus on three key emerging themes. First, there has been a significant reduction in support for voluntary sector infrastructural organizations with evidence of cuts of 50 percent or more in government funding, associated with a redirection of money towards frontline services. Historically, organizations that provide support to other sector organizations have been well funded in Northern Ireland. At the time writing (June 2012) most figures for the current financial year had still not been published. But, published figures show the public advice support services being particularly hard hit, with the Law Centre Northern Ireland losing more than half its funding and the Northern Ireland Association of Citizens' Advice Bureaux losing almost half. The community development agency, Community Change, has seen its funding reduced by more than £110,000, down from just over £198,000 in 2011/12 to just over £88,000 in the current financial year (Department for Social Development 2012).

Second, effective access to policy-making by interest groups continues to stall (Waterhouse Bradley 2012). At the same time, the formal compact structures have been renewed in the 2011 concordat, particularly the joint government voluntary sector forum. This forum has been made directly accountable to the Assembly for the first time in an attempt to give it a greater impact on individual government spending departments.

Third, while the new concordat is worded in almost the same terms as the 1998 compact, how partnership is understood by the local administration is vividly illustrated by a willingness among government ministers to act unilaterally without consultation to force funding bids from consortia of organizations in an effort to secure efficiency savings. While forced mergers remain rare, compulsory consortia have been instigated with housing associations and now the regional infrastructure bodies as a condition of receiving continuing government support. Frozen or decreasing budgets across most spending programs are accelerating the introduction of competitive tendering under public procurement rules for government contracts in policy areas like social care, housing, and welfare to work. We see the formation of a view within government that conceives of partnership as a matter of resource acquisition for the better achievement of government objectives. Although the Northern Ireland government still talks of partnership, it is a misnomer. This new environment is closer to a grab for the resources that third sector organizations can offer, whether these are legitimacy, or expertise, or gains in efficiency.

Civil Society in Ireland: A Return to the Grassroots

Structuring Civil Society in National Partnership

As a response to economic and political problems in the 1980s, the system of government was substantially changed to include a wide variety of interests in formal partnership arrangements at local and at national levels (Adshead and Quinn 1998). The national partnership structures were initially adopted as a response to the fiscal crisis in the 1980s. In this context, national wage bargaining was conducted against a background of fiscal restraint and the liberalizing and deregulation of the economy in a form of competitive neo-corporatism (Roche and Cradden 2003; Carney et al. 2011). The formal partners for the first three agreements (up to 2000) comprised the government, employers, trades unions, and farming interests. The success of these initial social pacts was underpinned by agreement among the partners over major economic and social objectives, and the need for compromise unified by the understanding that "essentially the purpose of the partnership is to set pay" (Adshead 2011, 85).

At the same time, the economic crisis of the 1980s had seen a resurgence of activity in civil society, particularly in the fields of unemployment, social welfare, and community development (Larragy 2006). These new organizations drew on older Irish traditions of social protest, were activist in orientation, and sought to adopt a range of tactics to achieve their goals (Daly 2008). Their analysis and goals tended to be based on a critique of the neo-liberal assumptions around which the national social partnership was constructed (Powell and Geoghegan 2004). Nevertheless, in 1996, representatives of these organizations were invited by the government to join the national partnership structures as the community and voluntary pillar (CVP) to become party to the fourth national partnership agreement, *Programme 2000,* changing their status from external critics to critical participants (Larragy 2006, 376; Meade 2005).

They were never party to the wage negotiations that were the core business of the national partnership. However, subsequent participation of the CVP was structured by a weak articulation of social rights in the Irish welfare state that meant that the role of civil society actors in representing the interests of people most reliant on welfare transfers in national policy debates was particularly important (Carney et al. 2012, forthcoming). A process of institutionalization among civil society actors was thus linked to a strategy of seeking influence within the economic and social policy decision-making structures in Irish governance to make long-term gains (Daly 2008; Meade 2005).

Deeply frustrated by the reality of working in the national partnership structures by the early 2000s, members of the pillar nevertheless at that time found it difficult to articulate alternative strategies (Meade 2005). Partnership was the only game in town for some. Others, notably the Community Workers' Cooperative – which, unable to sign up to the fifth agreement, the *Programme for Sustaining Progress,* 2003, had walked away from the partnership as part of an alliance of organizations, the Community Platform – subsequently found its funding cut despite a positive evaluation (Larragy 2006; Adshead 2011).

Critics of the role of civil society in Ireland's partnership structures have noted that the underlying thrust of the Irish state's policy towards civil society as "being one to move it from concerns with redistributive justice and social change towards the provision of services" (Kirby 2010, 177). Noting how community development has been reinvented as consumerist welfare provision, Geoghegan and Powell (cited in Kirby 2010) suggest that the interpretation of active citizenship as the exercise of self-reliance has had the effect of strengthening the state's hold over civil society, a process that Kirby (2010, 107) calls "bringing civil society to heel."

The former chief executive of the Equality Authority, who is also previous Chair of the Community Workers' Cooperative, has in addition suggested that the state has deliberately sought to marginalize dissent through an "overt, organized and aggressive agenda of control" (Crowley cited in Kirby 2010, 178). In Meade's (2005) analysis, partnership structures trapped civil society in a process of governance based on a particular analysis of social and economic development over which it had little bargaining power; this had the effect of denying Ireland's public sphere a range of critical voices.

This pessimistic account of incorporation and control, however, misses an important aspect of the impact of the community and voluntary pillar on social partnership in Ireland that it is necessary to consider in order to understand what has happened since the partnership structures collapsed in 2008. Both Meade (2005) and Adshead (2011) suggest that for some members of the CVP, being at the table was an end in itself. Some organizations, the National Women's Council of Ireland is cited as one, accepted subsequent invitations from the government to return to the partnership in a reconstituted pillar having earlier left as part of the Community Platform. It is arguable that their presence meant that the negotiations on the partnership agreements were unable to ignore the question of how the gains of the years of high growth in the Irish economy should be distributed beyond a carve-up in wage and taxation levels between private and public sector workers (Adshead 2011). The fact that this question was not satisfactorily resolved in this context helped undermine the consensus of both ends and means that had sustained the early years of the partnership's history and hence its legitimacy. By the 2008 banking collapse, there was a "total absence of consensus between the social partners over the causes of the crisis, its consequences and its remedy" (Adshead 2011, 90).

A Return to the Grassroots in the Face of Economic Collapse

In 2008 the Irish government precipitated the current debt crisis by guaranteeing all the debts of the collapsing banking sector, turning private debt into public debt. It walked away from the national partnership agreement as being no longer valid in the new circumstances. The 17 members of the CVP had to rapidly change from participating in long-term social planning to fire fighting cuts in services. This occurred in the most dramatic way possible when the government announced reductions in entitlements to free health care to the over 70s in the budget of October 2008, barely a month after the banking collapse.

Both the main national organizations for older people, Age Action Ireland and the Irish Senior Citizens' Parliament, had been full members of the CVP and had built up strong reputations for expert policy advice. Under their influence, the last partnership agreement had contained commitments to improve the situation of older people, including pensions, long-term care services, housing and health care that had been incorporated into the 2007–2011 Programme for Government. Within days of the budget announcement, however, the Senior Citizens' Parliament had mobilized a demonstration of 15,000 older people outside the Irish parliament building. At the time, the press described it as an "unprecedented" street protest. Age Action Ireland had facilitated a public meeting in a downtown Dublin venue in which government ministers were shouted down by angry pensioners, an event that received top billing in that evening's main television news. The result was a partial climb-down by the government at the time, and a subsequent unwillingness to tamper with the old age pension in later deficit reduction budgets.

The central civil society protagonists in these events had continued to sustain and nurture a wide membership base through the partnership period. At the time of the budget protests, the Senior Citizens' Parliament had 460 affiliated organizations representing about 100,000 people and Age Action Ireland has around 2,500 individual and community organization members in addition to about 300 corporate members. The twin-track approach of engaging fully with the partnership structures while at the same time, nurturing their membership and retaining their focus on lobbying, enabled them to switch tactics very quickly. Interview data gathered in 2011 suggests that both organizations saw lobbying as their core activity. The Parliament had been founded in 1993 as part of a European initiative to strengthen national interest group representation among older people across Europe and has had no other function; it was established with strong government support (officially launched by the President of Ireland) but later lost its core funding after receiving support from a large philanthropic foundation. Age Action Ireland has advocacy and information as their core provision and while it does provide services, these are perceived mainly as a means of income generation. For both, the partnership structures were treated as just another point of access to government and one that had its costs. One interviewee said:

> Our view was always that this was an added access point, but we would have to continue advocacy in terms of undertaking research, commenting on government papers or proposals, offering alternative views and so on.... I suppose people thought it was better to be in than out, but we were then seen as a privileged club and some people felt we were in a club and that was very unhelpful in representing the community and voluntary sector or older people. Because we were selected and brought in by government, there were no mechanisms for communicating with or involving the wider sector. It was another weakness – divorced from the political process and then divorced from our constituency. That's a pretty high price to pay for that."

Both these organizations had retained a strong insider/outsider status in respect to the partnerships, retaining their capacity to act outside these structures where necessary. Although the issue of access to health care evinced a great deal of public anger, they were able to mobilize their grassroots within days. They shaped public anger as a breach of the social contract between the state and older people and a breach of the trust that had underpinned the partnership process itself, decisively defeating in public opinion a government narrative around the necessity for national sacrifice in the face of the economic crisis.

But emerging evidence suggests that all 17 members of the CVP, including those that had tended to treat the partnership as the only game in town (Meade 2005) have adapted tactically to the collapse of the partnership structures in order to sustain their focus on representing the interests of people perceived to be particularly vulnerable to the effects of the recession (Carney et al. 2012, forthcoming). There has been a clear collective shift from partnership working to grassroots action, with a majority citing the protests over older people's access to health care as a template for action in the future. This is underpinned by the perception that the preservation of the rates of state old age pension since 2008 has provided evidence of the effectiveness of the mobilization tactics deployed in that campaign.[1]

The usual care should be taken not to generalize too readily from this evidence. The members of the CVP are not typical of the Irish voluntary and community sector, which is dominated by small and local associations (Acheson et al. 2004; Daly 2008). They were chosen by government because of their capacity to represent the interests of broad categories of citizens at a national level and it is arguable that this capacity has enabled them to respond to the collapse of partnership in the ways that they have. Meade's (2005) earlier account of the discomfort many of them expressed in feeling trapped in structures they were not sure would deliver for their constituencies may in retrospect be an indicator of their later response to the government's decision to collapse the partnership. While there is at present a paucity of evidence on the impact of the recession in Ireland on local voluntary action, the close embrace of community organizations and the state and the deepening crisis of poverty and unemployment as the recession has taken hold, have together turned advocacy into a fight for survival and a defence of threatened public services (Crowley 2012).

A further contextual factor should also be borne in mind. In contrast to Northern Ireland, there is no strong *sectoral* identity in Ireland with no equivalent of the Northern Ireland Council for Voluntary Action and no sense of a strategic partnership between the state and the *sector* as a single policy actor as has developed in the UK as whole. Donoghue and Larragy (2009, 122-123) note that a white paper on voluntary action published in 2000 was never followed up, partly as a consequence of fragmentation of responsibility between government departments, but also because of a lack of an "institutional home" within civil society for the idea of the *sector* as a contributor to a public sphere and public policy-making. The creation of the CVP and its invitation to participate in the national partnership structures was a pragmatic attempt by government to bring interest group representation inside. But the lack of an underlying narrative as to what the relationship between the *sector* as a whole and government was based on may have paradoxically left the organizations within the CVP freer to reinvent themselves once the structures disappeared.

Conclusion

The crucial difference between Ireland's two jurisdictions is the links between organized civil society and the citizen interests that they represent. In Northern Ireland, the UK model of strong horizontal policy towards the sector as a single policy actor was adapted in the context of the peace process. The partnership model has in practice locked voluntary and community organizations into a tight embrace, with a local administration seeking to use it to further a state-controlled remodeling of public services informed by a faith in markets to drive efficiency and innovation. The representation of interests in the public sphere has been further weakened by a political settlement that vests responsibility for social and economic reform in a state-run administration controlled by a compulsory coalition of competing ethno-religious blocks. De-investment in infrastructure and a redirection of available funds to direct service delivery against tightly defined targets is turning back over 20 years of development of a relationship originally founded on a mutual recognition of partnership as a basis for securing and underpinning the peace process. Together these factors have left community and voluntary organizations in Northern Ireland without plausible alternative narratives for a renewal of mission.

In Ireland, the immediate future of many community based and voluntary organizations is precarious in the extreme. But the collapse in national partnership structures has revealed a possibility for grassroots action around a defence of publicly funded welfare as organizations have started to adapt to the new times by reconnecting with their bases with which many have retained strong links. The historical role of grassroots civic action to counter structural deficiencies in the Irish welfare state model provides an alternative narrative for at least some organizations to turn to.

The emergence of many of these organizations in the last recession in the 1980s suggests that there is a history that activists can draw on. While there may be some evidence for cautious optimism for future voluntary and community organizations as bearers of interests in the public sphere in Ireland, this has to be set against the predominance of the view in national debates about the economic crisis that welfare is a cost that can be ill-afforded and is too generous (Considine and Dukelow 2011, 2012). Ireland shows little likelihood of turning from the neo liberal perspective and policies that fed the boom years between 1988 and 2008. In this context the partial success of the pensioner protests in 2008 may turn out to have been an aberration. In the absence of political debate about what sort of welfare state needs to survive in Ireland after the dust has settled, there are currently few opportunities for interest groups to contribute. In short, nobody in particular is listening.

These two contrasting Irish cases are suggestive in thinking about the fate of voluntary and community organizations in post-austerity welfare states. In the short term, the capacity to adapt as autonomous bodies capable of public interventions on behalf of citizens may depend on the extent to which third sector organizations remained connected to their constituencies and have been able to defend the structures that facilitate mobilization. In turn, features of national welfare states structure the relative importance of interest group representation in how the role of voluntary and community organizations is understood. Northern Ireland shows what happens when the link between voluntary action and interest group representation is weak, as voluntary organizations find themselves drawn into a remodeling of welfare institutions to fit reducing budgets and serve the interests of a state led strategy for market-based renewal. In Ireland, a much stronger tradition of mobilization around interests in civil society in a welfare state that only partially recognizes those interests leaves a space for voluntary and community organizations to imagine different futures.

NOTE

1.   In early September 2012, a campaign by disabled activists, including a 24 hour sit in by a group of wheelchair users at the Irish parliament, successfully blocked government plans to restrict access to independent living funds.

REFERENCES

Acheson, N. 2010. "Welfare State Reform, Compacts and Restructuring Relations between the State and the Voluntary Sector: Reflections on Northern Ireland Experience." *Voluntary Sector Review* 1 (2): 175-192.

Acheson, N., B. Harvey, J. Kearney, and A. Williamson. 2004. *Two Paths One Purpose: Voluntary Action in Ireland North and South*. Dublin: Institute for Public Administration.

Acheson, N. and C. Milofsky. 2008. "Peace Building and Participation in Northern Ireland: Local Social Movements and the Policy Process since the 'Good Friday' Agreement." *Ethnopolitics* 7 (1): 63-80.

Adshead, M. 2011. "An Advocacy Coalition Framework Approach to the Rise and Fall of Social Partnership." *Irish Political Studies* 26 (1): 73-93.

Adshead, M. and B. Quinn. 1998. "From Government to Governance: Irish Development Policy's Paradigm Shift." *Policy & Politics* 26 (2): 209-226.

Alcock, P. 2012. "New Policy Spaces: the impact of devolution on third sector policy in the UK." *Social Policy and Administration* 46 (2): 219-238.

Bode, I. 2006. "Disorganized Welfare Mixes: voluntary agencies and new governance regimes in Western Europe." *Journal of European Social Policy* 16 (4): 346-359.

Buckingham, H. 2012. "Capturing Diversity: a typology of third sector organisations' responses to contracting based on empirical evidence from homelessness services." *Journal of Social Policy* 41 (3): 569-89.

Cairns, B., R. Hutchinson, and M. Aiken. 2010. "'It's not what we do, it's how we do it': managing the tension between service delivery and advocacy." *Voluntary Sector Review* 1 (2): 193-208.

Carney, G., T. Dundon, and A. ni Léime. Forthcoming. "'Protecting the Vulnerable' in an Economic Crisis: A Participatory Study of Civil Society Organisations in Ireland." *Voluntary Sector Review* 3 (3).

Carney, G., T. Dundon, Å. ni Léime, and C. Loftus. 2011. *Community Engagement in Ireland's Developmental Welfare State: a Study of the Life Cycle Approach*. Galway: Irish Centre for Social Gerontology, National University of Ireland.

Considine, M. and F. Dukelow. 2011. "Ireland and the Impact of the Economic Crisis: upholding the dominant policy paradigm." In *Social Policy in Challenging Times: Economic Crisis and Welfare Systems*, ed. K. Farnsworth and Z. Irving, 181-198. Bristol: the Policy Press.

—. 2012. "From Financial Crisis to Welfare Retrenchment: Assessing the challenges to the Irish Welfare State." In *Social Policy Review 24: Analysis and Debate in Social Policy, 2012*, ed. M. Kilkey, G. Ramia, and K. Farnsworth, 257-276. Bristol: the Policy Press.

Crowley, N. 2012. *Lost in Austerity: Rethinking the Community Sector*. Birmingham and Southampton: Third Sector Research Centre Discussion paper C.

Daly, S. 2008. "Mapping Civil Society in Ireland." *Community Development Journal* 43 (2): 157-176.

Department for Social Development. 2012. *Government Funding Database: Government Grants to the Voluntary and Community Sector*. At http://govfundingpublic. nics.gov.uk/Home.aspx (accessed 16 May 2012).

Devine, P., G. Kelly, and G. Robinson. 2011. *An Age of Change? Community Relations in Northern Ireland*. ARK research update 72. Belfast: ARK publications.

Donnelly-Cox, G. and S. McGee. 2011. "Between Relational Governance and Regulation of the Third Sector: the Irish Case." In *Governance and Regulation in the Third Sector: International Perspectives*, ed. S.D. Phillips and S.R. Smith, 99-114. New York Abingdon: Routledge.

Donoghue, F. and J. Larragy. 2009. "Changing State-Civil Society Relations in Ireland." In *Policy Initiatives Towards the Third Sector in International Perspective*, ed. B. Gidron and M. Bar, 109-126. New York: Springer Publishing.

Farnsworth, K. and Z. Irving. 2011. "Varieties of Crisis." In *Social Policy in Challenging Times: Economic Crisis and Welfare Systems*, ed. K. Farnsworth and Z. Irving, 1-30. Bristol: The Policy Press.

Geoghegan, M. and F. Powell. 2009. "Community Development, the Irish State and the Contested Meaning of Civil Society." In *Power, Dissent and Democracy: Civil Society and the State in Ireland*, ed. D. O'Broin and P. Kirby, 95-110. Dublin: A. & A. Farmar.

Gidron, B. and M. Bar. 2009. "Introduction." In *Policy Initiatives Towards the Third Sector in International Perspective*, ed. B. Gidron and M. Bar, 1-20. New York: Dordrecht.

Gray, A.M. and D. Birrell. 2012. "Coalition Government and Northern Ireland: social policy and the lowest common denominator thesis." *Social Policy and Society* 11 (1): 15-26.

Horgan, G. 2006. "Devolution, Direct Rule and the Neo-Liberal Reconstruction of Northern Ireland." *Critical Social Policy* 26 (3): 656-668.

Kendall, J. 2010a. "Terra Incognita: Third Sectors and European Policy Processes." In *Handbook on Third Sector Policy in Europe: Multi-level Processes and Organized Civil Society*, ed. J. Kendall, 3-20. Cheltenham, Northampton MA: Edward Elgar.

—. 2010b. "The UK: Ingredients in a Hyperactive Horizontal Policy Environment." In *Handbook on Third Sector Policy in Europe: Multi-level Processes and Organized Civil Society*, ed. J. Kendall, 67-94. Cheltenham, Northampton MA: Edward Elgar.

Kirby, P. 2010. *Celtic Tiger in Collapse: explaining the weaknesses of the Irish model.* Basingstoke: Palgrave Macmillan.

Knox, C. 2003. "Democratic Renewal in Fragmented Communities: the Northern Ireland case." *Local Governance* 29 (1): 14-37.

Kuhner, S. 2012. "Welfare Retrenchment under Left and Right Government Leadership: towards a consolidated framework of analysis?" In *Social Policy Review 24: Analysis and Debate in Social Policy, 2012,* ed. M. Kilkey, G. Ramia, and K. Farnsworth, 137-164. Bristol: The Policy Press.

Larragy, J. 2006. "Origins and Significance of the Community and Voluntary Pillar in Irish Social Partnership." *The Economic and Social Review* 37 (3): 375-398.

Lister, R. 2010. "The Age of Responsibility: Social Policy and Citizenship in the Early 21st Century." In *Social Policy Review 23,* ed. C. Holden, M. Kilkey, and G. Ramia, 63-84. Bristol: The Policy Press.

McCall, C. and A.P. Williamson. 2001. "Governance and Democracy in Northern Ireland: The Role of the Voluntary and Community Sector after the Agreement." *Governance* 14 (3): 363-385.

Meade, R. 2005. "We hate it here, please let us stay! Irish Social Partnership and the Community/Voluntary Sector's Conflicted Experiences of Recognition." *Critical Social Policy* 25 (3): 3.

Morrow, D. 2012. "The Practice, Progress and Failings of Community Relations Work in Northern Ireland." Seminar paper given at the Institute for Social Science Research, University of Ulster, 23 May 2012. At http://www.youtube.com/user/IRiSSwatch/videos (accessed 24 May 2012).

National Council for Voluntary Organisations (NCVO). 2012. *Civil Society Almanac.* London: National Council for Voluntary Organisations.

Nolan, P. 2012. *Northern Ireland Peace Monitoring Report, Number one.* Belfast: Community Relations Council.

Northern Ireland Council for Voluntary Action (NICVA). 2012. *The State of the Sector VI.* Belfast: Northern Ireland Council for Voluntary Action.

Northern Ireland Executive. 2011. *Programme for Government and Budget 2011–2015.* Belfast: Northern Ireland Executive. At http://www.northernireland.gov.uk/index/programme-for-government-and-budget-v1.htm (accessed 15 May 2012).

Office of First Minister and Deputy First Minister (OfMDfM). 2005. *A Shared Future: Policy and Strategy for Good Relations.* Belfast: Office of First Minister and Deputy First Minister.

Powell, F. and M. Geoghegan. 2004. *The Politics of Community Development: Reclaiming Civil Society or Reinventing Governance.* Dublin: A & A Farmar.

Roche, W.K. and T. Cradden. 2003. "Neo-corporatism and Social Partnership." In *Public Administration and Public Policy in Ireland: Theory and Methods,* ed. M. Adshead and M. Millar, 69-87. London: Routledge.

Special European Union Programmes Body (SEUPB). 2008. *Peace III: EU Programme for Peace and Reconciliation, 2007–2013 Northern Ireland and the Border Region of Ireland, Operational Programme.* Belfast and Monaghan: Special European Union Programmes Body.

Taylor, M. 2012. "The Changing Fortunes of Community." *Voluntary Sector Review* 3 (1): 15-30.

Waterhouse-Bradley, B. 2012. Unpublished PhD thesis. Newtownabbey: University of Ulster.

CHAPTER 9

THE IMPACT OF THE ECONOMIC RECESSION ON SPAIN'S THIRD SECTOR

CARMEN PARRA

THE EFFECTS OF THE ECONOMIC CRISIS IN SPAIN

In the decade from 1997–2007, the Spanish economy experienced strong growth in terms of both GDP and employment. The Spanish authorities seemed unaware and unprepared that this economic cycle might come to a sudden end. Any recession was predicted to be progressive, with the so-called real estate boom restructuring the Spanish economy.

Nevertheless, the 2008 global economic crisis affected European economies as much as the US economy, and had serious consequences on the international financial sector as well (Torrero Mañas 2008a; 2008b, 50). At first, the Spanish economy seemed to avoid this shipwreck. Though the Bank of Spain established preventive restrictions and bank controls because of high credit and family indebtedness, these measures proved insufficient. By the end of 2009, the crisis had devastated the Spanish economy and it was uncertain when any sign of recovery would come (Torrero Mañas 2008b, 75). Even though the effects of the crisis on GDP were less dramatic in Spain than in other countries, the combination of effects on the finance, real estate, and productive sectors provoked such a deep impact on employment that Spain is expected to get out of this situation much later than other developed countries (OECD 2011).

In short, the economic crisis has produced devastating effects for Spain (Krugman 2009, 32). The most profound impacts are seen in the fall of the real estate sector, the battered financial sector (as a result of subprime mortgages coming from the United States), and the collapse of the economic model of growth on which the Spanish economy had been based (Shiller 2009, 24). The financial system has deteriorated, impeding the

Government-Nonprofit Relations in Times of Recession, ed. Rachel Laforest. Montreal and Kingston: Queen's Policy Studies Series, McGill-Queen's University Press. © 2013 The School of Policy Studies, Queen's University at Kingston. All rights reserved.

credit financing necessary to maintain corporate economic activity. At the same time, consumption has dropped due to families' high indebtedness, and unemployment has rapidly increased. Spanish internal and external economic activity has been considerably reduced (Recarte 2009, 56).

As for the public sector, falling incomes have led to important delays in the compliance of its obligations. This has created a significant feeling of insecurity among the institutions that have traditionally worked with the state (Obeso and Homs I Ferret 2009, 89).

Together with these economic effects are a series of social effects that have resulted from increased poverty from unemployment. The most affected groups are families with children, single-parent families, young people, and immigrants (Laparra and Ayala 2009). These populations confront the crisis from a situation of extreme fragility.

The social and economic dimensions of the Spanish crisis are framed within a global crisis that affects a large number of countries. While each country has its own unique context, there are a number of common elements. This allows us to identify this crisis as a global one, similar to the 1930s Depression. The parallels are revealed in various indicators. For example, both crises have their roots in dysfunctional financial mechanisms, which quickly spread throughout the world. Another commonality is the slow response by governments, who wanted to see "green buds" instead of the ongoing collapse of their economies. In neither situation were appropriate instruments adopted to face a situation that has surmounted all expectations and that is dragging entire regions to bankruptcy.

Economists now wonder whether it is possible to achieve a sustainable exit from the crisis by using the same economic approaches of the last two decades or, by contrast, if it is necessary to restructure the international economy to ensure a new global growth cycle, just as in the "New Deal" which set up the bases for economic growth until the 1970s (Homs I Ferret 2009, 40).

The Impact of the Crisis on the Third Sector

Not only has the international economic crisis had specific impacts on the Spanish economy, it has also had devastating effects on the third sector (Hanfstaengl 2010; Parra, Porta and Ruiz 2011, 6; Report of Observatorio del Tercer Sector 2010). Fewer private and public resources have been targeted to social policies, credit has been restricted, and economic traffic in general has reduced. At the same time, non-profit organizations have had to face greater needs. In other words, while fewer resources have been offered, greater resources have been demanded.

The impact of crisis on the non-profit sector comes at a very complex moment. Much of the sector is in a development and consolidation stage, where new strategic and structural measures are being put into place

(Parra, Porta and Ruiz 2011). Alongside new demands and new services, organizations are working to improve their policy and practice on transparency, accountability, and good governance.

The economic expansion period from 1997–2007 allowed an important rise in public budgets. This in turn resulted in the transformation of the welfare state. Both of these trends led to a favorable increase in the number of non-profit organizations. The economic situation allowed the third sector to consolidate and build a larger presence in society. Several factors helped the third sector to obtain benefits and reach a strong position that it would later have to abandon. Three aspects from this decade long growth period are noteworthy: the expansion of services offered by the welfare state; the relationship between the third sector, private companies, and government; and the relationship between government and non-profit organizations in the defense of social interests (De Castro Sanz 2010, 72).

Expansion of Services Offered by the Welfare State

The economic expansion that accompanied the Spanish economy until 2007 led to the restructuring of the third sector. Non-profit organizations widened their activities to reach a larger population while looking for new challenges (Rodriguez Cabrero 2005, 28). In this favorable economic period, numerous organizations became more professional by expanding their physical facilities, making important investments, increasing their staff, improving quality of services, and improving the transparency of their decision making. With public financing now almost nonexistent, those organizations that did not adequately carry out their transformation to its completion are now at a critical stage, with their future at risk.

Relationship between the Third Sector, Private Sector and Government

With an abundance of public resources available for the state's social services, the private sector saw a profit opportunity to act as suppliers of infrastructure and equipment. Businesses with little or no experience in the social sector took over this role from non-profit institutions who had traditionally been the leaders in this area. As a result, social services were subcontracted by private companies. Even though providing infrastructure and equipment for social services did not have huge benefits to the corporate sector, it was attractive enough to access new markets and ensure economic stability. This is the case, for instance, in the sector devoted to elderly, childhood or disabled care (Cayo Pérez-Bueno 2010, 124).

On the one hand, the private sector is considered to have interfered in areas traditionally developed by non-profit organizations. On the other hand, alliances and collaborations with companies are seen as a business opportunity in the face of the lack of public financing.

Relationship between Government and Non-profit Organizations when Defending Social Interests

Up to the time of the economic crisis, non-profit organizations had enjoyed the confidence of the government. The mere fact that an institution was devoted to culture, health, and education was seen as a good and responsive practice. However, after the crisis the government has imposed numerous controls on non-profit organizations that have diminished the third sector's autonomy. These controls include audits, increased control for workers, reduction of public aid, and increased demands for accountability on public money. New instruments and mechanisms have increased the need for interaction between non-profit and public sectors. Institutions whose revenues mainly came from public funds have been forced to integrate a series of mechanisms of state budgetary control that directly attack the liberty and the autonomy from which the sector had traditionally benefited.

Indeed, the Spanish non-profit sector is currently living through a very complex period. On the one hand, it is under the control of the public sector, which prevents it from acting on its own. On the other hand, it must comply with the commercial requirements of the private sector, which asks the third sector to increase its activity in order to have a larger market. Moreover, there is a duality in the functions of non-profit institutions. They are, at the same time, both services suppliers and defenders and promoters of social interests.

Generally speaking, this restructuring can be positive. However, whereas private sector relationships are based on market quotas, relationships established in the third sector are based on trust, making it difficult to substitute its interlocutors. For this reason, any change in course in the third sector demands a special approach where those institutions which are struggling should be helped to successfully overcome this difficult period of crisis.

Certainly, the current weaknesses in the third sector make it difficult for the sector to face future challenges. The crisis will oblige this sector to carry out a deep renewal in the years to come (Fundación Luis Vives 2011).

FIVE AREAS OF IMPACT ON THE SPANISH THIRD SECTOR

The economic crisis directly impacts the Spanish third sector in five areas: increase in social needs, reduction of government funding, reduced activity in the productive sector, difficulties in accessing credit, and decreased donations (Homs I Ferret 2009, 48).

Increase in Social Needs

According to a Cáritas report (FOESSA 2008), the number of groups facing the economic crisis from a position of extreme poverty – for example, single parents, immigrants, at-risk youth – has increased. Added to these groups are those affected by high indebtedness because of lack of employment income and minimal family support. Since 2007, for instance, the number of requests for food and other basic essentials has increased by 89.6 percent. Further, grants to pay rents and mortgages have increased by 65.2 percent. The increase in applications for social aid has led to a saturation of public social services. It has also provoked higher pressure on non-profit organizations, which can collaborate with the government but cannot be its substitute.

This reality leads us to the following conclusion: if a cohesive social level is to be kept within the European social model, social policies must be revised in order to establish basic protection of the most vulnerable populations. For example, general policies about minimum incomes should be revised and restructured as well as policies concerning basic pensions, social housing, and childhood protection. The economic crisis can spurn us forward toward a minimum threshold of general protection that will serve society well in the future (Laparra and Ayala 2009, 59). On the other hand, the third sector should be more transparent, with only those organizations that truly help social inclusion remaining on the market.

Reduction of Government Funding

Reductions in government budgets as a result of the economic crisis have had significant impact on non-profit organizations. The third sector has reduced its services and social programs, while trying to address the needs of more and more people with the same budget. This has endangered the quality and professionalism traditionally characteristic of the third sector. With the public sector focusing all its efforts on covering basic needs of the most vulnerable groups, non-profit organizations who had developed innovative prevention programs have received less support from government. Non-profit organizations now must restructure and adapt their activities. Thus, innovation has turned back to stagnation, with new instruments being more about subsistence then prevention.

The government's difficulties in adapting social programs to the new situation can be seen in the active policies of employment, including policies geared toward populations that typically have difficulty finding work such as former prisoners, people recovering from addictions, and young untrained immigrants. These policies are almost identical to those applied during the period of economic expansion, in spite of the important changes in the labor market, especially since 2007.

The most important responses have taken place within the unemployment policies and the "Plan España" (Lomeña Varo 2008, 22), which has strengthened the construction sector through public works. These actions led to an improvement of the relationship between passive policies (such as pensions, unemployment benefits, and aid to disabled) and active policies (such as initiatives to encourage job creation and consumption). The aim was to forge a way out of the crisis by changing the productive model and redirecting it towards a more competitive economy.

Reduced Activity in the Productive Sector

In Spain, non-profit organizations are a part of the so-called social economy. Depending on their field of action, some non-profit organizations survive thanks to productive activities that help them reduce their dependence on the public sector. This is the case of social enterprises geared to provide jobs for marginalized groups (Fundació un Sol Món, 2007) and of employment special centers (Parra 2010, 65; Martinez 2011, 25). These structures were developed in Spain in the 1990s in order to address social exclusion and disability. However, in the context of the economic crisis, these institutions have seen their labor activity reduced within a short period of time. This impact has been felt particularly by organizations that depended on private companies to subcontract services.

According to CEPES[1] (2011), in 2008 there was a daily average of 15 social economy companies that stopped their activity, losing 40,000 employees and putting 25 percent of jobs at risk. This loss of productivity stems from the fact that non-profit organizations develop their activities on sectors highly affected by the crisis, including construction, recycling, and social enterprises that employ vulnerable groups.

In the face of the economic crisis, social policies must include mechanisms that help stabilize the position of organizations which make up the social economy. These organizations are one of the most important social innovations to respond to the crisis. The social economy offers people employment and income that allow them to recover their self-esteem and self-organization capacities and reduce their vulnerability. Moreover, the cost of these kinds of measures are much lower than other programs since they create employment for workers who would otherwise receive unemployment subsidies and be a burden on public budgets.

In short, the social economy must be one of the sectors where government and the third sector work together to find alternatives to the unbalances created by a highly competitive labor market, and to seek a balance between economic profit and society's welfare.

Difficulties in Accessing Credit

In the wake of the economic crisis, governments are delaying payments to non-profit organizations for the social services they have provided. Further, there is a lack of transparency around the dates of those payments. This is causing important cash flow problems within the third sector. Organizations turn to banks for credit to pay debts. However, banks are not providing credit, so the situation is getting worse every day. Particularly now, cash flow is the weak point for non-profit organizations who are already highly indebted and who have scarce resources and little collateral to offer as guarantee for credit.

In a period of crisis, financing institutions have difficulty meeting the needs of non-profit organizations. Consequently, financial institutions have decided not to work with the third sector, despite the fact that arrears in the third sector are lower than in other economic sectors. Between 2006 and 2008, for instance, credit for third sector organizations decreased by 0.9 percent. In the face of this situation, the public sector must look for solutions to avoid the disappearance of non-profit organizations because of a lack of economic resources.

In Spain, non-profit organizations receive funds from the voluntary participation of citizens through the income tax. This public aid represents 0.7 percent of income tax revenue, and is allocated by choice of the taxpayer toward the infrastructure, equipment and construction expenses of either the Catholic church, or other non-specified non-Catholic organizations who carry out social projects. This kind of aid has been going on in Spain for twenty years. One of the consequences of the economic crisis is that this aid can no longer be used for staff hiring expenses or for maintenance costs. The aim is that only self-sufficient institutions continue.

Decreased Revenue from Donations

The participation of citizens in third sector financing has also been affected by the crisis. The reduction in the number of donations is not as important as the reduction in the amount donated. In fact, while the number of donors may have increased during the crisis, the amounts of donations have decreased. When individual donations fall, third sector institutions need alternative instruments for financing. To address this situation, the state is working on new projects to regulate sponsorship and patronage. The aim of these legal initiatives is to boost donations through tax deductions and coordinated collection to benefit an important number of third sector organizations.

A draft bill on patronage is currently in its final stages and will strengthen the ability of non-profits to seek private support beyond corporate sponsorships (Palencia-Jefler Ors 2001, 102). With governments now providing less funding, this new act will reward private sector support and pave the way for a new model of support to the third sector, with citizens and companies leading the way.

THE RESPONSE OF THE THIRD SECTOR TO THE SPANISH ECONOMIC CRISIS

Solutions to the crisis cannot only come from the public sector. On the contrary, the collaboration of non-profit organizations is necessary to obtain results which, unfortunately, will not be obvious in the short term. In order to start the recovery process, three main actions are necessary: merger of non-profit organizations, financing independence, and third sector professionalization.

Merger of Non-profit Organizations

One of the main characteristics of the Spanish third sector is its widespread dispersion. Unlike some countries, where non-profit organizations are predominantly organized into a few large foundations, Spain has a large number of small organizations spread over a number of different sectors.

This feature of dispersion is both a weak and a strong point in the present crisis (De Lorenzo García 2003, 78). Some small organizations with considerable local force can face the crisis better than mid-sized organizations that lack resources to address the new needs created by the economic collapse. However, small non-profit organizations who work locally may also have difficulty meeting public need; they have only minimal management, financing, and supporting organizations to develop their activities.

Currently, the third sector's challenge is to stay connected with the territory where it works and to preserve a local and personal identity as well as the confidence of its beneficiaries. At the same time, the third sector must integrate itself into wider organizations like associations and federations. Wider organizations allow non-profits to build up the capacity and resources they need to perform efficiently and be competitive within their activity sector. For example, organizations can reduce expenses by joint actions to share resources and synergies. Moreover, these alliances can foster the exchange of experience and good practices to improve results.

Though this approach has the support of both government and third sector organizations, networking, and the creation of alliances and mergers are happening at a slower speed than desired.

Financing Independence

Another feature of the Spanish third sector is the lack of organizational financial sustainability. As a result, third sector organizations are often dependent on public sector funding. Their survival depends on public grants and aid. When these organizations do not receive regular income, they become highly indebted to financing institutions because of public financing delays.

In response to this significant insecurity, the public sector should establish a regulatory frame to give more stability to organizations that collaborate with the government in the development of social programs. In order to do so, the following measures should be applied:

- sustainable, steady, and transparent budget contributions, independent from political changes;
- improved tax breaks for donations;
- multiannual programs and projects for need-driven, responsive initiatives;
- collaborative models between the public and private sectors, such as formal agreements in order to guarantee service delivery (for example, in education, health, culture, sports etc.);
- public-private partnerships based on complementarity, mutual confidence, and transparency; and
- reduction of the importance of subsidies.

All in all, the aim is to improve collaboration between the third sector and government in order to reduce uncertainties and to make shared activities more transparent.

The challenge of Spanish third sector organizations is to focus on capitalization by increasing investment capacity. Nevertheless, the Spanish financing sector must acknowledge and address the nonexistence of appropriate instruments to carry out risk capital operations for non-profit organizations. Numerous legal, foundational, and accounting difficulties create difficult barriers. Some instruments could be adapted from the private sector, but others require a specific design, for instance micro-credit instruments (Parra 2010, 74).

The solution to this problem lies in a new dialogue between financing institutions and the legislative branch to determine the basis of new laws that foster investment in the non-profit sector and minimize risks for investors.

Third Sector Professionalization

A further characteristic of the Spanish third sector is its lack of management professionalism. In a period of crisis, especially when the private sector has taken a more active role in social service delivery, this weakness becomes particularly apparent. In the past, characteristics such as proximity, quality, and employees' commitment and involvement were highly appreciated. But today's competitive context means that management capacity that is up to the task of the present social complexity has a higher value (Homs I Ferret 2009, 34). Unfortunately, the prestige of an excellent organizational legacy has become a secondary consideration for a society highly focused on economic results.

In this new context, the third sector has tried to professionalize its management systems and teams in order to compete with private companies. Training is a priority. Universities and training centers should follow models established by the European Union.

SOLUTIONS FOR THE SPANISH THIRD SECTOR

Having analyzed the weaknesses and challenges of the Spanish third sector, it is now possible to look for public and private solutions. From the third sector's perspective, the goal is to recover the sector's position and achieve results similar to those before the crisis. Five solutions are proposed: search for leadership, social innovation, networking, strengthening civil society, and development of new action instruments (Parra, Porta and Ruiz 2011, 22).

Search for Leadership

In times of crisis, the government cannot address the full spectrum of social needs created by the welfare state (health and free education for all). In this context, the third sector must step in to take a greater leadership role and address the social needs that are not met by either the private or public sectors alone.

The third sector has proved to be an effective solution for civil society to address social needs. The third sector has succeeded in this role to a greater extent than the private sector, since non-profit organizations have high rates of social cohesion in developed societies that are difficult to get in other fields. The current crisis has shown how difficult it is for the private sector to work as an actor in the welfare state. Clearly the market economy has generated deep unbalances. The question is, can the third sector bring new ideas to get out of the crisis?

The answer to this question implies accepting that the third sector has proved its capacity to compete with the private sector while being loyal to the values underlying its own existence. The third sector has also proved that profit is not people's only driving force and that certain qualities, including commitment and motivation, are what make non-profit organizations efficient. Finally, by applying the basic principle that the economy must be at the service of citizens' welfare, the third sector has also been able to activate material resources like donations and volunteers as well as immaterial resources like effort and innovation, that neither the state nor the private sector would have been able to mobilize.

The challenge for third sector organizations in this context is that they are too busy with the demands of daily activities to generate a theoretical discourse that addresses the important issues of this century. An articulate vision and analysis from the third sector is needed to demonstrate that the third sector perspective is an important contribution to the debate on how to recover from the economic crisis at both the national and international level. A new third sector-driven perspective would result in the restructuring of the present economic model, ending the differentiation between public, private, and non-profit sectors. A new model would facilitate the creation of a new social agreement defining the limits of each sector and protecting their respective fields of action.

To develop these new strategies, the active role of the third sector will be essential. Its experience, vision and contribution are critical. To be an effective actor in the debate, the third sector must openly state the need to support the sector's restructuring to better meet social needs. This is the basis of future economy.

The third sector has proposed measures to the government to devote more resources to the development of social policy and improve programs that focus on basic needs and vulnerabilities exposed by the economic crisis. Additionally, support measures have been suggested so that non-profit organizations can attend new social needs with greater success. These proposals constitute an important alternative for society as a whole and for leaders – to get out of the economic crisis with a more cohesive and equitable society, which should allow us to reach a new cycle of sustainable welfare.

Social Innovation

The increase in social needs due to the crisis requires social innovation. Services must be adapted to the new social order. Social innovation can develop more efficient services that maintain quality despite resource scarcity (Albaigès 2010, 12).

One example is the fight against poverty, a field which has required significant innovation given the challenges of creating behavior change from social exclusion to social integration. Investment in new technologies is important to improve the productivity of socially marginalized groups as well as their social integration in civil society.

Social innovation action must be directly focused on causes. Preventive and efficient strategies must be developed in order to obtain good results with few resources. To reach this aim it will be necessary to promote investment by developing research and analysis of solutions together with universities and research centers. These approaches help identify new methodologies and new focuses, with improved solutions. Investment in social research and development is needed. A social innovation approach requires effort from third sector organizations. Introducing new priorities in social policy will mean new challenges, including a reorientation of the distribution of public funding.

Searching for solutions at the root of issues, changing mentalities, and reconsidering structural barriers must be prioritized in the years ahead to obtain the desired results.

Networking

The wide dispersion of non-profit organizations makes it difficult to efficiently manage their activities as a cohesive sector. The current tendency is to create a gathering frame – a kind of virtual space or informal alliance – for different groups in order to bring stability to the system. Nevertheless, we are still far from reaching a level of vertical and horizontal integration that is solid enough to obtain visible results. This is the third sector's most urgent challenge and the one that can best contribute to successfully overcome the crisis.

Examples of better integration include the merger of organizations working on the same sector, the creation of purchasing and service pools for organizations sharing similar needs, and the formation of consortia to generate strong groups with investment capacity. In short, the idea would be to take the cumulative experience of the cooperative sector – highly developed in Spain – to the associative sector, while preserving features from the third sector such us proximity, social capital, and local work. In addition, management and organization structures typical of the private sector should be added, as well as new technologies. Together, these strategies would contribute to improved coordination and integration of the third sector.

Strengthening Civil Society

The third sector's strength rests on civil society's free will to get organized in order to meet social demands that are not covered by either the public or private sector. In order to launch programs to meet social demands, the third sector has progressively become a collaborator of both government – since it obtains public funds to carry out its activities – and the private sector.

For this reason, it is very important for the third sector to reinforce its relationship with civil society by constant mobilization on objectives, and by creating a close relationship with social interlocutors. We must always bear in mind that the strength of the third sector has always rested on its capacity to mobilize civil society, and not on its capacity to deliver services.

Therefore, a new balance and new ways of operating have to be found to make associative life compatible with modern management mechanisms and instruments that benefit society. Nonetheless, it is necessary to clearly differentiate the independence of the third sector and the public sector so they can live together in harmony (Aliena 2009, 22).

In the present context of important cultural change, we need to find new opportunities and mechanisms for citizen involvement in the resolution of social problems. Several examples of large scale civil mobilization have brought to the surface the demands of civil society for credibility, transparency, and opportunity for dialogue. This is the case of the "Indignant" movement that has mobilized young people throughout the world around the incompetence of politicians to face the world crisis.

Development of New Action Instruments

To face current challenges, new action instruments must be developed in the legal, financing, and management fields through new technologies.

Legal Field

The development of alliances between organizations has met serious difficulties because of problems with current associative legal rules. No model currently exists for a non-profit social company that offers legal security to its partners on issues of ownership and corporate responsibility. This is the reason why notaries and registrars make it difficult to register or legalize non-profit associations. In order to consolidate the third sector's function of offering social services without giving up its principles, new legislation is needed to adapt legal forms to third sector needs. Though the cooperative sector already has some of these instruments, the distinction between both sectors is more and more evident.

One of the government's challenges must be the creation of work integration social enterprises (WISES) – companies with non-profit sector characteristics that provide employment for socially disadvantaged groups. WISES, who did not gain legal recognition until 2007, play an important social function by providing work for people who would otherwise be outside the labour market.

Financing Field

Just as in the legal field, financing institutions pose problems to non-profit organizations since non-profits do not fit within the private financing mechanisms created for other kind of operations. For instance, the financing sector disagrees with the third sector's position on guaranteeing financial support. Further, the non-profit sector is relatively unknown by banks, and banks impose on non-profit organizations greater credit restrictions than on other sectors. This lack of trust results in the rejection of credit for the third sector organizations.

There are also legal difficulties. For example, governments, especially city governments, granted many subsidies to non-profit organizations to provide services. Now that governments can no longer pay, non-profit organizations have become insolvent institutions that are not suitable to request credit.

The development of new financial instruments adapted to the third sector's needs is urgent. Non-profit organizations require cash flow to pay suppliers. New instruments are needed to allow them to raise funds to consolidate and stabilize their organizations. Relationships between social investors and non-profit organizations need to be established on the basis of confidence and efficient achievement of the organization's social aims. Therefore, it will be necessary to develop initiatives to give transparency to the achievement of the social objectives of these organizations.

One of the financial proposals to rescue the third sector is the development of tailored risk capital programs. Once again, however, legal issues would currently prevent the implementation of such financing instruments in the non-profit sector. Another option developed in recent years is the creation of ethical financing. Ethical financing (SETEM 2004) consists of financing instruments held by citizens and based on a social net of organizations and people who participate in a special way to improve society. In Spain this alternative is still undeveloped. However, there is widespread agreement that these would be useful strategies for the third sector, especially to achieve a closer relationship with financing and corporate sectors (Alemany 2009, 90; Sasia and De la Cruz 2008, 86).

Management Field

The third sector needs new management and organizational instruments to facilitate greater visibility and transparency. Even though important progress has been made, it is necessary to consolidate this progress with further efforts toward local solutions, centralization, independence, and collaboration. In order to reach these objectives, innovation and strategic vision are required. These aspects can only be obtained through the professionalization and functional specialization of organizations. In addition, improved quality control mechanisms must be introduced. They will be necessary to establish rules and methodologies for specific procedures in order to carry out such programs.

New Technologies Field

In the new technologies field there is also a long way to go. The third sector tends to be skeptical about the potential of new technologies to improve social services. Nevertheless, beginning to experiment with new technologies will help them find a place within the non-profit sector. New technologies include, for example, web 2.0, e-education, and data bases of virtual jobs.

CONCLUSION

Not every non-profit organization has a global vision of the multiple effects generated by the present economic crisis. However, most of them have experienced the problems described in this paper. Most international institutions including the European Union, Organisation for Economic Co-operation and Development (OECD), and the International Monetary Fund (IMF), foresee that the crisis will likely endure in Spain beyond that of many other developed countries. The current and continuing negative effects of the crisis on the third sector should not be underestimated. The crisis causes us to deeply reconsider both individual organizational strategies as well as collective strategies to face problems and consolidate and strengthen the Spanish third sector.

This crisis is a challenge for the non-profit sector to improve and adapt to a new economic and social context. The third sector must overcome the crisis by growing in strength, and becoming one of the key actors of the social organization of the knowledge society.

NOTE

1.   CEPES: Confederación Española de la Economía Social.

REFERENCES

Albaigès, J. 2010. "La innovación en el Tercer Sector." In *La innovación social, motor de desarrollo de Europa*. Barcelona: Socialinnova Ed.
Alemany, J. 2009. *Dinero con conciencia: las finanzas éticas*. Madrid: Icaria Ed.

Aliena, R. 2009. "Los equilibrios del Tercer Sector, una filosofía del pluralismo de funciones." IV Foro del Tercer Sector. Revista Española del Tercer Sector nº 10: 10-35.

Cayo Pérez-Bueno, L. 2010. Estudios en Homenaje a Paulino Azúa Berra "Discapacidad, tercer sector e inclusión social." In *Colección Cermies* nº 47. Bilbao BBVA Ed.

Confederación Española de la Economía Social (CEPES). 2011. Estadisticas Estatales/Internacionales. At http://www.cepes.es/Estadisticas (accessed 10 February 2012).

De Castro Sanz, M. 2010. *Las relaciones entre el tercer sector y los poderes públicos.* Madrid: Obra Social Caja Madrid Ed.

De Lorenzo García, R. 2003. *Tejido asociativo y Tercer Sector.* Madrid: Centro de Estudios Ramón Areces Ed.

Fundació un Sol Món. 2007. ".Las empresas e inserción en España." In *Colección herramientas para la inclusión.* Barcelona: Obra Social Caixa Catalunya Ed.

Fundación Luis Vives 2011. At http://www.fundacionluisvives.org/actualidad/noticias/archivo/2011/05/24/.

Hanfstaengl, E.M. 2010. The Global Economic Crisis and its Impact on Civil Society Organizations. At http://ngosocdev.files.wordpress.com/2010/01/full-study-on-impact-of-global-crises-on-csos-2-25-10.pdf (accessed 30 April 2012).

Homs I Ferret, O. 2009. "Los restos del Tercer Sector ante la crisis." VI Foro Tercer Sector. Cuadernos de Debate nº 6. Caja Madrid. Obra Social Madrid.

Krugman, P. 2009. *El retorno de la economía de la depresión y la crisis actual.* Barcelona: Crítica Ed.

Laparra, M. and L. Ayala. 2009. *El sistema de garantía de ingresos mínimos en España y la respuesta urgente que requiere la crisis social.* Madrid: Cáritas. Fundación FOESSA.

Lomeña Varo, R. 2008. *El plan que pudo salvar España.* Madrid: Bubok Ed.

Martinez, J. 2011. *El empleo protegido: la importancia de los centros especiales de empleo.* Madrid: CIES Ed.

Obeso, C. and O. Homs I Ferret. 2009. "Impactos de la crisis en las relaciones laborales en España." Información Comercial Española. Revista de Economía 850: 89-108.

Organisation for Economic Co-operation and Development (OECD). 2011. Country Statistical Profiles. At http://stats.oecd.org/Index.aspx?DataSetCode=CSP2010 (accessed 10 February 2012)

Palencia-Jefler Ors, M. 2001. *Fundraising: El arte de capatar recursos.* Madrid: Insituto de Filantropía y Desarrollo Ed.

Parra C. 2010 *Empresas con conciencia.* Barcelona: Viceversa Ed.

Parra, C., F. Porta, and C. Ruiz, C. 2011. "Tercer sector, economía social y economía solidaria en España." In *El impacto de la crisis económica en la economía social y solidaria.* Barcelona: J.M. Bosch Ed.

Recarte, A. 2009. "El informe Recarte 2009." In *La economía española y la crisis Internacional.* Madrid: La Esfera de los Libros, Ed.

Report of Observatorio del Tercer Sector. 2010. "El ámbito económico-financiero de las entidades del tercer sector: retos y propuestas de acción." Colección Debates OTS nº 14. Barcelona.

Rodriguez Cabrero, G. 2005. "Los retos del tercer sector en España en el espacio social europeo." *Revista Española del tercer sector* (1): 63-95.

Sasia P.M. and C. De la Cruz. 2008. *Banca ética y ciudadanía*. Madrid: Trotta Ed.

SETEM. 2004. *Finanzas éticas: un análisis de la situación española*. Madrid: Setem Ed.

Shiller, R.J. 2009. *El estallido de la burbuja. Cómo se llegó a la crisis y cómo salir de ella*. Barcelona: Gestión 2000 Ed.

Studies of Fundación (FOESSA). 2008. Fomento de Estudios Sociales y Sociología Aplicada. VI Informe sobre exclusión y desarrollo social en España. Madrid: Fundación FOESSA Ed.

Torrero Mañas, A. 2008a. *Revolución en las finanzas (Los grandes cambios en las ideas. Represión y liberalización financiera)*. Madrid: Marcial Pons Ed.

—. 2008b. *La crisis financiera internacional y económica Española*. Madrid: Encuentro Ed.

CHAPTER 10

NO CONNECTIONS BETWEEN SEPARATE SPHERES? ECONOMIC RECESSION AND THE THIRD SECTOR IN GERMANY

BJÖRN SCHMITZ

INTRODUCTION

The dramatic bankruptcy of Lehman Brothers in 2008 is seen as the starting point of the global financial and economic crisis, even if other factors and causes date back to the time before the crash. The current crisis was first a financial one, as risky financial instruments failed and left banks with cripplingly high credit. As a result, financial institutions lost their financial stability and sometimes were unable to repay their debts. Most countries tried to stabilize this situation by facilitating government funds for banks, providing fresh money to keep the frozen credit market going again. Governments have also taken additional measures, promoting consumerism and trying to stimulate investment, even as institutional trust was failing. In many countries, these interventions resulted in a massive increase of debt and even until now, the impact on the third sector is unclear. Countries all over the world are affected differently by the current economic situation. Most indicators show that Germany is manoeuvring well through the crisis. After outlining the current status of the German economic situation, this chapter will describe the government response to the crisis, both toward the economy and the third sector. The chapter will then describe the German third sector, with a special focus on social welfare associations and foundations. The chapter concludes

Government-Nonprofit Relations in Times of Recession, ed. Rachel Laforest. Montreal and Kingston: Queen's Policy Studies Series, McGill-Queen's University Press. © 2013 The School of Policy Studies, Queen's University at Kingston. All rights reserved.

with some remarks concerning future prospects of the third sector, with a focus on social entrepreneurship as well as social innovation promotion programs.

ECONOMIC SITUATION IN GERMANY

In general, Germany has remained relatively unscathed by the global economic crisis. We can demonstrate this through three basic indicators of economic health. First, the Gross Domestic Product (GDP), which is seen as the key indicator for prosperity or economic decline. Second, the unemployment rate, another important indicator of economic well-being. And third, stock market changes, which illustrates the potential of organizations (of course only those organizations dealing their shares at the market) to grow or decline. While stock markets can often say more about the future, GDP expresses what has happened in the past.

Gross Domestic Product

The Gross Domestic Product is still the most common indicator for economic prosperity, and an important orientation point. GDP figures are closely connected to how the wealth of a nation is perceived even if it is neglects how wealth is distributed. However, the GDP serves as a very powerful indicator and an important orientation point. Table 1 gives an overview of percentage GDP change in the previous year for a selection of industrialized countries. The table clearly illustrates that after moderate increases in 2008, most countries faced negative economic growth in 2009. However, most economies recovered quickly and turned to positive growth in 2010, albeit with smaller growth than in the years before the crisis.

Like most other countries, Germany's economy started growing again after the dip in 2009. What is more, the growth rates for Germany were on the same level as before the crisis. This distinguishes Germany from many other countries, including UK, the US or France. From the perspective of GDP, the crisis did not last long for most countries. Clearly however, while governments helped overcome negative growth, their efforts left them with a tremendous increase in national debt.

Unemployment and Income

Traditionally, Germany has been perceived as very inflexible and bureaucratic in workforce contracting as well as hiring and release legislation. Many have argued that these factors were a major influence on Germany's

TABLE 1
Nominal GDP Growth Rates

	Average 1986-96	1997	2000	2006	2007	2008	2009	2010	2011
Australia	7.2	5.3	7.8	7.9	9.1	9.0	0.5	7.8	7.7
Canada	5.0	5.5	9.6	5.6	5.5	4.6	-4.5	6.2	5.4
France	4.3	3.2	5.6	4.9	4.9	2.7	-2.0	2.2	3.7
Germany	5.2	2.1	2.8	4.0	4.7	1.7	-3.3	4.1	4.2
Greece	16.0	10.7	8.0	8.5	7.5	4.3	-0.8	-2.1	-2.6
Iceland	11.7	8.0	8.1	13.8	12.0	13.3	0.8	3.0	4.2
Ireland	8.4	15.7	16.2	9.3	6.8	-4.9	-11.2	-3.6	-1.3
Japan	4.0	2.1	1.1	1.1	1.6	-2.2	-6.6	1.8	-2.2
Korea	16.5	9.8	9.9	5.0	7.3	5.3	3.8	10.1	5.6
Netherlands	4.5	7.0	8.2	5.2	5.8	4.3	-4.1	3.4	2.2
Portugal	12.6	8.5	7.3	4.3	5.6	1.6	-2.0	2.3	-1.1
Spain	8.7	6.3	8.7	8.3	7.0	3.3	-3.1	0.8	2.1
Sweden	6.3	4.3	5.9	6.3	6.2	2.5	-3.6	6.8	5.8
United Kingdom	7.2	6.2	5.1	5.9	5.8	2.9	-3.5	4.2	4.8
United States	5.8	6.3	6.4	6.0	4.9	2.2	-1.7	3.8	4.0
Euro area	6.1	4.1	5.5	5.2	5.3	2.3	-3.2	2.6	3.1
Total OECD	9.2	8.0	7.4	5.9	5.4	2.8	-2.5	4.3	3.9

Source: Author's compilation based on data from OECD 2012b.

high unemployment rates in the late 1990s and until 2005. Since then, various policy changes have been put in place, including lowering payments for unemployment benefits and cutting unemployment benefits when the unemployed are not actively seeking new work. However, workforce legislation is still very strict and laying off still has high barriers for organizations. For example, staff terminations for operational reasons have to fit with socially acceptable criteria instead of mere staff performance targets. Nevertheless, Table 2 shows that after 2008, unemployment rates in Germany were low in comparison to many other countries.

During the first year of the economic crisis, many organizations faced a dramatic decrease in demand due to lack of trust and uncertainty concerning the national economy. To prevent broader lay-offs, the German government provided massive support to short-time work. Short-time work (known as *Kurzarbeit* in Germany) is a special means whereby workers agree to reduced hours or not working at all, and instead gets reduced payment without losing their job. Labour legislation ensures that, in some cases, government funds compensate for the reduced wages. In short, during the height of the economic crisis, most workers kept their jobs, but earned less money. Unemployment statistics remained essentially unchanged, and workers returned to their full time contracts when economic demand increased again in late 2010 and 2011. For organizations, the advantage was not to lose good workers, and to maintain the

TABLE 2
Harmonized Unemployment Rates
(percentage of civilian labour force, seasonally adjusted)

	2009	2010	2011		
			Jun	Jul	Aug
Canada	8.3	8.0	7.4	7.2	7.3
Finland	8.2	8.4	7.8	7.8	7.8
France	9.5	9.8	9.8	9.8	9.9
Germany	7.7	7.1	6.1	6.0	6.0
Greece	9.5	12.6	16.7	..	..
Ireland	11.8	13.7	14.4	14.6	14.6
Italy	7.8	8.4	8.0	8.0	7.9
Japan	5.1	5.1	4.6	4.7	4.3
Korea	3.6	3.7	3.3	3.3	3.1
Norway	3.1	3.5	3.3	3.2	..
Spain	18.0	20.1	21.0	21.1	21.2
Sweden	8.3	8.4	7.4	7.3	7.4
United Kingdom	7.6	7.8	8.0	..	..
United States	9.3	9.6	9.2	9.1	9.1
OECD-Total	8.4	8.6	8.3	8.2	8.2

Source: Author's compilation based on data from OECD 2012b.

ability to react quickly to an increase in production. For workers, the reduced income was difficult, but not as grave as it would have been if they had lost their jobs altogether. Unlike Germany, some countries such as Ireland and Spain, saw their unemployment rates skyrocket during the economic crisis.

Unemployment rates show a relatively strong economic situation in Germany. However, unemployment rates say little about the income structure of the working population. A study of OECD countries showed that the income gap between poor and rich people in Germany has grown faster than in most other industrialized countries (OECD 2012a). According to this study, the 10 percent of the German working population with the highest income earned eight times more than the 10 percent of the working population with the lowest income. In the early 1990s, the relation was 6 to 1. In total numbers, an average income in the high income population is €57,300 in comparison to €7,300 in the low income population. The reason for this change is seen in the advancement of wages and salaries. Additionally, part-time and temporary contracts have significantly grown. According to the Federal Statistical Office, 12.6 million people were threatened by poverty in 2009 because of their low monthly budget. Further, the number of people who earn less than €9.15 gross per hour has increased by 2.3 million between 1995 and 2010 (Kalina and Weinkopf 2012).

Stock Market

Stock market indexes like the Dow Jones or DAX are seen as economic indicators for the biggest and most important organizations of an economy. Furthermore, stock market indexes help speculate the future prospects of those organizations and the economy as a whole. When the economic outlook is pessimistic, the indexes will drop. For example, after the 9/11 attacks in the US, and after the bankruptcy of Lehman Brothers in 2008, the stock market reacted dramatically.

In Germany the central index DAX has dropped by approximately 50 percent from its high in 2008 until its low in mid 2009. After mid 2009, the DAX recovered slowly and almost reached its former high, but then had to face another decrease due to the European debt crisis. Figure 1 shows this development.

Apart from being an indicator for current economic progress and future prospects, the stock market has a crucial function in providing liquidity for organizations and investors, including foundations with investments in securities and shares. In April 2009 the International Monetary Fund estimated that because of the financial crisis, the value of securities and shares had decreased by four thousand billion US dollars. This massive loss has had a major impact on further investments and liquidity for many companies. In Germany, however, the third sector has not been seriously affected since investments, especially for foundations, are governed by risk-averse legislation (IMF 2009).

Taken together, the economic indicators of GDP, unemployment rates, and stock market indexes show that Germany has survived the economic crisis on relatively stable footing. The current economic situation is very robust with good future opportunities. Nevertheless some threats have to be mentioned. The European debt crisis also affects Germany and it is hard to predict what challenges lie ahead. Like many other countries, Germany has also increased its debt. However, Germany is trying to reduce its necessary new debts, and it is unpredictable where budget cuts will appear. As we will see later, budget cuts for most of the German third sector require changes to legislation.

GOVERNMENT REACTIONS TO THE ECONOMIC CRISIS IN GERMANY

Despite the impact on national debt, the German government reacted to the crisis by supporting financial institutions with money. The main focus was to re-establish trust among the financial institutions to assure the continuation of financial flows and investments. After the Lehman Brothers crash many financial institutions were uncertain whether their investments and balance sheet items were safe. They were unwilling

FIGURE 1. German Central Index DAX from 2007 to 2012

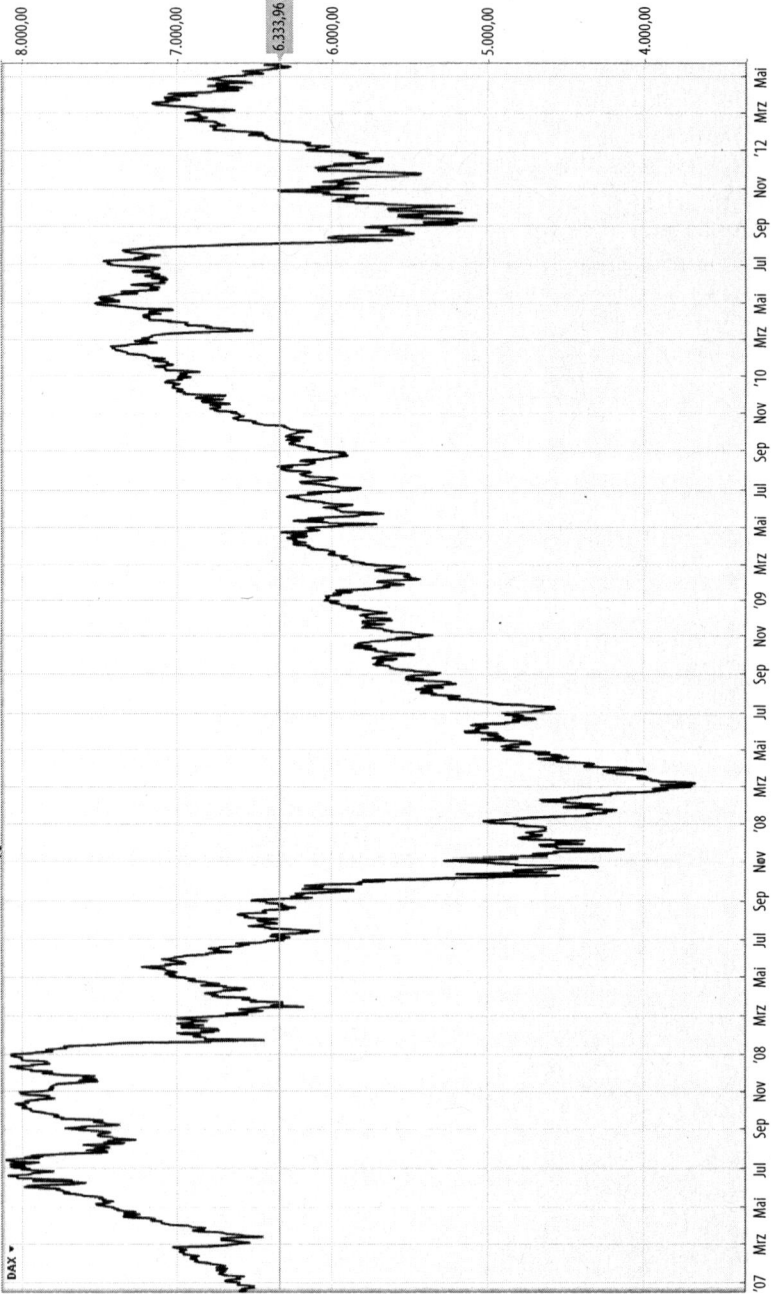

Source: DAX development since 2007 (source: http://www.boerse-frankfurt.de).

to lend money to other organizations because they could not be sure if a specific bank was close to collapse or if they would lose their money. Berlin's rescue program was to give credit guarantees up to €480 billion between banks, and €80 billion for fresh capital for financial institutions. Savings deposits were given unlimited assurance. Furthermore, the problem of lack of transparency in the financial sector was tackled by new regulations.

To protect financial institutions and assure payments, the German government also started programs to revive the German economy, investing €50 billion. At the core of these initiatives was an €18 billion program for education and infrastructure by the federal government. Another initiative focused on vehicle taxes. New vehicles were no longer taxed for their cylinder capacity but for their carbon dioxide emissions. Furthermore new car sales were encouraged by the so called "scrapping premium" (*Abwrackprämie*). Owners of older cars were given this premium when buying a new car emitting less carbon dioxide. To finance these programs, the federal government added €37 billion in new debt to the planned budget.

The economic crisis did not provoke any response to third sector regulations. Since the German economy was faring quite well after a short dip, the danger for the third sector now lies in the huge governmental debts and shortfalls of available funds. Donations and fees might decrease due to higher private debts, and investments in the stock market may lead to losses. Another threat is the low interest rates for investments.

THE THIRD SECTOR IN GERMANY

To understand the impact of the economic crisis on the German third sector, we must first understand several aspects about the sector. It should be noted first that in general, data quality on the third sector is poor. There is little longitudinal data, and available data sets are not comparable due to different definitions of the third sector. Germany does not have a nonprofit legal form for tax exemption. Instead, charitable status may be attributed if several conditions are fulfilled.

The Economic Contribution of the Third Sector

According to 2007 data from the statistical register for enterprises (statistisches Unternehmensregister), there are 2.3 million people working in the third sector in Germany, or 9 percent of the total workforce with national insurance in Germany. Current research estimates 2.3 billion hours of voluntary work in the sector, which would correspond to another million full-time workers. From an organizational perspective, 3 percent of all organizations are included in the third sector, for a total of 105,000 organizations. The average size of third sector organizations is bigger than those in either the private or public sectors. From an economic perspective, the third sector contributes 4.1 percent to the national GDP, or €90 billion. Third sector organizations in Germany are predominantly active in health care, veterinarian care, social care, religious congregations and associations, civic and advocacy organisations, education and research, and culture and recreation (Fritsch et al. 2011).

The German third sector is characterized by two distinguishing criteria. Firstly, the third sector in Germany is dominant in social services. A total of 38 percent of all third sector jobs are in social services, which exceeds the European average of 27 percent (Center of Civil Society Studies 2005). Secondly, third sector organizations are intensely interwoven with the public sector. In numbers, 65 percent of all third sector revenue is from government funding, while only 3 percent comes from philanthropy and 32 percent from fees. These proportions have remained consistent since 1995, when nursing insurance was introduced. Most of the government funding derives from mandatory insurance that employers pay when earning income. In other words, government spending for third sector services does not come from taxes like VAT. As a result, citizens have a legal claim to receive the services of the third sector when they are in need.

Third sector organizations which offer specified services receive a set reimbursement for their services. Both organizational reimbursements as well as insurance payments are highly regulated. The percentage and amounts of insurance contributions are protected by law, and the amount paid for services is regulated and fixed by specific legislation. This gives great stability and predictability for third sector organizations; a change in funds being charged for services would only change when legislation changes.

The relationship of third sector organizations with government varies across fields, dramatically determined by the mandatory insurance. The greatest expenditures are in health and social services, totalling up to 61 percent of all third sector expenditures (Center of Civil Society Studies 2005). Table 3 gives an overview of the employment and funding structures of different fields of the German third sector.

For organizations within the German third sector, tax-exemption is not related to legal status. Rather, an organization qualifies for tax-exemption by fulfilling two basic requirements. First, they are not allowed to distribute potential profits. Second, their activities must contribute to public welfare. The government provides a list of several areas where tax-exemption status is possible because contributions to public welfare are expected. For example, according to §52 paragraph 2 of *Abgabenordnung* (Regulation of Taxation) among others these are: support of science and research, education, art and culture, international understanding, monument conservation, environmental and countryside conservation, support of homeland, traditions, protection of animals, and development cooperation.

TABLE 3
Structure of the German Third Sector

Field	Employment	Volunteers	Expenditures	Revenue from:			Total Revenue (millions*)
				Government	Philanthropy	Fees	
Culture and recreation	5%	33%	9%	20%	13%	66%	12,232
Education and research	11%	1%	9%	75%	2%	23%	12,281
Health	30%	7%	35%	94%	0%	6%	47,566
Social services	38%	8%	26%	65%	5%	30%	35,929
Environment	1%	5%	1%	22%	16%	62%	1,031
Development and housing	6%	2%	5%	57%	0%	43%	7,545
Civic and advocacy	2%	5%	1%	58%	7%	36%	2,036
Philanthropy	0%	2%	7%	10%	3%	86%	8,972
International activities	1%	2%	1%	51%	41%	8%	837
Religious worship	3%	19%	2%	95%	0%	5%	2,167
Professional and unions	4%	4%	5%	2%	1%	97%	6,972
Not elsewhere classified	-	13%	-	-	-	-	-
Totals	**100%** FTE	**100%** FTE	**100%** millions*	**65%**	**3%**	**32%**	**137,567**
	1,480,850	**1,211,474**	**137,547**				
Totals as a percent of:							
Economically active population	3.6%	3.0%					
Gross Domestic Product			4.0%				

updated: 1/18/2005

* Local currency.
"-" = Data not available.
Source: Center of Civil Society Studies 2005.

The Role of Free Welfare Associations

The health care and social services fields are dominated by Free Welfare Associations (FWA) (Zimmer et al. 2004), which represent the "most powerful share of the German nonprofit sector" (Zimmer 2000, 102). There are six "peak associations of free welfare work" (*Spitzenverbände der freien Wohlfahrtspflege*) which serve as umbrella organizations under which FWAs are organized (Zimmer and Toepler 2000). These organizations include the religiously affiliated Caritas (*Deutscher Caritasverband*), Diakonie *(Diakonisches Werk der Evangelischen Kirche in Deutschland)*, and the Jewish Welfare (*Zentralwohlfahrtsstelle der Juden in Deutschland*), as well as the politically affiliated (social democratic) Worker´s Welfare Service *(Arbeiterwohlfahrt)*. These umbrella organizations also include

Parity–Association of Non-affiliated Charities (*Deutscher Paritätischer Wohlfahrtsverband*), as well as Red Cross Germany (Vilain 2002; Zimmer and Toepler 2000). In 2008, these organizations employed 80 percent of the entire third sector workforce, having 1,541,829 paid employees (54 percent part-time). From a national perspective, these six organizations account for almost 4 percent of the overall German labour force (BAGFW e.V. 2008). These organizations offer all kinds of social services and health care, including care centres, youth welfare services, health services, unemployment consulting, assistance to immigrants and refugees, and training and educational programs (Zimmer and Toepler 2000).

FWAs are responsible for offering the social services ensured by German legislation according to the "principle of subsidiarity" (Zimmer et al. 2004). Until legislation changes in the 1990s, the FWAs and their affiliated organizations were the preferred recipients of government funds allocated for social services contracts, available to nonprofit, public or for-profit providers (Priller et al. 2000; Thränhardt 2003; Zimmer et al. 2004). This preferential position for FWAs in social service provision had been incorporated in German law since the 1960s (Zimmer et al. 2004). The receipt of funding was independent from efficiency or effectiveness indicators (Vilain 2002), as FWAs were guaranteed independence and self-determination (Zimmer 1999). The only criterion for FWAs to receive government funding was that private income (e.g., from fees, donations, bequests etc.) make up a 30 percent share of their total financial base (Zimmer et al. 2004).

Foundations   .

Apart from government funding, foundations play another vital and strategic role in third sector funding. From a budget point of view, foundations are not as powerful in Germany as in other industrialized countries like the US, but their influence is growing fast. The following table shows the growth of foundations. Figures are estimates from the *Bundesverband Deutscher Stiftungen e.V.* (Association of German Foundations). Because German foundations have no formal register or obligation for transparency, little is known about their growth or financial status.

Table 4 illustrates that the German foundation sector is growing steadily. Even during the economic crisis, there was no detectable slowdown in growth. Growth in total numbers does not reveal specific information about the number of new foundations; many foundations have either dissolved or merged. Despite this caveat, it is interesting to see that the number of foundations in Germany has almost doubled within 11 years. This growth is accompanied by growth of foundation capital and yearly budgets and number of employees. Excluding volunteers, there are 40-50,000 employees in the foundation sector. In 2009, the total estimated

TABLE 4
Growth of the German Foundation Sector

Year	Number of Foundations (estimate)	Growth from Previous Year	Relative Growth (percent)
2011	18,946	+784	+4.31
2010	18,162	+790	+4.55
2009	17,372	+966	+5.56
2008	16,406	+957	+6.19
2007	15,449	+1048	+7.28
2006	14,401	+911	+6.75
2005	13,490	+820	+6.47
2004	12,670	+477	+3.91
2003	12,193	+901	+7.98
2002	11,292	+789	+7.51
2001	10,503		

Source: Bundesverband Deutscher Stiftungen 2011.

assets of all German foundations was €100 billion, with annual earnings of about €7 billion. In comparison to the US, these numbers are relatively small. The Bill & Melinda Gates Foundation, for example, has a capital of US$31 billion alone.

The boom in foundation growth can be explained by a legislation change. The 2007 government's "Help for Helpers" initiative paved the way for strengthening the role of foundations. With this initiative, the exemption limit for tax free donations was increased to one million per year. Since then donations have risen significantly. Both new and more mature foundations have more capital to work with. The Association of German Foundations expects that foundation capital will quadruple in the next 25 years. However, each sector will not profit equally from the increase in capital. Table 5 shows the fields where German foundations operate.

TABLE 5
Fields of Operation of German Foundations 2011

Field	Number of Foundations (percent)
Culture and recreation	15.1
Education	15.3
Science and research	12.9
Social purposes	30.8
Environment	3.8
Private purposes	4.2
Other tax-exempt purposes	17.9
Total	100.0

Source: Bundesverband Deutscher Stiftungen 2011.

Foundations in Germany have not been hit hard by the crisis. In fact, the foundation sector is booming despite the crisis. Their investments are relatively stable due to conservative investment law. Legislation does not allow risky investments to ensure capital preservation (*Kapitalerhaltungsgrundsatz*). For example, foundations are not allowed to invest in shares or make other risky capital market investments such as speculation or gambling. Foundations have to make investments with the expectation of a positive return on investment (Schlüter, Stolte and Manteuffel 2007). Furthermore, capital earnings must be used directly in the same fiscal year. As a result, the foundations capital has not been affected significantly by the downturn of the stock market. However, low interest rates for investments which lower the amount of earnings available for charitable and other purposes, remains a current problem.

RESPONSE OF THIRD SECTOR ORGANIZATIONS

Since the 1990s, the German government has faced limited and decreasing financial resources especially due to the German reunification. In this context, the preference toward FWAs and their relationship with government has changed. Reducing costs of social welfare has been a priority. The government has made major cuts in public expenditures and triggered a crisis of the German welfare state (Dahme 2008; Zimmer 2000). At the same time, the government introduced stronger competition among providers of social services and health care, thereby eliminating the quasi-monopoly of the FWAs (Thränhardt 2003; Zimmer et al. 2004). State wide and regional providers began competing to win grants and contracts through bidding procedures (Grunwald 2001).

This new context had tremendous impact on FWAs. They were forced to change their operations and become more efficient and effective, to search for new funding sources, and to establish new and more business-like management strategies. These changes put pressure on the workforce. Management systems in need of renovation included financial oversight, quality management, and reporting (Dahme and Wohlfahrt 2007; Zimmer and Freise 2003; Ridder and Neumann 2001). Most of these tools came from the for-profit sector and got adapted to third sector organizations needs (Vilain 2002). Interesting enough, these changes came at the same time that commercialization of nonprofits was being debated in the US (Weisbrod 1998; Dees, Emerson and Economy 1998; Young and Salamon 2003). Parallel to this, the debate on social entrepreneurship arose (Emerson and Twersky 1996; Drayton 2002 and 2005; Bornstein 2004; Bishop 2006; Nicholls 2006; Mair, Robinson and Hockerts 2006; Mair and Martí 2006). As a result, some of the FWAs responded by implementing new strategic thinking as well as innovative structures

(Schmitz and Scheuerle 2012). This process of social innovation support is also reinforced by the recent establishment of a new funding program. In January 2012, the KfW (*Kreditanstalt für Wiederaufbau*) started a program to support the organizational growth process of social innovations initiated by social entrepreneurs. The KfW is a development bank with a wide range of programs, predominantly supporting small and medium-sized organizations. Funding for the KfW comes from the German government. Further, the bank is predominantly controlled by the Ministry of Finance. Hence, the program for social entrepreneurship support is a result of administration policies. Financial support is only given as a supplement to the funds of a partner investor and is connected to a range of conditions. For example, the partner investor is not allowed to own or control more than 49 percent of the social entrepreneurship organization, or to shift the risk of the investment to the social entrepreneur, her/his organization, or a closely related entity (family member or associates). Furthermore, the partner investor has to support the social entrepreneurship venture with knowledge and other nonfinancial support and has to report to the KfW according to a cooperation agreement. The maximum amount given from the KfW per organization is €200,000.

The KfW program does not support start-ups but rather organizations in a more mature phase of their development. What is more, the support is given to organizations that demonstrate an earned-income model that helps the organization to become financially self-sustainable. In short, the government is interested in organizations tackling social problems in a financially self-sustainable way so that less governmental financial support is needed. What this means for the mature welfare organizations remains unclear. What can be said is that because of this KfW program, social entrepreneurship organizations will grow and might become competitors for the older and bigger organizations. This may lead to further policy changes that result in cuts to government budgets. That said, most mature organizations seem well positioned to perform well in terms of innovation and diversification (Schmitz and Scheuerle 2012).

At a broader level, the European Commission is already heavily supporting social innovation. Five recent research projects are trying to evaluate the necessity and promotion of social innovations in Europe. These are: WILCO (Welfare Innovations at the Local level in favour of Cohesion); IMPROVE (Poverty Reduction in Europe–Social Policy and Innovation); WWWforEurope (Welfare, Wealth and Work for Europe); INNOSERV (Social Platform for Innovative Social Services);and TEPSIE (The Theoretical, Empirical and Policy Foundations for Building Social Innovation in Europe). In addition to these research projects, the European Commission is supporting the practice field of social innovation. Social innovations are seen as necessary to tackle the social problems ahead.

CONCLUSIONS AND FUTURE PROSPECTS

In summary, the third sector in Germany has weathered the economic crisis well. No long term recession is apparent. The income streams for social service providers are very stable due to legislation, and foundations invest their capital very conservatively, not accepting risky investments. What is more, the nonprofit job market is currently booming. According to a 2011 survey conducted by the German institute *Wissenschaftsladen Bonn*, nonprofits and non-governmental organizations are increasingly searching for staff. There are approximately 70 percent more job opportunities in those organizations in Germany at the end of 2010 than there were in 2006. In numbers, 22,000 job offers were made in the past five years. Employees with a background in humanities and social sciences were in particularly high demand (77 percent), whereas people with a background in engineering and natural sciences comprised only 23 percent of job offers. Interestingly, temporary contracts were most often for engineers and natural scientists and less likely for people from the humanities. Despite the current stability of the German third sector, there are considerable dangers that can affect the sector in the years to come. The greatest danger lies in the enormous increase in debt because of the fiscal stimulus spending that was put in place to face the economic downturn. Debt levels have increased by 15 percent since 2009. As a result, social budgets may soon be cut.

Since the Reagan Administration, budget cuts have been put forward to explain the trend toward social entrepreneurship and earned-income strategies (Galaskiewicz and Bielefeld 1998; Light 2000; Dees, Emerson and Economy 1998; Ryan 1999; Salamon 1999). In Germany, we also see a trend towards social entrepreneurship. However, without huge budget cuts in the past, and only limited shrinkage in funding for the third sector, budget cuts seem to be only a part of the explanation.

Legislative changes that lead to cuts to the budget for social services would likely provoke protests. Egalitarian social security is a deeply rooted ideal in Germany. Instead, social innovations might be preferred, including social entrepreneurship initiatives which may be more efficient and less capital-intensive than conventional solutions. This approach has tremendous consequences for mature nonprofit organizations like the free welfare associations. The funding structure of mature organizations might weaken while more efficient approaches will be preferred. Older organizations might also react with their own innovations and earned income strategies (Schmitz and Scheuerle 2012). The current policy discussions supporting social innovation approaches hint that this might be the direction the government will turn in the future.

In addition to these investments in social innovation, other changes brought on by the economic crisis and the accompanying social problems are heavily debated. Distrust in the economic system has led to value changes. One such indicator is the increasing demand for sustainable and organic products. New organizational forms may arise, allowing stronger participation of stakeholders. Stakeholders will invest their time and energy into organizations where they can influence their direction, including social organizations like nonprofits or social entrepreneurship organizations. Because of more people in vulnerable situations and the aging population, greater demands for nonprofit services can be expected. Even if Germany has come through the crisis relatively well, the road ahead is full of uncertainties.

REFERENCES

BAGFW e.V. 2008. "Bundesarbeitsgemeinschaft der Freien Wohlfahrtspflege." Einrichtungen und Dienste der Freien Wohlfahrtspflege Gesamtstatistik – Organizations and services of free welfare work annual statistics. At http://www.bagfw.de/uploads/media/GS_BAGFW_091221_web_01.pdf (accessed 20 May 2012).

Bishop, M. 2006. "The Rise of the Social Entrepreneur: Whatever He May Be." *The Economist* 378 (8466), special edition, 11-13.

Bornstein, D. 2004. *How to Change the World, Social Entrepreneurs and the Power of New Ideas*. New York: Oxford University Press.

Bundesverband Deutscher Stiftungen. 2011. *"Verzeichnis Deutscher Stiftungen 2011 Bd. 1-4,7., erweiterte und überarbeitete Auflage."* Berlin: Bundesverband Deutscher Stiftungen.

Center of Civil Society Studies. 2005. "The civil society sector at a glance: Germany." The Comparative Nonprofit Sector Project. John Hopkins Institute for Policy Studies. John Hopkins University. At http://www.ccss.jhu.edu/pdfs/CNP/CNP_Germany_WrkExp.pdf (accessed 12 August 2010).

Dahme, H.J. 2008. "Krise der öffentlichen Kassen und des Sozialstaats." *Aus Politik und Zeitgeschichte* 12 (13): 10-16.

Dahme, H.J. and N. Wohlfahrt. 2007. "Vom Korporatismus zur strategischen Allianz von Sozialstaat und Sozialwirtschaft: Neue 'Sozialpartnerschaft' auf Kosten der Beschäftigten?" In Dahme, H.J., A. Trube, and N. Wohlfahrt. *Arbeit in sozialen Diensten: flexibel und schlecht bezahlt?*, 22-34. Baltmannsweiler: Schneider Hohengehren.

Dees, G.J., J. Emerson, and P. Economy, eds. 1998. *Enterprising Nonprofits – A Toolkit for Social Entrepreneurs*. New York: John Wiley and Sons.

Drayton, B. 2002. "The Citizen Sector: Becoming as Entrepreneurial and Competitive as Business." *California Management Review* 44 (3): 120-132.

——. 2005. "Social Entrepreneurs: Creating a Competitive and Entrepreneurial Citizen Sector." At www.changemakers.net/library/readings/drayton.cfm (accessed 20 December 2011).

Emerson, J. and F. Twersky, eds. 1996. *New Social Entrepreneurs – the Success, Challenge and Lessons of Non-profit Enterprise Creation*. San Francisco: The Robers Foundation.

Fritsch, S., M. Klose, R. Opfermann, N. Rosenski, N. Schwarz, H.K. Anheier, and N. Spengler. 2011. ZIVIZ – Zivilgesellschaft in Zahlen, Abschlussbericht Modul 1.

At http://www.ziviz.info/fileadmin/download/zivilgesellschaft_in_zahlen_ abschlussbericht_modul_1.pdf (accessed 20 May 2012).

Galaskiewicz, J. and W. Bielefeld. 1998. *Nonprofit Organizations in an Age of Uncertainty*. New York: Aldine De Gruyter.

Grunwald, K. 2001. *Neugestaltung der freien Wohlfahrtspflege. Management organisationalen Wandels und die Ziele der Sozialen Arbeit*. München and Weinheim: Juventa.

International Monetary Fund (IMF). 2009. "Stabilizing the Global Financial System and Mitigating Spillover Risks." In *IMF: International Financial Stability Report*, April.

Kalina, T. and C. Weinkopf. 2012. *Niedriglohnbeschäftigung 2010 – Fast jede/rVierte arbeitet für Niedriglohn. IAQ-Report 2012-01*. At http://www.iaq.uni-due.de/ iaq-report/2012/report2012-01.pdf (accessed 5 April 2012).

Light, P. 2000. *Making Nonprofit Work*. Washington, DC: The Brookings Institute.

Mair, J. and I. Martí. 2006. "Social Entrepreneurship Research: A Source of Explanation, Prediction, and Delight." *Journal of World Business* 41: 36-44.

Mair, J., J. Robinson, and K. Hockerts, eds. 2006. *Social Entrepreneurship*. Houndmills: Palgrave Macmillan.

Nicholls, A., ed. 2006. *Social Entrepreneurship: New models of Sustainable Social Change*. Oxford: Oxford University Press.

Organisation for Economic Co-operation and Development (OECD). 2012a. *Divided We Stand-Why Inequality Keeps Rising*. OECD Publishing.

—. 2012b. Statistics from A to Z. At http://www.oecd.org/document/0,3746, en_2649_201185_46462759_1_1_1,00.html (accessed 20 May 2012).

Priller, E., A. Zimmer, H.K. Anheier, S. Toepler, and L.M. Salamon. 2000. "Germany: Unification and Change." In *The Third Sector in Germany. Münsteraner Diskussionspapiere zum Nonprofit-Sektor*. At http://www.aktive-buergerschaft. de/fp_files/Diskussionspapiere/2002wp-sband03.pdf (accessed 20 May 2012).

Ridder, H.G and S. Neumann, S. 2001. "Personalwirtschaft im Umbruch? / Human Resource Management on the move?" *Zeitschrift für Personalführung* 11 (3): 243-261.

Ryan, W.P. 1999. "The New Landscape for Nonprofits." *Harvard Business Review* 77 (1): 127-136.

Salamon, L.M. 1999. *America´s Nonprofit Sector*. New York: The Foundation Center.

Schlüter, A., S. Stolte, and E. Manteuffel. 2007. *Stiftungsrecht – Erscheinungsformen und Errichtung der Stiftung, Stiftungsaufsicht, Verwaltung des Stiftungsvermögens, Besteuerung von Stiftung und Stifter, Internationales Stiftungsrecht*. München: C.H. Beck.

Schmitz, B. and T. Scheuerle. 2012. "Founding or Transforming? – Social Intrapreneurship in three German Christian based NPOs." *Journal of Social Entrepreneurship Perspectives* 1 (1): 13-36.

Thränhardt, D. 2003. "Engagement und Effizienz. Wohlfahrtsverbände im Wandel." In *Wohlfahrtsverbände im Wandel – Qualitätsmanagement und Professionalisierung*, ed. W. Lange and U. Hunger, 7-19. Münster: Civil Society Network.

Vilain, M. 2002. "Nonprofit Management – Current Challenges for Personnel Management in German Welfare Organisations." At http://www.stiftungsver-bund-westfalen.de/download/Vilain_Nonprofit-Management_-_Current%20 Challenges.pdf (accessed 22 May 2012).

Weisbrod, B.A., ed. 1998. *To Profit or Not to Profit – The Commercial Transformation of the Nonprofit Sector*. Cambridge: Cambridge University Press.

Young, D.R. and L.M. Salamon. 2003. "Commercialization, Social Ventures, and For-profit Competition." In *The State of the Nonprofit America*, ed. L.M. Salamon, 423-336. Washington: The Brookings Institution.

Zimmer, A. 2000. "Welfare Pluralism and Health Care: The Case of Germany." In *The Third Sector in Germany. Münsteraner Diskussionspapiere zum Nonprofit-Sektor*. At http://www.aktive-buergerschaft.de/fp_files/Diskussionspapiere/2002wp-sband03.pdf (accessed 20 May 2012).

Zimmer, A. and M. Freise, M. 2003. "Personal Management in Nonprofit-Organisationen / Human Resource Management in Nonprofit Organizations." In *Wohlfahrtsverbände im Wandel – Qualitätsmanagement und Professionalisierung*, ed. W. Lange and U. Hunger, 107-134. Münster: Civil Society Network.

Zimmer, A. and S. Toepler. 2000. "Government Policy and Future Issues. Federal Republic of Germany." In *The Third Sector in Germany. Münsteraner Diskussionspapiere zum Nonprofit-Sektor*. At http://www.aktive-buergerschaft.de/fp_files/Diskussionspapiere/2002wp-sband03.pdf (accessed 20 May 2012).

Zimmer, A., J. Gärtner, E. Priller, P. Rawert, C. Sachße, and R. Graf Strachwitz. 2004. "The Legacy of Subsidiarity: The Nonprofit Sector in Germany." In *Future of Civil Society: Making Central European Nonprofit Organizations Work*, ed. A. Zimmer and E. Priller, 681-711. Wiesbaden: VS-Verlag.

CHAPTER 11

THE NATIONAL COMPACT: CIVILIZING THE RELATIONSHIP BETWEEN GOVERNMENT AND THE NOT-FOR-PROFIT SECTOR IN AUSTRALIA

JOHN BUTCHER

INTRODUCTION

Australia is a curious case. Nineteenth century European explorer-naturalists thought of the island continent as a "separate creation" where a demanding environment forced organisms to evolve unique forms, adaptations and survival strategies in isolation from the rest of the world. The same might be said of Australia's political culture and patterns of public administration which have evolved in response to the nation's social and political ecology – more "Ozminster" than "Westminster," despite the inevitable tides of globalization washing our shores (Evans 2010, 262). Consider the following:

- In its April 2012 *World Economic Outlook*, the International Monetary Fund (IMF) noted that projected growth in domestic GDP and domestic demand is forecast at 3.0 percent in 2012 and 3.5 percent in 2013 (compared to the average for advanced economies of 1.4 and 2.0 percent respectively) (IMF 2012, 191).
- Unemployment is trending steady at 5.2 percent (ABS 2012), interest rates are low (by Australian standards) and inflation will be in the 2-3 percent range over the next two years despite strong domestic demand (RBA 2012).

Government-Nonprofit Relations in Times of Recession, ed. Rachel Laforest. Montreal and Kingston: Queen's Policy Studies Series, McGill-Queen's University Press. © 2013 The School of Policy Studies, Queen's University at Kingston.

- Meanwhile, the IMF notes that a planned return to surplus by 2012/13 "will increase fiscal room and take pressure off monetary policy and the exchange rate," while an on-going mining boom will provide opportunities to "build fiscal buffers further over the medium term and contribute to national saving" (IMF 2011).
- In his April 2012 *Economic Note*, the Treasurer observed that, "We have very low debt and our public finances are in great shape – reflected in Australia being awarded the coveted AAA credit rating from all three global ratings agencies for the first time in our history" (Swan 2012a).

Taken together, these indicators give credence to the government's claims that Australia is in an enviable economic position by comparison with the rest of the world (Wright 2012). The outside observer would be forgiven for thinking that any government presiding over such an economic "good news story" would be in a position of political strength.

But this is where the topsy-turvy world of Australian politics turns politics as usual on its head. Unlike the economy, the federal Labor minority government has staggered along in almost perpetual crisis, burdened by questions of legitimacy, political miscalculation, scandals, and a relentlessly negative campaign by the opposition.

In spite of all this, the government continues to pursue a broad structural reform agenda, including a suite of needed reforms affecting Australia's not-for-profit sector.[1] The fate of this reform agenda is, however, coupled with the fortunes of the minority Labor government and the uncertain prospect that it will survive long enough to fight the next scheduled election on its own terms in late 2013. The sector itself exhibits ambivalence towards this reformist government, notwithstanding the fact that much of the reform agenda enjoys broad sector support.

In this chapter we consider how this seemingly contradictory state of affairs has come to pass and where it might end up. The chapter is in two parts. Part 1 deals with the impact of the global financial crisis on the Australian policy and political scene as well as its direct and indirect impacts on Australia's not-for-profit sector. Part 2 sets out the recent history of the not-for-profit policy space with particular emphasis on the National Compact and associated reform initiatives undertaken by Labor governments led, successively, by Prime Ministers Kevin Rudd and Julia Gillard.

Part 1 – The Australian Response to the Global Financial Crisis

Unlike other countries profiled in this volume, Australia's was one of the few developed economies to avoid a recession during the global financial crisis (Ellis 2011).[2] This was owed largely to four factors: (1) a strong mining sector coupled with sustained demand for commodities; (2) a massive federal stimulus program; (3) the underlying strength of the economy; and (4) a well-regulated financial sector.

The 2007 general election returned the Australian Labor Party (the ALP), led by Kevin Rudd, to power after eleven years in opposition. The new government was of a reformist caste with a sweeping policy agenda, including plans to initiate a suite of reforms to better support constructive engagement between the federal government and the not-for-profit sector. Within the government's first year in office the deepening global financial crisis loomed as an existential threat to the Australian economy.

The fundamentals of the Australian economy were sound, and these provided a strong platform from which to mount a response to the worsening global economic downturn. Firstly, the government had a healthy balance sheet by virtue of having inherited a $21 billion+ surplus from the outgoing Liberal-National Coalition government led by John Howard (Wanna 2009, 584). Secondly, as the United States' sub-prime mortgage market began to collapse in February 2007, Australian GDP rose against the global trend to a high of 4.2 percent in the September quarter of 2007 and unemployment fell to a low of 4.1 percent in the March quarter of 2008 (McGregor-Lowndes 2011, 1).

On the domestic front, the government announced an initial stimulus package in 2008 of $10 billion, followed by a second stimulus package in 2009 of $42 billion.[3] In the process, the government incurred a deficit for the second time since 1997 (the Coalition government incurred a deficit of 0.1 percent in 2002). The resultant deficit of 4.3 percent of GDP exceeded a previous high of 4.0 percent in 1993 (also under a Labor administration), a fact exploited by the opposition, which portrayed the government's stimulus measures as gross profligacy and the Labor administration "addicted to tax and spend" government (Hockey 2011a, 2011b).[4]

Despite the opposition's hyperbole, Australian government net debt is low by international standards (Commonwealth of Australia 2011; Colonial First State 2010). Furthermore, the success of the government's stimulus response has been attested by senior industry analysts and expert commentators (Stiglitz 2010; Long 2010; ABC 2009; Stafford 2009), and by overseas agencies such as the World Bank and the OECD (Hutchens 2011; Colebatch 2009). Australia not only dodged the global financial crisis "bullet," but according to the Australian Treasurer Wayne Swan, in 2012 Australia's economic fundamentals are enviable, with "growth around trend, low unemployment, contained inflation, a sturdy financial sector, strong government finances, a huge investment pipeline and a triple A credit rating from all three international ratings agencies" (Swan 2012b).

Impact of the Global Financial Crisis on the Not-for-profit Sector

The direct effects of the global financial crisis on Australia's not-for-profit sector are largely a matter of conjecture. According to one survey of 263 not-for-profit organizations, sector income from investments, fund-raising, and corporate donations declined in the face of economic uncertainty.[5] However, the same survey found that funding from federal and state/territory governments (representing around 45 percent of the total income for responding not-for-profits) remained stable in 2009, thus providing an important bulwark against a loss of revenue from other sources.

By 2009, owing to better than expected economic conditions, the mood in the sector was reported to be "markedly more optimistic, with a growing number anticipating a return to growth" (PwC, FIA and CIS 2010). It should be noted, however, that these findings are indicative only for about 10 percent of Australia's large and diverse not-for-profit sector. Of the estimated 600,000 not-for-profit organizations in Australia, only about 59,000 are regarded as "economically significant" and therefore likely to rely on government grants or contracts for a major share of their income (Productivity Commission 2010, 53-85).

The direct effects of the global financial crisis on Australian social policy are harder to discern. There was no notable rush by the federal government to reign in social spending or to cut social entitlements. That said, declining tax revenues along with deteriorating business and consumer confidence certainly meant there was far less room for discretionary expenditure unless it clearly served the task of supporting the economy. Rather, what prevailed was what detractors and supporters alike characterized as a classical Keynesian response (Garnett and Lewis 2011).[6]

The then head of the Treasury department had advised the government in 2008 to "go hard, go early, go households" (Garnett and Lewis 2011, 183; Uren and Taylor 2010). Accordingly, the government's response to the global financial crisis – the *Nation Building, Economic Stimulus Plan* – included measures to sustain domestic demand such as direct cash payments to Australian households, and a series of targeted infrastructure programs aimed to both support employment and generate broad community benefits. The latter included investment in education, social housing, community infrastructure, road and rail infrastructure, and domestic energy efficiency.

Other direct and indirect measures were taken in an attempt to moderate demand for essential social services provided by the not-for-profit sector. The federal government provided $11 million in Temporary Financial Assistance Grants to support charitable and non-profit organizations that experienced a decrease in donations; doubled funding for emergency relief and financial counselling; and provided an additional $50 million for no income loans, matched savings, and affordable credit (ALP 2010).

Apart from its direct effects, the global financial crisis also served to highlight the social and labour force implications of Australia's "two speed" economy in which a booming resource extraction sector makes up the "fast lane" and in the "slow lane" are all the rest.[7] The influx of well-paid "fly-in, fly-out" mining industry workers has also fuelled increases in the cost of living in regional centres, leading to significant disadvantage for people on fixed incomes and those who are reliant on the private rental market. This has in turn placed further pressures on not-for-profit community services that have not only experienced a growing demand for services, but who struggle to attract and retain staff in the face of competition from a cashed-up mining sector. The situation is not helped by the fact that workers in the community services sector have been historically underpaid, a fact recently given formal recognition by Australia's paramount industrial tribunal, Fair Work Australia.[8]

Political Crisis

The mobilization of the economic stimulus package was a major distraction for the new government and quickly became the centre of policy concern, to some extent crowding out other aspects of its legislative and policy program. The scale of the stimulus package and the speed with which it was rolled out severely stretched the capacity and capability of federal government departments, their state government partners,[9] and affected industry sectors. Through 2009 and 2010, despite having "saved" Australia from the worst effects of the global financial crisis, there was controversy about apparent deficiencies in the administration of high profile components of the stimulus package. Coupled with the political optics of a rapid return to budgetary deficit and the inability to secure support for a number of the Rudd government's signature policies,[10] these deficiencies fed an opposition narrative of a confused and inept Labor administration (Abbott 2011).

By mid-2010 the government had reached a point of policy and political paralysis. Prime Minister Kevin Rudd's approval ratings were described as being "in freefall." At the urging of influential members of the Labor caucus, Rudd was challenged for the leadership by his then Deputy, Julia Gillard.[11] Realizing he did not have the numbers to win a caucus ballot for the leadership, Rudd resigned and on 24 June 2010, Julia Gillard became Australia's first female Prime Minister, saying, "a good government had lost its way" (McKew 2012; Levy 2010). Twenty-three days later, amid rising public unease over the unseating of a sitting Prime Minister in only his first term – an historic first for Australia – Gillard called a general election for 21 August 2010.

The election resulted in a hung parliament in which Labor and the opposition commanded an equal number of seats in the House of

Representatives. The balance of power rested with the cross-benches and, after 17 days of tough negotiation, a Greens MP and three independents reached agreements under which they would guarantee supply for a Labor administration.

Minority government has not been smooth sailing for the Prime Minister or for Labor. The government's political woes have been exacerbated by a series of policy reversals,[12] political scandals[13] and a leadership challenge brought on by the former prime minister, Kevin Rudd.[14]

The government's relationship with the not-for-profit sector has been strained by the politics of minority government. While parts of Australia's not-for-profit sector might not welcome the return of a federal Coalition government, relations with the federal Labor government at the political level have the distinct appearance of being cordial, yet reticent.

Although the government has largely followed through on its undertakings with regard to policy reforms (see Figure 1) the government has disappointed the not-for-profit sector on a number of "hot button" social policy issues such as legislation to curb problem gambling, the treatment of asylum seekers, and indigenous policy. These are all examples of policy arenas where the minority government is effectively wedged between the aspirations of progressive voices in the sector and the white bread politics of so-called middle Australia.

The not-for-profit sector was particularly critical of the government's determination to return the budget to surplus in 2012/13 (Commonwealth of Australia 2011) arguing, along with the support of the Australian Greens, that the government should instead invest in social programs of benefit to the most vulnerable in Australian society (Goldie 2012; Scott 2012). On this too, however, the government was wedged politically.

A key theme in the opposition's narrative of the government's economic incompetence is that Labor has not delivered a budget surplus since it was first elected in 2007 (conveniently ignoring the small matter of the global financial crisis). Returning the budget to surplus, therefore, is a mark of Labor's desperation to re-establish its credentials for economic management. Having staked its economic reputation on achieving a surplus in 2012/13, and having worn the opprobrium of the opposition, the media, and the electorate for past policy reversals, Labor found itself locked-in.

Clearly, the commitment to a surplus in 2012/13, coupled with declining revenues and the imposition of mandatory savings requirements on government entities, placed additional fiscal pressure on government. Although the government announced in April 2012 its intention to commence a National Disability Insurance Scheme in 2013, significant new spending initiatives in other areas considered by the not-for-profit sector to be a priority – such as a national dental scheme, an increase in benefits for job-seekers, or a major overhaul of school education – would have to await less straitened fiscal conditions.

FIGURE 1
Political and Policy Trajectory of Rudd/Gillard Governments 2007–2013

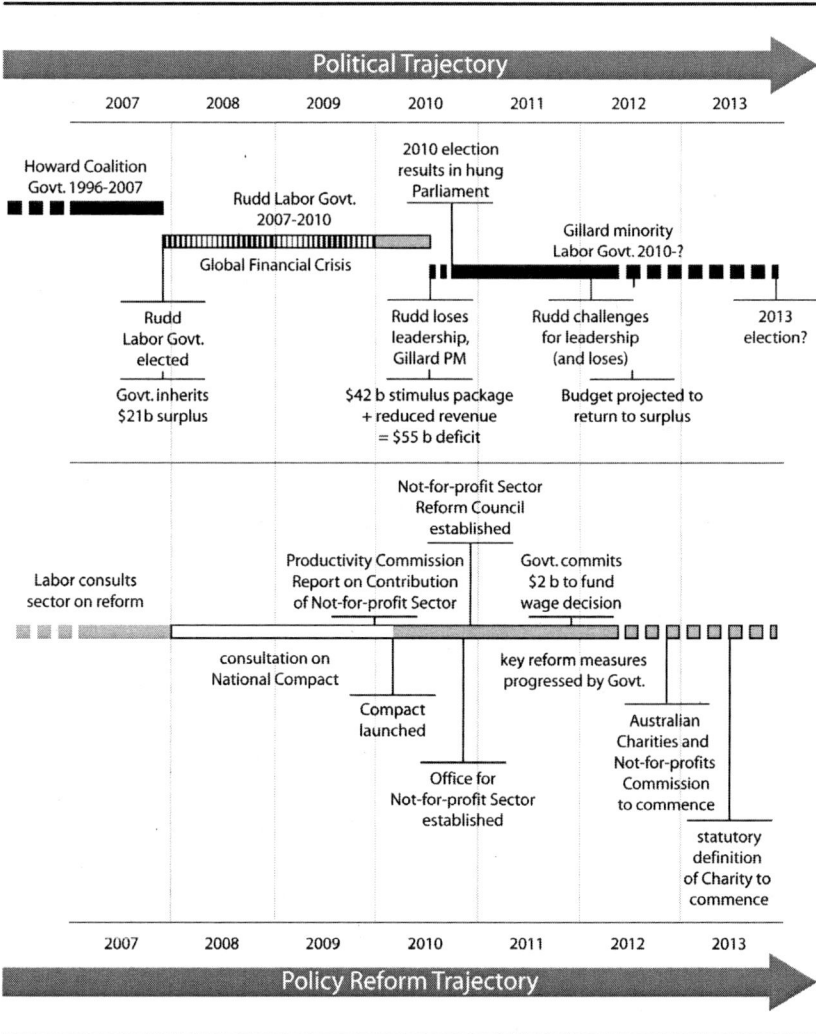

Political Trajectory

| 2007 | 2008 | 2009 | 2010 | 2011 | 2012 | 2013 |

Howard Coalition
Govt. 1996-2007

Rudd Labor Govt.
2007-2010

2010 election
results in hung
Parliament

Gillard minority
Labor Govt. 2010-?

Global Financial Crisis

Rudd
Labor Govt.
elected

Govt. inherits
$21b surplus

Rudd loses
leadership,
Gillard PM

$42 b stimulus package
+ reduced revenue
= $55 b deficit

Rudd challenges
for leadership
(and loses)

Budget projected to
return to surplus

2013
election?

Not-for-profit Sector
Reform Council
established

Labor consults
sector on reform

Productivity Commission
Report on Contribution
of Not-for-profit Sector

Govt. commits
$2 b to fund
wage decision

consultation on
National Compact

key reform measures
progressed by Govt.

Compact
launched

Australian
Charities and
Not-for-profits
Commission
to commence

Office for
Not-for-profit Sector
established

statutory
definition
of Charity to
commence

| 2007 | 2008 | 2009 | 2010 | 2011 | 2012 | 2013 |

Policy Reform Trajectory

Source: Author's compilation.

PART 2 – AN AUSTRALIAN COMPACT

The broad policy aims underpinning the not-for-profit sector reform agenda were formulated prior to the global financial crisis – as early as 2006 – when Labor was still in opposition. In the course of the 2007 election, Labor announced its intention to consult with the not-for-profit sector about a compact along the lines of agreements in the UK and Canada and pledged to task the government's premier economic research and advisory body, the Productivity Commission, to undertake a study of the contribution of Australia's not-for-profit sector.

The launch of the Australian National Compact in March 2010 marked an important milestone towards fulfillment of Labor's promise to "repair" the relationship between the federal government and the not-for-profit sector (Gillard and Wong 2007). The National Compact, like its better-known predecessors the English Compact and the Canadian Accord (see Laforest, and Rochester and Zimmeck in this volume), is a formal, deliberate policy instrument designed to establish new rules of engagement between government and the not-for-profit sector. It would also be an important plank in a broader policy agenda for social inclusion.

Then Prime Minister Kevin Rudd hailed the National Compact as an expression of the government's desire "to embrace new ways of governing – including forming innovative partnerships with the Third Sector to tackle the nation's long-term challenges" (Commonwealth of Australia 2011). The following discussion explores the political events and the policy antecedents that shape the policy discourse on which the National Compact is founded together with the trajectory of sector reform in uncertain political times.

The Howard Experiment with Market Governance

In many respects, the Liberal-National Coalition government led by John Howard (1996–2007) could be characterized as an exemplar of neo-liberal and managerialist discourses (Mendes 2009). Howard had declared that the increasing demand for greater choice was a driving force behind the transformation of economic, political, and social life (Howard 1998).

In its first two terms the Howard government's enthusiasm for market-based approaches to public administration drove a massive program of public asset sales, the privatization of government business functions, and the outsourcing of a variety of corporate support services (Aulich and O'Flynn 2007a, 160-63; Aulich and O'Flynn 2007b).

The same logic was applied to the delivery of human services, beginning in 1998 with the creation of a quasi-market to replace a long-standing system of (primarily) publicly operated employment services (Thomas 2007). Branded as the Job Network, the new system was "one of the first comprehensive attempts internationally to apply market mechanisms to the provision of subsidized employment services" (Productivity Commission 2002, XXII).[15] The Job Network thus became the template for the expansion of third party contracting and the creation of quasi-markets in areas such as family relationship and migration services (Butcher and Freyens 2010, 16; Wanna, Butcher and Freyens 2009, 160-67).[16]

The Howard government's competitive tendering and contracting practices came straight from the new public management playbook (Aulich 2005, 59-60) and placed a premium on vertical integration and control, particularly financial controls (Halligan 2008, 16-18). For those not-for-profit sector organizations participating in the newly established human services quasi-markets, it was – to paraphrase Dickens – the best of times, and the worst of times. Many not-for-profit service providers experienced a phenomenal expansion of their market-share. They also endured the imposition by funding bodies of often onerous and intrusive reporting requirements, together with pressures to work in ways that sometimes conflicted with their values and mission (Meagher and Healy 2003; Nevile 1999).

Rapid growth also served to accentuate endemic capacity and capability deficits within the sector. Whereas larger not-for-profits participating in these new markets responded by becoming more "professional" and "businesslike" (O'Shea, Leonard and Darcy 2007), many small to medium sized organizations struggled to overcome high transaction cost barriers and so were excluded from participation in competitive tendering (Butcher and Freyens 2010). Those parts of the sector unable to compete in their own right in the new human service markets either languished in a capacity doldrums or were forced into various consortium arrangements with other sector partners – often on unequal terms (Butcher and Freyens 2010).

Howard's Relationship with the Sector

Although the Howard government lauded the contribution to society and communities of the churches, community groups, social clubs, philanthropic and charitable organizations, its broad approach to the sector was *laissez-faire*. Although it was prepared to acknowledge a role in "facilitating linkages between individuals, communities, voluntary associations and business" and accepted the need to be alert to potential threats to voluntary activity (Howard 1998), the government considered it unnecessary to intrude into the essentially private activities of not-for-profit organizations. Further, despite being increasingly dependent on the not-for-profit sector as an agent of service delivery, the federal government offered little in the way of practical support for capacity development.

Although Howard considered his government reformist in relation to economic and fiscal policy, it was unapologetically socially conservative (Singleton 2005, 4-5). While the government cultivated relationships with large charitable organizations that were broadly sympathetic with elements of its social policy agenda, such as the Salvation Army (Manderson 2011, 234; Boucher and Sharpe 2008), it was – despite its proclaimed libertarian leanings – intolerant of sector advocacy and policy activism, at least on the part of those not-for-profits with which it had contractual relationships (Mendes 2008, 130; Mendes 2005, 147). In this regard, the inclusion in funding agreements of so-called "gagging clauses" which enjoined contracted not-for-profit service providers from commenting on public policy was a major source of concern for the sector (Sawer 2002; Melville 2003; Maddison, Denniss and Hamilton 2004; Mendes 2005; Staples 2006; Hamilton and Maddison 2007).

Beyond Market Governance

By the government's fourth term (2004–07) a "re-balancing" of policy emphasis was already underway – away from the nostrums of new public management towards coordination, at least in the sense of inter-agency coordination and cooperation, and working across portfolio boundaries (Halligan 2008, 16-17). Nevertheless, its attitude towards the not-for-profit sector continued to reflect a preoccupation with a principal-agent paradigm in which government is a sovereign purchaser of services from non-state suppliers in contestable markets. Even so, the practical challenges of program design, policy implementation, and service delivery in complex environments forced the incorporation of relational elements into funding agreements with not-for-profit service providers, albeit within stringent accountability frameworks (Butcher and Freyens 2010, 28-29). However, any significant progress towards inter-sectoral cooperation would have to await a change of government. That came in 2007, when Kevin Rudd's Labor Party won the election.

Civilizing the Relationship

In a 2006 essay the then Labor Opposition Leader (and soon to be Prime Minister) Kevin Rudd called on Labor to "reclaim the centre of Australian politics" and to "form fresh political alliances" in order to counter the "market fundamentalism" of the Howard government (Rudd 2006, 46-50). Rudd's call-to-arms signaled the nascence of Labor's future policy agenda for the not-for-profit sector. By 2007, there was a palpable public weariness with a decade of policy preoccupation with conservative economic ideology (Brown 2007; Langmore 2008). The emergent interest in collaborative, or network governance created a policy window within which Labor could attempt to differentiate its political brand.

In the lead-up to the November 2007 general election, the Federal Labor Party released its policy platform document, *An Australian Social Inclusion Agenda*, in which it flagged the establishment of a Social Inclusion Board comprised of community leaders to provide input into a Social Inclusion Unit located in the Department of the Prime Minister and Cabinet (DPMC)

(Gillard and Wong 2007, 5-6). Labor would take a "whole of government approach" in which "partnerships with State and local governments, the not for profit and private sectors" would be the *modus operandi* of government (Gillard and Wong 2007, 6).

Labor acknowledged the capacity pressures on the not-for-profit human services resulting from an increased reliance on purchaser provider contracts (Gillard and Wong 2007, 10) and asserted the necessity of "rebuilding trust and reciprocity" while criticizing the Howard government for having:

> attacked both the right and capacity of community sector organizations to advocate and [rejecting] their contribution or role in public policy development or debate. The breakdown of the relationship between the community sector and government diminishes Australia's democracy but also undermines our capacity to effectively combat disadvantage. (Gillard and Wong 2007, 11)

Accordingly, Labor undertook to remove restrictive clauses in funding agreements that constrained the sector's advocacy role and to establish "a truly independent and effective voice for the community sector" (Gillard and Wong 2007, 11).

Labor argued that under Howard there had been a "breakdown" in the relationship between government and the sector (Gillard and Wong 2007, 10), a claim affirmed by a well-placed official who remarked on the "absolute breakdown" of the relationship between government and the sector and the "complete disconnect" about their respective positions despite being engaged in contracts more than ever before.[17] To repair the relationship, Labor offered to consult the sector about whether "a compact, such as those that operate in Canada and the UK, could or should be developed in Australia, and what might be included in such a partnership" (Gillard and Wong 2007, 11). Parliamentary Secretary for Social Inclusion and the Voluntary Sector, Ursula Stephens, confirmed Labor's commitment to, "building (and in some cases re-building) trust, strong relationships and partnerships," adding, "We want to be partners in this journey, not contract managers" (Stephens 2008).

In 2007, then Shadow Minister for Social Inclusion, Julia Gillard, outlined the foundations of a strategy to instill cooperation and trust in the government's relationship with the sector in a speech to the Sydney Institute. Gillard argued that the traditional "welfarist approach" needed to be replaced with investment in human capital so as to bring disadvantaged Australians into the mainstream market economy (Gillard 2007, 103). Gillard acknowledged the provenance of Labor's approach to social inclusion in references to the Blair Labour government in the UK and to Canadian efforts (Gillard 2007, 108). She affirmed that Labor wanted to "modernize" policy thinking in this space by acknowledging the not-for-profit sector as an important driver in the social economy, and by committing to a model of governance exhibiting both vertical and horizontal integration (Gillard 2007, 111). Recall that after Rudd's resignation, Gillard replaced him as Prime Minister in June 2010.

From Vision to Implementation

During the 2010 election campaign, the government announced its intention to pursue important reforms for the not-for-profit sector. A re-elected Gillard Labor government would:

- establish an Office of the Not-for-Profit Sector within the Prime Minister's department "to drive and coordinate the policy reform agenda within government" and provide secretariat support to the Council;
- establish a Not-for-Profit Sector Reform Council made up of representatives from across the sector to "provide an important government-to-sector interface through which those most affected by these reforms can help shape their implementation";
- commission a "scoping study" for a national "one-stop-shop" regulator for the not-for-profit sector to remove the complex regulatory arrangements currently in place and streamline reporting arrangements;
- build on work already underway through the Council of Australian Governments[18] in relation to the implementation of a National Chart of Accounts "to improve consistency in financial reporting by organizations to funding agencies and departments, and harmonizing fundraising legislation across States and Territories"; and
- cut "red-tape" by streamlining tendering and contracting processes, in part by developing "a new, common form contract or 'master agreement' for use between the Australian Government and non-profit organizations" and through a cross-agency review "of the efficiency and effectiveness of tendering, contracting and acquittal arrangements between the Australian Government and non-profit organizations" (Australian Labor Party 2010).

Keen to make progress on these measures, the government tasked the Treasury to develop a series of discussion papers on the roles and functions of a national regulator (Treasury 2011a), a proposed statutory definition of charity (Treasury 2011b), options for better targeting not-for-profit tax concessions (Treasury 2011c), and not-for-profit governance arrangements (Treasury 2011d). Amid this flood of discussion papers, there was growing feeling within the sector that the National Compact had been left behind, as well as disquiet about the policy role being played by Treasury – a role some regarded as marking a shift in the emphasis of reform from collaboration towards compliance.

However, government officials stress that the National Compact is the "foundation stone" for the reform measures now in train. Therefore, any attempt to assess the impact to date of Labor's reform agenda must begin with the eight priorities for action enunciated in the National Compact. A cursory survey of the government's actions to date against these action statements provides evidence of the foundational nature of the compact and the government's resolve to pursue an ambitious reform agenda (see Table 1).

There is little doubt that, whatever the sector's misgivings about the likely impact of the National Compact, it was considered a sign of good faith from the new Labor government. To the extent that some looked upon the National Compact as a Holy Grail that would bring enlightenment to a benighted policy domain, it was destined to disappoint, owing in part to a stubborn persistence of the very attitudes, behaviours, and practices that the compact was meant to address. But the National Compact was never intended to be the end game of the reform process. Rather, it was an important milestone along the reform pathway – a guiding framework for a new conversation between the sector and government.[19] To move beyond the mendicant mentality fostered under the previous government requires a new kind of relationship, as well as the careful unpicking of institutionalized behaviours and long-standing practices.

Whither Labor's Reform Agenda?

The success of the not-for-profit reform agenda ultimately depends on the political fortunes of the Gillard minority government. Ironically, the government's current malaise has its roots in the Rudd government's response to the global economic downturn. For despite the fact that the economic stimulus package almost certainly prevented Australia going into recession, the opposition has successfully purveyed to the public an impression of a venal government beset by policy and implementation failure – impressions that the messy spectacle of leadership struggles in the Labor Party has done nothing to allay. Rudd's sacking, followed by near defeat at a general election in 2010 and the further leadership challenge of February 2012 have severely damaged the Labor brand. This might ultimately lead to the unraveling of the not-for-profit reform agenda if there is a change of government at the next election, due in late 2013.

Despite Labor's attempts to articulate a broad "fairness agenda" (Carey, Riley and Crammond 2011, 54), serial crises and political instability have hindered its ability to sustain a coherent political narrative and establish deep institutional underpinnings. This stems in part from a disjuncture between the respective policy discourses articulated by Rudd and Gillard. On the one hand, the Rudd discourse emphasized civil society, joined-up government, inter-sectoral cooperation, and participatory governance

TABLE 1
Labor's Not-for-profit Sector Reform Agenda, Actions to Date

National Compact (March 2010) Priorities for Action	*Not-for-profit Sector Reform Initiatives*
Document and promote the value and contribution of the sector.	Productivity Commission Report into the Contribution of the Not-for-profit Sector, published in January 2010.
	Government has accepted "in-principle" all but one of the recommendations relating to the Commonwealth. The one exception is recommendation 9.5 to establish social innovation funds at the program level. While innovation is critical, the government believes it should be pursued in other ways.
Protect the sector's right to advocacy irrespective of any funding relationship that might exist.	Restrictive "gagging clauses" have been removed from federal government contracts.
	Government encourages the establishment of a new peak organization, the Community Council for Australia, to act as a voice for the sector (launched March 2010).
Recognize sector diversity in consultation processes and sector development initiatives.	Not-for-profit Sector Reform Council appointed with a membership representing diverse perspectives (December 2010).
	The Council is leading the co-creation of a Consultation and Policy Development Code that will "provide a framework for how the Government and the not-for-profit sector should work together to achieve better outcomes for all Australians."
Improve information sharing including greater access to publicly-funded research and data.	The new national regulator, the Australian Charities and Not-for-profits Commission (ACNC), will establish and maintain a public information portal from 1 October 2012.
	The Australian Bureau of Statistics is working with the Reform Council on improvements to statistical data on the not-for-profit sector including a framework for measuring the contribution of the sector.
Reduce red tape and streamline reporting.	A Standard Chart of Accounts agreed by Council of Australian Governments for commencement on 1 July 2010.
	The Department of Finance and Deregulation has developed a standard short form contract template for procurement purposes and is developing streamlined funding processes and simplified funding agreement templates for low risk grants.
	ACNC will implement a "report-once, use-often" reporting framework for charities from 1 October 2012.

… continued

TABLE 1
(Continued)

National Compact (March 2010) Priorities for Action	*Not-for-profit Sector Reform Initiatives*
Simplify and improve consistency of financial arrangements including across state and federal jurisdictions.	The ACNC to commence on 1 October 2012 (Exposure Draft—Australian Charities and Nonprofits Commission Bill released December 2011).
	Consultation paper on a legislative definition of charity (October 2011) for commencement 1 July 2013.
	Discussion paper on harmonization of charitable fundraising (February 2012).
	Negotiations with state and territory governments on national regulation and a single national definition of "charity" to be progressed through the Council of Australian Governments.
Act to improve paid and unpaid workforce issues.	A National Volunteering Strategy (30 November 2011) sets the direction for volunteering and supports organizations to adapt to and accommodate emerging forms of participation.
	In May 2011, Fair Work Australia, the national workplace relations tribunal, concluded that employees in the social and community services industry do not enjoy remuneration for work of equal value by comparison with workers in state and local government employment.
	On 10 November 2011, the Gillard government announced its preparedness to provide over $2 billion to fund its share of any wage increases awarded.
	On 1 February 2012, Fair Work Australia made an order for equal remuneration for work of equal or comparable value to be phased in from 2012 to 2020.
Improve funding and procurement processes.	Appointment of Compact Advocates at the Deputy Secretary level in federal government departments to ensure adoption of Compact principles and commitment to priority action areas.
	Department of Finance and Deregulation to commence work on a common grant template including standard terms and conditions and supplementary conditions (early 2012).

Source: Author's compilation.

– aspirations never fully realized by a government whose decision-making and policy formulation was centralized and hierarchical (Marsh, Lewis and Fawcett 2010, 157). The Gillard discourse, on the other hand, has consistently emphasized a "participatory economy" (as opposed to participatory government), an idea that has become a central organizing theme of her government.

Claiming the "dignity of work" as "a deep Labor conviction," Gillard recently proclaimed:

> The party I lead is – politically, spiritually, even literally – the party of work.... The party of work not welfare, the party of opportunity not exclusion, the party of responsibility not idleness. (Gillard 2011)

This appears to signal a contemporary Australian analogue of an observed shift in British Labour ideas away from social democracy towards "liberal conservatism," characterized by Driver and Martell as an adherence to a "conservative prescriptive moral communitarianism" coupled with a "positive celebration of the dynamic market economy" (1997, 43). Such a shift leaves little room for Labor to differentiate its policy brand in the Australian political marketplace.

Until recently, there have been few statements from the opposition's benches about their intentions should they form the next government. However, a June 2012 speech by Kevin Andrews, Shadow Minister for Families, Housing and Human Services (and a former minister in the Howard government) signalled the opposition's intention to "reverse the nanny state" (Andrews 2012). Andrews described Labor's Australian Charities and Not-for-profits Commission as "monolithic," and a "power grab by government," and derided the rationale for its establishment as "mischief." The Coalition would instead establish "a small Commission as an educative and training body," attached, initially, to the Australian Taxation Office. The new body would have no regulatory role.

Andrews also sounded a warning about "unnecessary state control of the civil sector" and the danger that a sector dependent on government funding would be politicized and co-opted as "another arm of government." A future Coalition government would promote philanthropy, "restore a culture of personal responsibility" and simplify reporting and contractual requirements, Government would support and empower the work of not-for-profit organizations, not direct them "as an arm of the State" (thus signalling, possibly, some relaxation of the Coalition's past embrace of marketization). This messaging suggests a "smaller government" agenda comprising a generous portion of State paternalism with just a dash of principal-agent theory.

The apparent consensus among professional pollsters is that a Labor comeback is "possible, but not likely" (Munro 2012). Provided the Gillard government survives to fight an election in late 2013, it should have at least bedded-down the bulk of its not-for-profit reform agenda by that time. At this juncture it cannot be said with certainty whether a Coalition government will continue the not-for-profit sector reform path set by Labor, re-fashion it in some way, or abandon it altogether.

What we do know is that the Leader of the Opposition, Tony Abbott, sees the political discourse in Australia as a contest between advocates of "bigger government" (i.e., Labor) and "empowered citizens" (Abbott 2012). The opposition has flagged its intention to repeal key structural reform measures (principally, Labor's carbon and mining taxes) and to focus on the "bottom line" by accelerating debt retirement, delivering successive budget surpluses, and the "consolidation" of the federal public sector (Hockey 2012). It is ironic that, despite its role in "empowering citizens," there is little public discussion or awareness of Labor's not-for-profit sector reform initiatives. This renders the sector vulnerable in the face of a future Coalition administration's "smaller government" agenda.

NOTES

1. This chapter uses the term not-for-profit sector in preference to the usual North American nomenclature, *nonprofit sector*, or the common British terms *voluntary sector* or *third sector*. This reflects common usage in Australia both within the sector itself and in government. This is the terminology that is used in Australian government policy documents and in legislation as well as in most sector and academic commentary. This is not simply a concession to Australian convention, but serves the interests of researchers who might choose to investigate further the history and context of the events described here.

2. Australia was one of only three countries not to go into recession since 2008, according to *Euromoney* which, in 2011, conferred the "Finance Minister of the Year" award on Australian Treasurer Wayne Swan (Ellis 2011).

3. Source: http://www.economicstimulusplan.gov.au/pages/theplan.aspx.

4. Source: http://www.tradingeconomics.com/australia/government-budget.

5. A survey of not-for-profit organizations undertaken in 2009 by PricewaterhouseCoopers (PwC), the Fundraising Institute Australia (FIA) and the Centre for Social Impact (CSI) found that around 60 percent of respondents reported a decline in income (PwC, FIA and CIS 2010).

6. Here it is important to remind readers that in Australia's federal system of government, states and territories have constitutional responsibility for the delivery of public health, education, social housing, child and family services, services for people with disabilities, services for the aged, and a host of other social welfare services. These are funded by federal transfers in the form of National Partnership Payments and delivered within the terms of National Partnership Agreements. State and territory governments, in fact, have a larger exposure to the not-for-profit sector than does the federal government

in terms of regulatory responsibility, the making of grants, and contracted service delivery. For further information go to: http://www.federalfinancialrelations.gov.au/content/national_partnership_agreements/.

7. The continuing high demand for Australian mineral resources coupled with the volatility of American and European markets have also served to boost the Australian dollar, thereby placing further stress on an already struggling manufacturing sector.

8. For further information about the decisions of Fair Work Australia in relation to the Equal Remuneration Case, go to: http://www.fwa.gov.au/index.cfm?pagename=remuneration&page=introduction.

9. It should be noted that the states and territories have their own policy frameworks governing relations with the not-for-profit sector and while general economic conditions (and structural conditions) in each jurisdiction have a bearing on the level of government investment in the sector, it is not clear that the global financial crisis figures as strongly as historical and institutional factors in shaping the nature of that relationship.

10. Key among these were a radical overhaul of hospitals funding, the establishment of an emissions trading scheme, and the imposition of a resource super profits tax. The former met trenchant resistance from some state governments, and the latter saw the mobilization of a vociferous campaign on the part of climate change skeptics and Australia's largest mining companies.

11. Canadian and British readers might be surprised to learn that the rules of both the Australian Labor Party and the Liberal Party of Australia allow for the calling of a leadership ballot in which the party leader (and therefore the Prime Minister or Leader of the Opposition) is elected by a simple majority of the Parliamentary Party rather than by a convention of the party membership.

12. High profile policy "back-flips," such as the decision to introduce a carbon tax despite an unequivocal undertaking during the election not to do so, and the abandonment of a commitment to a key independent MP to legislate mandatory pre-commitment legislation to curb problem gambling, have been portrayed by the opposition and in the media as cynical and opportunistic and have fed a public perception of the government as inconsistent and untrustworthy.

13. Two particular issues have had major political repercussions for the government. The first involves unresolved allegations against a government MP concerning misuse of a union credit card prior to his entering Parliament. The second involves the Speaker of the House of Representatives, who defected from the opposition Liberal Party in return for the speakership and subsequently stood aside following allegations of fraud and sexual harassment.

14. The opposition has relentlessly attacked the integrity and legitimacy of the Prime Minister, sowing public distrust of her role in sacking Kevin Rudd. Gillard's standing with the electorate was further eroded in February 2012 when Kevin Rudd announced his intention to challenge Gillard for the leadership. Although the ballot of the Labor caucus confirmed Gillard as Leader and Prime Minister with 71 votes to 31 for Rudd, it also served to revive public disquiet over Rudd's sacking and fuel public antipathy towards the government.

15. Tenders were invited from for-profit and not-for-profit providers for employment services contracts valued at $1.7 billion (1998–2000). With the second tendering round in 1999 the total value of employment services contracts offered to the market had grown to $3 billion (Productivity Commission 2002, 4.8-4.9). Considine (2001, 119-120) points out, the establishment of a competitive quasi-market for publicly-funded employment services commenced in 1994 under the Keating Labor government, with one-third of public assistance for the long-term unemployed contracted to both for-profit and not-for-profit providers in the expectation that competition would lead to service improvement.

16. It should be noted that the federal government was not necessarily leading the charge in this regard. Australian state governments, which have constitutional responsibility for the provision of a wide range of health and human services, had also made major forays into third party service provision.

17. Personal communication, 11 May 2011. This analysis is informed by interviews with over 40 respondents who, to protect their confidentiality, cannot be identified.

18. The Council of Australian Governments, or COAG, is the peak intergovernmental forum in Australia. Its role is to "initiate, develop and monitor the implementation of policy reforms that are of national significance and which require cooperative action by Australian governments" (Source: http://www. coag.gov.au/about_coag/index.cfm).

19. Personal communication, 11 May 2011.

REFERENCES

Abbott, T. 2011. *Towards a Stronger Economy*. Liberal Party of Australia. At http://www.liberal.org.au/Latest-News/2011/03/31/Towards-a-Stronger-Economy.aspx (accessed 30 April 2012).

—. 2012. Address to the House of Representatives – Address in Reply, Parliament House, Canberra. At http://www.tonyabbott.com.au/LatestNews/Speeches/tabid/88/articleType/ArticleView/articleId/8709/Address-to-the-House-of-Representatives--Address-in-Reply-Parliament-House-Canberra.aspx (accessed 30 May 2012).

Andrews, K. 2012. Coalition's Approach to the Charitable Sector, "Empowering Civil Society," Address to the Menzies Research Centre, Melbourne. At http://kevinandrews.com.au/media/public-speech/coalition-approach-to-the-charitable-sector (accessed 19 June 2012).

Aulich, C. 2005. "Privatisation and Outsourcing." In *Howard's Second and Third Governments*, ed. C. Aulich and R. Wettenhall, 57-76. Sydney: UNSW Press.

Aulich, C. and J. O'Flynn. 2007a. "From Public to Private: The Australian Experience of Privatisation." *Asia Pacific Journal of Public Administration* 29 (2): 151-169.

—. 2007b. "John Howard: The Great Privatiser?" *Australian Journal of Political Science* 42 (2): 365-381.

Australian Broadcasting Corporation (ABC). 2009. "Initial Praise for Govt Stimulus Package." Australian Broadcasting Corporation. At http://www.abc.net.au/news/2009-02-03/initial-praise-for-govt-stimulus-package/282008 (accessed 30 April 2012).

Australian Bureau of Statistics (ABS). 2012. 6202.0 – Labour Force, Australia, March 2012. At http://www.abs.gov.au/ausstats/abs@.nsf/mf/6202.0 (accessed 30 April 2012).

Australian Labour Party (ALP). 2010. Strengthening the Non-Profit Sector. At http://www.alp.org.au/getattachment/88a7eb81-8b47-4315-ad6e-c1c13c169365/historic-reforms-to-australia-s-not-for-profit-sec/ (accessed 1 March 2012).

Boucher, G. and M. Sharpe. 2008. *The Times will Suit Them: Postmodern conservatism in Australia*. Crows Nest, NSW: Allen & Unwin.

Brown, P. 2007. "Coalition Focus on Economy a Big Blunder, Poll Finds." *The Age*, 1 December. At http://www.theage.com.au/articles/2007/11/30/1196394625553.html (accessed 21 February 2012).

Butcher, J. and B. Freyens. 2010. "Competition and Collaboration in the Contracting of Family Relationship Centres." *The Australian Journal of Public Administration* 70 (1): 15-33.

Carey, G., T. Riley, and B. Crammond. 2012. "The Australian Government's 'Social Inclusion Agenda': the intersection between public health and social policy." *Critical Public Health* 22 (1): 47-59.

Colebatch, T. 2009. "OECD praise for Canberra's stimulus package." *The Age*, 17 September. At www.theage.com.au/business/oecd-praise-for-canberras-stimulus-package-20090916-froi.html#ixzz1sub3xM23 (accessed 30 April 2012)

Colonial First State. 2010. 2010/11 Australian Budget: Better than all the rest. Economic Research Note, Colonial First State Global Asset Management. At www.cfsgam.com.au/uploadedFiles/CFSGAM/PdfResearch/100512%20Budget2010.pdf (accessed 30 April 2012).

Commonwealth of Australia. 2011. Budget Paper No. 1: Statement 7: Asset and Liability Management. At www.budget.gov.au/2011-12/content/bp1/html/bp1_bst7-01.htm (accessed 30 April 2012).

Considine, M. 2001. *Enterprising States: The Public Management of Welfare to Work*. Cambridge: Cambridge University Press.

Driver S. and L. Martell. 1997. "New Labour's Communitarianisms." *Critical Social Policy* 17 (52): 27-46.

Ellis, E. 2011. "Finance minister of the year 2011: Swan confounds his domestic skeptics." *Euromoney*, 20 September. At www.euromoney.com/Article/2897778/Category/17/ChannelPage/10690/Finance-minister-of-the-year-2011-Swan-confounds-his-domestic-sceptics.html?single=true (accessed 24 February 2012).

Evans, M. 2010. "The Rise and Fall of the Magic Kingdom: Understanding Kevin Rudd's domestic statecraft." In *The Rudd Government: Australian Public Administration 2007–2010*, ed. C. Aulich and M. Evans, 261-278. ANZSOG with ANU E Press. At http://epress.anu.edu.au/wp-content/uploads/2011/02/ch14.pdf (accessed 30 April 2012).

Garnett, A. and P. Lewis. 2011. "The Economy." In *The Rudd Government: Australian Public Administration 2007–2010*, ed. C. Aulich and M. Evans, 181-198. ANZSOG with ANU E Press. At http://epress.anu.edu.au/wp-content/uploads/2011/02/ch10.pdf (accessed 30 April 2012).

Gillard, J. 2007. "The Economics of Social Inclusion: Address to the Sydney Institute on 12 July 2007." *The Sydney Papers* 19 (3): 102-112.

—. 2011. "The Dignity of Work": Address to the Sydney Institute Annual Dinner. At www.pm.gov.au/press-office/dignity-work-address-sydney-institute-annual-dinner (accessed 15 February 2012).

Gillard, J. and P. Wong. 2007. *An Australian Social Inclusion Agenda*. Australian Labor Party. At http://dare2dream.westernsydneyinstitute.wikispaces.net/file/view/ALP+Social+Inclusion+Agenda+2007.pdf (accessed 14 February 2012).

Goldie, C. 2012. "Policy priorities for 2012: jobs and services." *The Drum*, 6 February. Australian Broadcasting Corporation. At http://www.abc.net.au/unleashed/3812406.html (accessed 30 April 2012).

Halligan, J. 2008. "The Search for Balance and Effectiveness in the Australian Public Service." In *Howard's Fourth Government*, ed. C. Aulich and R. Wettenhall, 13-30. Sydney: UNSW Press.

Hamilton, C. and S. Maddison. 2007. "Non-government Organisations." In *Silencing Dissent: How the Australian Government is Controlling Public Opinion and Stifling Debate*, ed. C. Hamilton and S. Maddison, 78-100. Crows Nest, NSW: Allen & Unwin.

Hockey, J. 2011a. Joe Hockey Doorstop – worst Budget deficit in Australian history. Liberal Party of Australia. At www.liberal.org.au/Latest-News/2011/04/29/Joe-Hockey-Doorstop.aspx (accessed 30 April 2012).

—. 2011b. Interview with Peter Van Onselen, 18 September 2011. At www.joehockey.com/media/transcripts/details.aspx?s=293 (accessed 29 May 2012).

—. 2012. Post Budget Address, National Press Club: Joe Hockey. At http://www.liberal.org.au/Latest-News/2012/05/16/Post-Budget-Address.aspx (accessed 30 May 2012).

Howard, J. 1998. Address by the Prime Minister, The Hon. John Howard MP, to the World Economic Forum Dinner. At http://parlinfo.aph.gov.au/parlInfo/download/media/pressrel/DG005/upload_binary/dg0052.doc;fileType%3D application%2Fmsword (accessed 19 February 2012).

Hutchens, G. 2011. World Bank chief praises Australia. *Sydney Morning Herald*, 15 August. At www.smh.com.au/national/world-bank-chief-praises-australia-20110815-1itdu.html#ixzz1sue8QJgn (accessed 30 April 2012).

International Monetary Fund (IMF). 2011. *World Economic Outlook (WEO) – Slowing Growth, Rising Risks*. International Monetary Fund. At www.imf.org/external/pubs/ft/weo/2011/02/index.htm (accessed 30 April 2012).

—. 2012. *World Economic Outlook April 2012 – Growth Resuming, Dangers Remain*. International Monetary Fund. At www.imf.org/external/pubs/ft/weo/2012/01/pdf/text.pdf (accessed 30 April 2012).

Langmore, J. 2008. "It's not the economy, stupid." *The Drum*, 4 February. At www.abc.net.au/news/2007-12-04/its-not-the-economy-stupid/976802 (accessed 21 February 2012).

Levy, M. 2010. "Labor Party was losing its way under Rudd: Gillard." *The Age*, 24 June. At www.theage.com.au/national/labor-party-was-losing-its-way-under-rudd-gillard-20100624-z10q.html#ixzz1t79jVavK (accessed 30 April 2012).

Long, S. 2010. "Economists' open letter backs fiscal stimulus." *PM*, Australian Broadcasting Corporation, 16 August. At www.abc.net.au/news/2010-08-16/economists-open-letter-backs-fiscal-stimulus/946372 (accessed 30 April 2012).

Maddison, S., R. Denniss, and C. Hamilton. 2004. *Silencing Dissent: Non-government organizations and Australian Democracy*. Discussion Paper Number 65, Canberra: The Australia Institute.

Manderson, D. 2011. "Possessed: The unconscious law of drugs." In *The Drug Effect: Health, Crime and Society*, ed. S. Fraser and D. Moore, 225-39. Melbourne: Cambridge University Press.

Marsh, D., C. Lewis, and P. Fawcett. 2010. "Citizen-centred Policy Making under Rudd: Network governance in the shadow of hierarchy?" In *The Rudd Government – Australian Commonwealth Administration 2007–2010*, ed. C. Aulich and M. Evans, 143-160. Canberra: ANZSOG with ANU E-Press. At http://epress.anu.edu.au/anzsog/rudd/pdf/ch08.pdf (accessed 30 April 2012).

McGregor-Lowndes, M. 2011. An Examination of Tax Deductible Donations Made By Individual Australian Taxpayers in 2008-09, Working Paper No. CPNS 54. At http://eprints.qut.edu.au/43323/1/Working_Paper_54_v6_Draft.pdf (accessed 13 February 2012).

McKew, M. 2012. United we stand, divided we fall. *Sydney Morning Herald*, 26 February. At www.smh.com.au/opinion/politics/united-we-stand-divided-we-fall-20120225-1tvur.html#ixzz1t7AUUmQM (accessed 30 April 2012).

Meagher, G. and K. Healy. 2003. "Caring, Controlling, Contracting and Counting: Governments and Non-profits in Community Services." *Australian Journal of Public Administration* 62 (3): 40-51.

Melville, R. 2003. *Changing Roles of Community-Sector Peak Bodies in a Neo-Liberal Policy Environment in Australia*. Wollongong, NSW: Institute of Social Change and Critical Inquiry, Faculty of Arts, University of Wollongong.

Mendes, P. 2005. "Welfare Reform and Mutual Obligation." In *Howard's Second and Third Governments*, ed. C. Aulich and R. Wettenhall, 135-151. Sydney: UNSW Press.

—. 2008. *Australia's Welfare Wars Revisited: the players, the politics and the ideologies*, 3rd ed. Sydney: UNSW Press.

—. 2009. "Retrenching or Renovating the Australian Welfare State: the paradox of the Howard government's neo-liberalism." *International Journal of Social Welfare* 18 (1): 102–110.

Nevile, A. 1999. *Competing Interests: Competition policy in the welfare sector*. Discussion Paper Number 21. Canberra: Australia Institute and Anglicare Australia. At https://www.tai.org.au/index.php?q=node%2F19&pubid=21&act=display (accessed 30 April 2012).

O'Shea, P., R. Leonard, and M. Darcy. 2007. "Does 'Competition' Kill 'Social Capital'?" *Third Sector Review* 13 (2): 49-69.

PricewaterhouseCoopers (PwC), the Fundraising Institute Australia (FIA) and the Centre for Social Impact (CSI). 2010. *Managing for Recovery: The state of the not-for-profit sector 2009*. At http://www.pwc.com.au/about-us/corporate-responsibility/assets/Managing-Recovery-Feb10.pdf (accessed 13 February 2012).

Productivity Commission. 2002. *Independent Review of the Job Network*. Inquiry Report No. 21. Canberra: Commonwealth of Australia. At www.pc.gov.au/__data/assets/pdf_file/0018/54333/jobnetwork.pdf (accessed 17 February 2012).

—. 2010. *Contribution of the Not-for-Profit Sector*. Canberra: Commonwealth of Australia. At www.pc.gov.au/projects/study/not-for-profit/report (accessed 30 April 2012).

Reserve Bank of Australia (RBA). 2012. Statement by Glenn Stevens, Governor: Monetary Policy Decision, Media Release Number 2012-09. At www.rba.gov.au/media-releases/2012/mr-12-09.html (accessed 30 April 2012).

Rudd, K. 2006. "Howard's Brutopia: the battle of ideas in Australian politics." *The Monthly* (Nov): 46-50. At www.themonthly.com.au/monthly-essays-kevin-rudd-howard-s-brutopia-battle-ideas-australian-politics-312 (accessed 15 February 2012).

Sawer, M. 2002. "Governing for the Mainstream: Implications for Community Representation." *Australian Journal of Public Administration* 61 (2): 31-49.

Scott, S. 2012. Prime Minister Julia Gillard rejects demands from Greens leader Christine Milne to scrap Budget surplus. *The Courier-Mail*, 17 April 2012. At www.couriermail.com.au/news/national/pm-rejects-surplus-cut/story-e6freooo-1226328155713 (accessed 30 April 2012).

Singleton, G. 2005. "Issues and Agendas: Howard in Control." In *Howard's Second and Third Governments*, ed. C. Aulich and R. Wettenhall, 3-18. Sydney: UNSW Press.

Stafford, P. 2009. "Business leaders praise Rudd Government's stimulus package." SmartCompany. At www.smartcompany.com.au/politics/20090204-business-leaders-praise-rudd-governments-stimulus-package.html (accessed 30 April 2012).

Staples, J. 2006. *NGOs out in the Cold: The Howard Government Policy Towards NGOs.* Discussion Paper 19/06, Democratic Audit of Australia, Australian National University. At http://democratic.audit.anu.edu.au/papers/20060615_staples_ngos.pdf (accessed 21 February 2012).

Stephens, U. 2008. "Rudd Government's Social Inclusion Agenda." Speech to Australian Council for International Development Forum. At http://ministers.deewr.gov.au/stephens/rudd-governments-social-inclusion-agenda (accessed 22 February 2012).

Stiglitz, J. 2010. "In praise of stimulus." *The Age*, 9 August. At www.theage.com.au/business/in-praise-of-stimulus-20100808-11q8e.html#ixzz1sudStxHN (accessed 30 April 2012).

Swan, W. 2012a. *Treasurer's Economic Note.* At http://ministers.treasury.gov.au/wmsDisplayDocs.aspx?doc=economicnotes/2012/013.htm&pageID=012&min=wms&Year=&DocType=4 (accessed 30 April 2012).

—. 2012b. *Treasurer's Economic Note.* At http://ministers.treasury.gov.au/ministers/wms/content/economicnotes/2012/attachments/005_Treasurer's_Economic_Note.pdf (accessed 30 April 2012).

Thomas, M. 2007. *A Review of Developments in the Job Network.* Research Paper no. 15. Parliamentary Library, Department of Parliamentary Services. At http://www.aph.gov.au/library/pubs/rp/2007-08/08rp15.pdf (accessed 17 February 2012).

The Treasury. 2011a. *Consultation Paper – Scoping Study for a National Not-For-Profit Regulator.* 25 February. Canberra: Commonwealth of Australia. At www.treasury.gov.au/contentitem.asp?NavId=037&ContentID=1934 (accessed 30 April 2012).

—. 2011b. *Consultation Paper – A Definition of Charity.* 28 October. Canberra: Commonwealth of Australia. At www.treasury.gov.au/contentitem.asp?NavId=037&ContentID=2161 (accessed 30 April 2012).

—. 2011c. *Consultation Paper – Better Targeting of Not-For-Profit Tax Concessions.* 27 May. Canberra: Commonwealth of Australia. At www.treasury.gov.au/contentitem.asp?NavId=037&ContentID=2056 (accessed 30 April 2012).

—. 2011d. *Consultation Paper – Review of Not-for-profit Governance Arrangements.* 8 December. Canberra: Commonwealth of Australia. At www.treasury.gov.au/contentitem.asp?NavId=037&ContentID=2252 (accessed 20 April 2012).

Uren, D. and L. Taylor. 2010. "How Rudd bet the house." *The Australian*, 19 June. At www.theaustralian.com.au/politics/how-rudd-bet-the-house/story-e6frgczf-1225881236755 (accessed 30 April 2012).

Wanna, J. 2009. "Commonwealth of Australia January to June 2009." *Australian Journal of Politics and History* 55 (4): 584-592.

Wanna, J., J. Butcher, and B. Freyens. 2009. *Policy in Action: The Challenge of Service Delivery*. Sydney: UNSW Press.

Wright, J. 2012. Australian economy leads the world. *Sydney Morning Herald*, 18 April. At www.smh.com.au/opinion/political-news/australian-economy-leads-the-world-20120418-1x6ac.html#ixzz1sqJfVXzI (accessed 30 April 2012).

CHAPTER 12

SOUTHERN CIVIL SOCIETY ORGANIZATIONS IN TUMULTUOUS TIMES: GLOBAL RECESSION AND ITS CONSEQUENCES

BARBARA LEVINE AND EVREN TOK

INTRODUCTION

This chapter provides an appraisal of how the current global economic recession is impacting civil society and non-governmental organizations (CSO/NGO),[1] especially those in the developing world, and assesses their potential to make a significant contribution to social and economic development in the developing South. Due to the global economic downturn, many CSOs have been experiencing significant, and in some cases, drastic declines in their resources; their ability to respond to the needs of their constituents and client groups have also been reduced.[2] Simultaneously, CSO-government relations have been altered significantly, paving the way to a relationship characterized by instability, tension, and ambiguity.

This chapter recognizes that the causes of reduced financing for Southern CSOs are multiple and are the result of a near-catastrophic coincidence of pressures. The global economic crisis as experienced by developing country governments, CSOs, and citizens has been exacerbated by commodity price volatility, soaring food and energy costs, debt consolidation, significantly reduced aid flows from traditional rich donor countries, and environmental disasters (e.g., drought or floods due to climate change, war, and civil strife). The global economic crisis multiplies the negative effects of these other crises. Sadly, "it appears that the burden of coping has been borne disproportionately by poor and

Government-Nonprofit Relations in Times of Recession, ed. Rachel Laforest. Montreal and Kingston: Queen's Policy Studies Series, McGill-Queen's University Press. © 2013 The School of Policy Studies, Queen's University at Kingston. All rights reserved.

vulnerable men, women and children. This reality is poorly understood" (Global Pulse 2010).

Complicating the situation is the fact that, according to an author like Hossain (2011; 2010; Hossain et al. 2010), the global risk context is one of complex, compound shocks that are multi-sectoral and fast-moving, and that manifest themselves differently according to country context. While CSOs everywhere may find themselves reeling from the severity and speed of the changing environment, the challenges they face may be quite diverse. Their strategies will depend on the details of their specific local, country, or regional contexts (Hossain et al. 2010; McCord 2010).

The chapter begins by looking at the changing nature and contours of the multilateral development system. We examine the impacts of the recent global recession as well as the emergence of new actors that became vocal in reforming the historically established Western domin- ated aid structure. The first section points out some of the implications of these broader changes on CSOs in the South. Next, the chapter analy- ses CSO responses in the context of global recession by presenting and evaluating the available data from a United Nations study conducted by Hanfstaengl (2010) as well as the compilation of various reports by CSOs themselves. The case of the civil society sector in South Africa provides a specific country-level illustration. The chapter concludes by reflecting on policy prospects, suggesting that the ends and means pursued by governments and CSOs may be more divergent than they have been in the past. In other words, given the immensity of the problems, more CSOs will be advocating for more social spending and new programs that create jobs and provide social safety nets. Given governments' lim- ited resources and often formulaic responses (debt reduction, reduction of size of government, deficit control), it is suggested that there may be more confrontation among state and civil society actors than has been the case in the past decade.

CHANGING TIMES: SHIFTING TRENDS IN THE MULTILATERAL SYSTEM, DEVELOPMENT AID, AND CSOS

Prior to the onset of the 2008 economic crisis, official development assist- ance (ODA) to developing countries was marked by renewed international vigour. Beginning in 2000, an era of aid optimism was sparked by the signing of the UN Millennium Declaration, where international leaders pledged to steadily increase aid commitments to 0.7 percent of GDP in a unified attempt to reduce extreme poverty by 2015 (UN 2012). The international call for poverty reduction was reaffirmed in 2005 during the G8 meeting at Gleneagles, which generated significant international attention and clearly identified Africa as the main focus of donor efforts. General concerns surrounding the effectiveness of past and future aid simultaneously sparked a movement towards a decisively results-based aid agenda. Reinforced in the 2005 Paris Declaration for Aid Effectiveness and the 2008 Accra Accord, results-based programming became a defining feature of the international aid platform, as donors sought to produce tangible results from their continued aid efforts. The Paris Declaration on Aid Effectiveness and the Accra Accord are political compacts signed by both donor and recipient countries in an effort to promote aid effectiveness through partnership and cooperation. While neither agreement is binding, both the Paris Declaration and the Accra Accord embody commitments, mostly on the part of donors, to reform aid delivery strategies according to the standards outlined within the compacts (Rogerson 2011). Both agreements have been signed by 137 countries and territories, including all 24 DAC members, 113 non-DAC and Southern countries, as well as 27 international organizations and 14 CSOs (OECD 2012). Significantly, international CSOs fought hard to be included in the Accra Accord and were recognized eventually as legitimate development actors in their own right.

By 2008, the onset of the global financial crisis had replaced the era of aid optimism with scepticism and general fatigue surrounding the development undertaking. At the same time, the financial crisis had sparked a rise in domestic tensions for donor governments, as increasing unemployment and deteriorating local conditions appeared to place international assistance on the backburner. In response to domestic tensions and in an effort to offset the effects of the financial crisis on domestic conditions, governments launched a series of fiscal stimulus packages aimed at jumpstarting economic growth, subsequently incurring large debt loads and reducing public expenditure to finance growing debt. In essence, this combination of domestic pressure and increasing levels of sovereign debt caused absolute levels of ODA to decline (UNCTAD 2012). This further focused aid spending on "value for money" programs that promised immediate results, where ODA was increasingly used as a catalyst to generate additional development finance resources (i.e., often through the private sector) (Deutscher 2010; OECD 2011).

The focus on result-based aid programming and the overall decline in aid budgets prompted an adjustment of traditional CSO programs. Typically, CSOs had tended to focus on the long-term work of building social and community capital. Given the international shift towards result-based programming, many CSOs saw their funding redirected to NGOs working in humanitarian and relief work, or alternatively, began to see their programs skewed to delivering concrete, immediate results that may not be sustainable.[3]

At the same time, new non-traditional donors (e.g., China, India, Brazil, Eastern Europe) are gaining more importance, in parallel to the relative decline of traditional DAC donors.[4] For some developing countries, these new donors are becoming the most important source of foreign development finance. That said, as demonstrated in Reality of Aid's 2010 special report on South-South Cooperation, these new donor relationships also pose new challenges with regards to civil society participation and human rights. Many of these new donors have never worked easily with civil society actors in their own countries. How would they conceive of CSOs as legitimate development actors in countries receiving aid to mitigate the worst extremes of the global recession and the economic and social crises mentioned above? Furthermore, the new emphasis in the official discourse on the private sector as a "development partner and actor" poses many additional risks and raises multiple questions including, who benefits, and, whose rules prevail?

Given these exceptional pressures, what are the responses and strategies of Southern CSOs, especially in the context of diminished resources? A recent UN survey as well as CSOs' own reports paint a partial picture of the strategies and tactics they have currently adopted in an effort to ride out the global economic storm. A series of crucial research questions emerge in relation to the current situation and prospects of the CSO in the South. For instance, will CSOs emerge from this period stronger and more confident than before, better able to deliver goods and services to those who need them, with more resources to broaden and deepen social development programming for the poorest? Will they be in a stronger position to influence policy and decision-making, especially at the global level, and to democratize the decision-making of the emerging institutions of global governance? Based on the data collected so far from CSOs themselves, the answers to these questions are disappointing. Up to this point, it appears that CSO coping strategies have thus far been partial, short-term, and insufficient when they need to be far-reaching, transformative, and original.

AN ANALYSIS OF CSOs BEFORE AND DURING THE GLOBAL RECESSION

Even before the 2008 recession, CSOs have found themselves challenged to prove their legitimacy in the face of multiple critiques, much of it ideological or political (Edwards 2009). As CIVICUS and other CSO umbrella organizations have documented, just as CSOs' voice and influence have grown, so too have attempts to restrict the space for independent citizen action. Governments from Russia to Ethiopia to Uganda and the US have formulated tighter laws, regulations, and registration processes for NGOs to counter their growing influence. Critics are quick to charge that only a small percentage of CSO funds go to the intended recipients in communities in need, or that foreign funders are driving the agendas of domestic CSOs and subverting local "democratic" processes. They claim, sometimes correctly, that a significant portion of funding goes to cover operational and marketing costs, and to pay for the salaries of highly-paid staff and consultants. To be fair, NGOs are under a significant amount of pressure to maintain and raise funding, and to show their success in diversifying funding. Furthermore, these criticisms do not always reflect a balanced or nuanced understanding of the way CSOs are involved in the development enterprise. CSOs do more than deliver direct services; they may be involved with research, advocacy, public education, policy influence and dialogue, technical assistance, and training.

CSOs are also routinely criticized for a lack of accountability and transparency, or for a failure to be professional, democratic, or technically savvy (Van Rooy 2004). There have been several studies carried out by donor governments, universities, and CSOs themselves that document disappointingly little influence of "policy champion" NGOs on government policies, laws, rules and behaviour, especially in Africa (Robinson and Friedman 2009; Felsen and Besada 2011).[5] This perception by the state that CSOs are weak exacerbates a vicious cycle so that in times of crisis there is limited inclusion of CSOs in the process of preparing and implementing crisis responses. A recent report published by the Regional Center for Public Administration Reform (RCPAR) and the United Nations Development Programme (UNDP) underlined that unfortunately, the exclusion of civil society not only decreases policy effectiveness, but also causes mutual distrust between CSOs and government, hence contributing to a lack of collaboration the next time crisis strikes (2011).

While it is unclear whether, or to what degree, these criticisms have affected the decline in funding to CSOs following the 2008 economic crisis, CSOs have recently sought to redefine and increase their role in development by actively addressing the concerns of their critics. Indeed, Mutasa (2008) notes that the international community is "witnessing a steady shift in attitudes of both the government and civic groups ... [as] for the sake of accountability, there [has been] a growing realisation that civil society needs to engage government officials, donors, politicians and parliamentarians more determinedly" in an effort to reduce opposition and increase mutual support and accountability. This shift became particularly pronounced in 2008, when CSOs broadened their participation in cooperative international measures during the Aid Effectiveness High Level Forum in Accra. At the forum, CSOs criticized the lack of transparency surrounding official donor spending, while simultaneously suggesting that CSOs should also accept donor calls for transparency in CSO activities (Hanfstaengl 2010). As a result, it appears that while the workings of CSOs are not without difficulties, CSOs have actively sought to quiet the voices of their critics by increasing participation in international initiatives and adopting mutually accountable standards with official donors.

Many have signed on to national and global civil society codes of ethics, others are making efforts to enhance accountability upwards to donors and downwards to members and clients or service recipients. CSOs are broadening networks and cooperative arrangements in novel ways to further their influence with governments, multilateral institutions, the private sector, and other civil society stakeholders in both developed and developing countries. (The most recent effort is the Open Forum to enhance the aid effectiveness agenda of the Paris Declaration at the Fourth High Level Forum on Aid Effectiveness in Busan). This evolution from within the sector, in fact, demonstrates that CSOs are committed to offering a serious critique of the West's understanding of development and to presenting an "alternative" form of development. As authentic development partners, CSOs envision their role as being to engender a bottom-up dynamic and a restructuring of society. However, to achieve any kind of scale, they need suitable financial, legal, and cultural supports, as well as recognition from public authorities. They are also aware, especially those close to the communities with which they work, that most government proposals to deal with the current economic recession fall far short of what is required and fail to address the social consequences of the current multiple crises (Africa Training and Research Center in Administration for Development 2011). Consequently, where the public sphere fails to respond effectively and is unable to mobilize resources and energy from or for the community level, there is the potential that CSOs will join efforts with broader social movements and new social actors to press government for citizens' social and economic rights.

In the midst of these pressures and dynamics, many CSOs are struggling to survive and thrive. In an effort to illuminate how CSOs are managing (or not) to ride out the global economic downturn, the United Nations Secretariat (UNS) initiated a study guided by a CSO Steering Committee, which included two members of the NGO Committee for Social Development (Marianists International and the Sisters of Charity Federation), along with Friedrich Ebert Stiftung (FES), and the UN Non-Governmental Liaison Service. Thus, a global survey was undertaken in the fall 2009 on the impact of the inter-related environmental, financial, and economic crises on CSOs and the constituencies they serve. A critical initial finding of the survey was that a considerable number of CSOs reported substantial reductions in their funding in the wake of the global financial and economic crisis, and they are concerned that this threatens their ability to deliver the services and activities that are vital for the wellbeing of people (Hanfstaengl 2010).

According to the findings of the survey (Hanfstaengl 2010), of the 640 CSOs that responded, 33 percent were from Africa, 23 percent were from Asia, including China, 16 percent were from Western Europe, 13 percent from the US and Canada, 9 percent from Latin America, 3 percent from Eastern Europe, 2 percent from Japan, Australia, New Zealand, and 1 percent from Ukraine and Russia. Surveyed CSOs provide a wide range of services. With regard to development programs, most of the responding CSOs work primarily in the areas of education (309), gender (296), poverty eradication (285), human rights (254), and health care (236).

The findings of the survey indicated that CSOs globally encountered a stark decline of resources. Although some CSOs have seen increased funding, overall the survey finds a worsening financial situation for CSOs in the period 2008–2009. For example, 153 CSOs (24 percent) reported budget decreases in 2008, 214 (33 percent) in 2009 and 160 CSOs (25 percent) expected reductions in 2010. The main reasons given by CSOs for the decline were decreased grants from existing sources as a result of the world economic crisis. Disturbingly, most of the reductions have occurred in sub-Saharan Africa.

CSOs have seen reductions by individual contributors, private foundations, international institutions, and governments – although not necessarily by all categories at once. Whereas 378 responding CSOs still indicated an increase from 2008 onwards, 582 responses saw a decrease in the different categories of funding: 147 responses saw a decline in direct personal contributions, 104 CSOs experienced reductions by private foundations, 95 by international institutions, 87 by governments, and 71 by corporations.

The data presented in the survey confirm that 2008 and 2009 marked a special challenge for CSOs worldwide. Most of the responding CSOs reported budget decreases in those years that were threatening to compromise their ability to deliver services and activities. Civil society organizations around the world that participated in this study reported that most government proposals in the form of fiscal packages and retrenchment to deal with the global crises did not sufficiently address their social consequences. The CSOs themselves are faced with the challenge of stepping into this gap, as demand for services is increasing. The surveyed CSOs revealed that the amount and scope of requests for support by the constituencies and partners of civil society organizations are growing. In fact, Hanfstaengl (2010) indicated that more than half of the responding CSOs reported increasing demand for services.

Not surprisingly, an important objective of this survey was to find out if the scope of requests by the constituencies and partners of civil society organizations changed due to the global crises. According to Hanfstaengl (2010), this hypothesis is largely confirmed by the results of the survey. CSOs project further increases in requests for emergency relief, as well as for support to provide basic social services for the next two years. They consistently report that the large increase of requests is due to increasing job losses and unemployment (Anderson 2010; Hanfstaengl 2010).

In this context of crisis, what are some of the CSO strategies to cope with the reduction of revenues and drying up of resources? As one would expect, a majority of CSOs (64 percent) have had to substantially reduce the number of staff, while nearly three-quarters (72 percent) have had to narrow the scope of work or reduce services. Not only do these strategies reduce CSO impact in the present, they are likely to diminish their resilience for the future.

However, not all strategies have been defensive. According to the same survey, many CSOs report that they have started additional fundraising campaigns, or have explored current or new opportunities in their countries or within their constituencies. As illustrated in Figure 1 question F, CSOs have extended their use of Internet tools. Decreasing resources have also led CSOs to seek networking opportunities with other locally based CSOs to address common problems. Another study also confirms that 80 percent of the organizations have developed better collaborative networks to address declining funds, and 78 percent have also started additional fundraising campaigns (Stahl 2010).

FIGURE 1
CSO Strategies to Cope with Decreasing Revenue in Sub-Saharan Africa

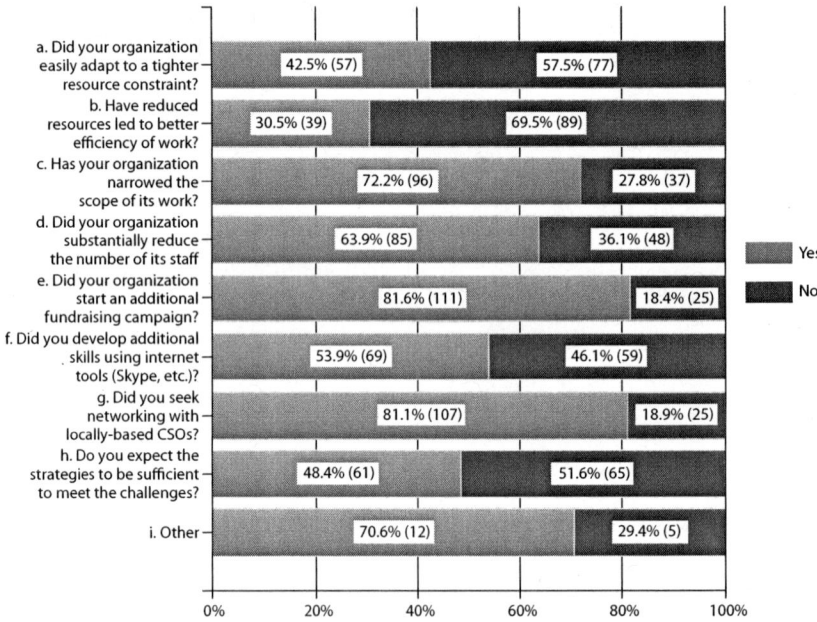

Source: Hanfstaengl 2010.

The findings of a recent conference entitled "How civil society and local governments are fighting the global crisis" (Skopje Conference 2011) suggest that local governments have a special role to play in collaborating with CSOs to complement and strengthen their services. Similarly, Anderson's white paper (2010) touches on the need for collaboration between CSOs and local governments in order to weather the impacts of the crisis. By and large, sub-Saharan African CSOs involved in the Hanfstaengl survey are experiencing difficulties in adapting themselves to crisis-ridden situations. Furthermore, decreasing resources do not mean that available resources are used more efficiently. Most of the responding CSOs do not expect their strategies to cope with the financial shortfall to be sufficient to meet the challenges. The sub-Saharan African results are echoed in other regions. In Latin American and Caribbean countries, slightly more than half of the respondents reported that they had to narrow their scope of work while in Asian countries, 58 percent of CSOs had to both narrow their scope of work and reduce their staff. Other worrying negative impacts on the sector will likely be increased competition among NGOs for funding from an increasingly smaller pie, and reduced autonomy.

Data from the survey suggest that the change of funding sources has been most acute in sub-Saharan Africa. From 2008 to 2010, the sharpest decreases were experienced in the funding provided by direct personal contributions. Given the impact of the economic recession on individual households, this result isn't surprising. The next significant decrease is the support of international institutions, followed by support from private foundations. At this point, we come across a puzzling contradiction. It is often reported that the private sector, in the form of large philanthropic foundations funded by some of the richest people in the world today, is playing a growing role in development as an important funder and partner of the not-for-profit sector (Economist 2011; Economist 2006; Economist 2004). For example, according to one estimate, total private donations[6] in 2008 amounted to USD 233 billion, compared with USD 121 billion in official development assistance (CGP 2010, 6). But the results of the Hanfstaengl 2010 survey appear to contradict this argument. So while donors and recipients are looking to the private sector as an engine for growth in partner countries, the reality appears to be much bleaker. especially in the case of the African continent.

The Case of South Africa

South Africa is an illustrative case. Thabo Rapoo, executive director of the Center for Policy Studies in South Africa, argues that many non-profit organizations are on the brink of collapse due to a lack funding (Rapoo 2010). The sector has already lost many activists and leaders to more lucrative positions in government and business or to burn-out and retirement, while many organizations struggle to remunerate their remaining staff. These challenges are compounded by funding inconsistencies and a shift in donor preferences away from long-term program and core support, towards short-term project support. Funds for projects rarely allow CSOs to invest in their own staff and volunteers, so that many CSOs are "thin" when it comes to management and administrative support to their staff and beneficiary groups. Professional development and training for boards, staff, and volunteers are unusual and mostly ad-hoc. As a result, CSOs are increasingly finding themselves in a negative cycle, where the absence of human capital development within the organization has made it more difficult for CSOs to compete for funding that would allow them to hire permanent professional staff (CIVICUS 2011).

In addition to the recent global financial crisis, several other factors add to the problems faced by CSOs. Not only are donors increasingly interested in funding corporate social investment or business development projects as opposed to policy research and activist organizations, but many donors including private donors are focusing on fewer countries. This move to corporate social investment is particularly problematic due to the tensions between developmental goals and corporate incentives. Too often, the choice of CSO partners is haphazardly made by public relations consultants in the absence of clear and transparent guidelines. Given that corporations engage in corporate social responsibility as a means to improve company image, firms tend to view their involvement with CSOs as temporary strategies rather than long-term relationships, diminishing the incentive for firms to actively seek specific CSOs and programming to receive sustained funding (CIVICUS 2011). In fact, the implications of this situation for South Africa are quite paradoxical in the sense that CSOs were once upon a time seen as the motors of the post-apartheid democratization process; now they are the victims of this same process.

Rapoo (2010) argues that the global economic recession has been a major factor, precipitating the funding cuts by virtually all international donors in South Africa. Some of the major foreign donor funding agencies (such as the Mott Foundation, Kellogg Foundation, and DANIDA) have slashed their global funding drastically, in some cases reportedly by as much as 30 percent. It is also argued that the current round of donor funding cut-backs has created a terminal situation the likes of which was only witnessed back in the early 1990s. Between 1992 and 1994, approximately 1000 non-profit organizations in South Africa found themselves deep in financial crisis due to donor funding cuts, with 200 to 400 organizations eventually collapsing. Donors had decided at that time to welcome the new post-apartheid democratic order, under the leadership of Nelson Mandela, by shifting the bulk of their funding away from the non-profit sector and toward bilateral funding relations with the new government. This was based on the erroneous assumption that, given its popular legitimacy and democratic credentials, the new democratic government would have the necessary institutional (i.e., technical, managerial, and administrative) capacity to deliver services efficiently and effectively to the underprivileged. It has become clear now that government cannot possibly meet all the needs of the poor on its own, even with the best of will and financial resources. The government needs civil society organizations to assist, as well as watch over it.

CSO Coping Strategies and Concluding Observations

The decrease in available funding because of the global economic recession has meant that CSOs have had to find numerous coping strategies. They have developed collaborations with other organizations, and intensified fundraising particularly from hitherto unexplored areas such as local philanthropy. For instance, most African governments have not yet reached their goal of spending one percent of GDP on research and development. According to a study conducted in 2009 by the United Nations Economic Commission for Africa (UNECA), a plan for an African Science Philanthropy Initiative has been initiated. According to Makoni (2012), this was envisaged as a common pool where African donors could bring together their funding, which would then be allocated to various development related projects. Certainly, the interest in steering African philanthropy towards science is a good sign, but the effort remains small and sporadic.

Similarly, the East African Organization of Grantmakers' conference in April 2012 with the theme "Philanthropy, Leadership, and Governance in East Africa" is a stimulating undertaking, which encourages potential progress on corporate, community, family, and individual types of philanthropy (East African Association of Grantmakers 2012).

In the case of Latin America, the Latin American Donor Index disseminated by the Avina Foundation and Inter-American Development Bank (2010) argues that "Philanthropy in the region should review and strengthen its role as a strategic social investor and review the role of receptors and channels of funds and donations to build partnerships and synergies between both to effectively stimulate innovation and social change" (IDB 2010). Nevertheless, the report indicates that although it recognizes an increase in local philanthropy (defined as donations originating from the region) it cautions that only after consolidating the data from 2009 and 2010 would it be "possible to estimate the scope of the international economic crisis in Latin America's philanthropy" (IDB 2010).

CONECTAS, a Brazilian based human rights NGO, provides a vivid illustration of how CSOs might cope in a hostile funding climate. After five years of initial support, CONECTAS learned that UNF (United Nations Foundation) could no longer continue its funding. CONECTAS encountered a harsh challenge of replacing a major, institutional donor with a range of smaller funders and mostly project-based support (CONECTAS 2011). Despite the challenges of raising funds from national sources, CONECTAS aspired to attract two local funders in 2010–2011. One funding document mentions plans to invest time and resources in communicating directly with the Brazilian corporate sector.

In other circumstances in which philanthropy is absent, some CSOs have had to scale back their interventions, for example by closing down nutrition centers or reducing the amount of education support they offer. Others have reduced the number of staff they employ, leaving "one person to do the work of three." Still others have increased their use of internet tools. In short, CSOs are overstretching themselves in order to fulfill their mandates, or narrowing their mandates, or both.

According to Hossain (2010), there are currently four challenges for civil society: a) breach its own boundaries, to address cross-cutting issues at their source; b) amplify the voice of those directly affected; c) influence a fairer policy response at local, national, and global levels; and d) fertilize debate, to grow new understandings of how the global economy should work, and for whom.

Compared to these challenges, the responses by many CSOs, especially in developing countries, are, sadly, only partial, fragmented, and often defensive. Given the scope of the crises, there needs to be a new, dynamic response from the civil society sector that is dynamic and transformative. In other words, what is most urgently needed is the vision and the analysis that would see CSOs combining real resources on the ground through mergers and strategic alliances to better serve vulnerable groups, demonstrate long-lasting results, and influence policies.

A key study by Jackson identifies a roadmap and vibrant agenda on how this could be achieved. Jackson argues that it is time for CSOs to "regroup, recalibrate and reload" (2010, 2). Where jurisdictions permit, he urges CSOs to reconstruct their partnerships with government to include greater power symmetry and longer-term program funding. This indeed is not an easy task, especially in the increasingly competitive funding environment. It is also true that this strategy may result in the depoliticization of CSOs or the delegitimization of CSOs that aim for transformation in the system. In other circumstances, CSOs have to redouble their efforts to raise private donations, diversify the mix of revenue sources, and create hard, physical assets (office buildings, daycare centres, various other kinds of social infrastructure) that will help get them through tough economic times. Jackson adds that civil society as a sector "should lobby to change laws and regulations in a direction that would enable foundations and endowments to make program-related investments" (2010, 5). And where possible, CSOs should take greater control of the evaluation agenda, using tools such as the Expanded Value Added Statement[7] and ensuring more stakeholder participation in the design and analysis of results.

The experiences of CSOs reveal that there are mixed signals and conflicting perceptions regarding the role of private sources in compensating for shrinking state budgets. There is a need to systematically analyze the constellation of NGOs and foundations. Current research and measures are inadequate; a more systematic understanding and measurement indicators are needed.

While this chapter is primarily about CSO strategies and coping tactics in the short-term, the authors urge civil society organizations to remind the international community with one voice of the need for long-term transformation of global governance structures at the macro level, not just within civil society organizations. A positive recent example is UNCTAD's first Public Symposium, held 18 and 19 May 2009 in Geneva, which highlighted the "human face" of the global economic crisis and provided a platform for civil society organizations to voice their concerns and offer ideas firmly anchored in grassroots realities (UNCTAD 2009). At this event, civil society in Africa expressed its disappointment with the global multilateral response to the crisis, observing that the current stimulus packages may not be adequate to address the challenges that African economies face.

Finally, the situation of CSOs suggest that home governments have to be more effective in mobilizing resources for social development in the face of increasingly severe social problems. As the data show, CSOs – which are frequently among the first-line responders during crisis – suffer from diminishing resources at the same time as vulnerable populations are at greater risk. While there is much discussion in the global media about the need for mechanisms to bail out the banking system, there is barely a whisper about the need for safety mechanisms to maintain the health of civil society organizations.

NOTES

We would like thank Brian Tomlinson, Rachael Calleja and Eloisa Martinez for their valuable comments on the earlier versions of this chapter.

1. In the international development literature CSO/NGO is the most widely used term to refer to non-profit and voluntary sector organizations. For the sake of conceptual clarity, we use CSO as the umbrella concept throughout this chapter in lieu of non-profit and voluntary organizations.
2. It is very difficult to speak of civil society around the world as a homogeneous group. Global civil society is comprised of hundreds of thousands of organizations in incredibly diverse circumstances in nearly 200 countries. The majority of CSOs are small, often unregistered, and reliant on volunteers and few paid staff. Others (especially some well-known international and national NGOs like Oxfam, CARE and BRAC) have multi-million dollar budgets, complex and sophisticated global structures, and considerable experience interacting with political elites and economic decision-makers.
3. At this point, a legitimate question is to what extent the increasing allocation of funds for humanitarian relief has meant decreasing resources of the Southern CSOs for development work? Currently, the evidence at hand signals that CSOs face serious trade-offs and limitations.
4. According to the OECD Stat Extracts, total ODA was approximately $120 billion in 2011. Non-DAC donor aid was approximately $15 billion in 2011, up from an average of $4 billion per annum between 2004–2006 prior to the onset of the financial crisis (OECD 2009). However, there are concerns

regarding non-DAC donors as they do not use the DAC definition of ODA and often count large amounts of export credits.
5.   According to Brian Tomlinson, formerly of the Canadian Council for International Cooperation (a national umbrella organization of Canadian development NGOs), more nuanced research needs to be done on this topic. He points out that "any assessment must take into account the political environment within which CSOs work in the South" (Personal Interview with Brian Tomlinson on 16 July 2011, Ottawa, Canada). During times of crisis he notes that governments with weak legitimacy may feel threatened by CSOs and respond by severely restricting the public space available to civil society.
6.   Includes foundations, corporations, private and voluntary organizations, volunteerism, universities and colleges, and religious organizations.
7.   Expanded Value Added Statement (EVAS) is an innovative tool to account for economic, social, and environmental factors. It provides a way to account for traditionally non-monetized factors (such as volunteer hours) to provide a better picture of social value creation. For further information please see: http://www3.carleton.ca/cedtap/stories/evas.pdf.

REFERENCES

African Training and Research Center in Administration for Development in Collaboration with Hans Seidel Foundation. 2011. Seminar on Decentralization, Local Governance and Poverty Alleviation. At http://www.cafrad.org/Workshops/Tanger26-28_09_11/cpen.pdf (accessed 1 July 2012).
Anderson, K. 2011. "Accountability as Legitimacy: Global Governance, Global Civil Society and the United Nations." Washington College of Law Research Paper No. 2011-28.
Anderson, S. 2010. "Civil Society Responses to the Global Economic Crisis." White Paper Prepared for Funders Network on Transforming the Global Economy (FNTG). At http://www.fntg.org/whitepaper2010.php (accessed 30 June 2012).
Center for Global Prosperity (CGP). 2010. Annual Report. At http://www.hudson.org/index.cfm?fuseaction=published_articles_and_op-eds. (accessed 20 August 2012).
CONECTAS. 2010. Organizational Assessment Report. At www.conectas.org/arquivos/multimidia/PDF/94.doc (accessed 14 March 2012).
Deutscher, E. 2010. Development Co-operation Report 2010. Paris: Organisation for Economic Co-operation and Development.
East African Association of Grantmakers (EAAG). 2012. Annual Conference on Philanthropy, Leadership and Governance blog, 25-27 July 2012. At http://eaagblog.wordpress.com/2012/04/24/faq-east-africa-philanthropy-awards/ (accessed 1 July 2012).
Economist. 2004. The Birth of Philantrocapitalism. At http://www.economist.com/node/5517656 (accessed 1 July 2012).
—. 2006. The New Powers in Giving. At http://www.economist.com/node/7112702 (accessed 1 July 2012).
—. 2011. Giving for Results, Lessons of Philanthropy. At http://www.economist.com/node/18679019 (accessed 1 July 2012).

Edwards, M. 2009. *Civil Society*. Cambridge: Polity Press.

Felsen, D. and H. Besada. 2011. "Non-State Collaborative Alternatives to Traditional Multilateral Government Aid: The Role of the Third Sector." The North-South Institute's Ottawa Conference on Multilateral Development Cooperation, 20-21 June.

Global Pulse. 2010. Voices of the Vulnerable: Recovery from the Ground Up. New York: United Nations Secretary General's Office/Global Pulse. At http://www.unglobalpulse.org/sites/all/files/reports/Voices-ofthe-Vulnerable.pdf (accessed 30 June 2012).

Hanfstaengl, E.-M. 2010. Impact of the Global Economic Crises on Civil Society Organizations. New York: NGO Committee for Social Development. At http://ngosocdev.wordpress.com/2010/01/28/174 (accessed 28 July 2011).

Hossain, N. 2010. Complex Global Shocks and the New Challenges for Civil Society. At http://www.fimcivilsociety.org/f/library/FIM%20 paper%20 Naomi%20Hossain.pdf (accessed 26 October 2011).

—. 2011. "Beyond Silos: Complex Global Shocks and the New Challenges for Civil Society." *IDS Bulletin* 42: 4-14.

Hossain, N., R. Fillaili, G. Lubaale, M. Mulumbi, and M. Rashid. 2010. Social Impacts of Crisis: Findings from community-level research in five developing countries. Mimeo. Brighton: Institute of Development Studies. At www.ids. ac.uk/go/news/now-available-the-social-impact-ofcrisis-one-year-on-reports (accessed 1 July 2012).

Inter-American Development Bank (IDB). 2010. Philanthropy Trends in Latin America. At http://www.lacdonors.org/biblio/Tendencias%20Filantropicas %20en%20America%20Latina/avina_articulo_2010_09_eng.pdf (accessed 1 July 2012).

Jackson, E. 2010. "Regrouping, Recalibrating, Reloading: Strategies for Financing Civil Society in post-Recession Canada." *The Philanthropist* 23: 2-5.

Makoni, M. 2012. Where are the Africa's Science Philanthropists? At http://www. researchresearch.com/index.php?option=com_news&template=rr_2col&view =article&articleId=1165276 (accessed 1 July 2012).

McCord, A. 2010. "The Impact of the Global Financial Crisis on Social Protection in Developing Countries." *International Social Security Review* 63: 31-45.

Mutasa, C. 2008. Accountability and Policy Dialogue. African Forum & Network on Debt & Development (AFRODAD). At http://www.dpwg-lgd.org/cms/ upload/pdf/accountability.pdf (accessed 30 June 2012).

Organisation for Economic Co-operation and Development (OECD). 2009. StatExtracts: Country Profiles. At http://stats.oecd.org/Index. aspx?DatasetCode=CSP2009 (accessed 20 August 2012).

—. 2011. The Role of the Private Sector in the Context of Aid Effectiveness: Supporting more Effective Partnership for Development in Busan. At http://www. oecd.org/dataoecd/39/35/48156055.pdf (accessed 18 May 2012).

—. 2012. Countries, Territories, and Organisations Adhering to the Paris Declaration and AAA. At http://www.oecd.org/document/55/0,3746,en_2649_ 3236398_36074966_1_1_1_1,00.html (accessed 18 May 2012).

Rapoo, T. 2010. "Funding Crisis for Research NGOs in South Africa Looming Larger Than Ever." Centre for Policy Studies. At http://www.cps.org.za (accessed 30 June 2012).

Regional Center for Public Administration Reform (RCPAR) and United Nations Development Program (UNDP). 2011. Economic Crisis Responses from a Governance Perspective in Eastern Europe and Central Asia: Regional Report.

Robinson, M. and S. Friedman. 2009. "Thematic Evaluation of Support by Danish NGOs to Civil Society in Ghana and Ethiopia." IDS paper 383. Ministry of Foreign Affairs of Denmark.

Rogerson, A. 2011. Key Busan Challenges and Contributions to the Emerging Development Effectiveness Agenda. Overseas Development Institute: Background Note. At http://www.odi.org.uk/resources/docs/7299.pdf (accessed 18 May 2012).

Skopje Conference. 2011. "How Civil Society and Local Governments are Fighting the Global Crisis." Skopje, Croatia: Association of Local Democracy Agencies (ALDA). At http://www.uzuvrh.hr/vijestEN.aspx?pageID=2&newsID=430 (accessed 1 July 2012).

Stahl, D. 2010. Grassroots Aid Groups Struggle to Stay Afloat. At http://ipsterraviva.net/UN/currentNew.aspx?new=7194 (accessed 26 October 2011).

United Nations (UN). 2012. Millennium Development Goals: Background. At http://www.un.org/millenniumgoals/bkgd.shtml (accessed 30 June 2012).

United Nations Conference on Trade and Development (UNCTAD). 2009. UNCTAD Deliberations on the Global Economic Crisis and Development. At http://www.unctad.org/en/docs/gdsmisc20091_en.pdf (accessed 30 June 2012).

—. 2012. Official Development Assistance and Debt Relief. At http://dgff.unctad.org/chapter4/4.3.html (accessed 30 June 2012).

United Nations Economic Commission for Africa (UNECA). 2009. Economic Report on Africa. At http://new.uneca.org/Portals/ngm/CrossArticle/1/Documents/15YearReviewofBPfA.pdf (accessed 20 August 2012).

Van Rooy, A. 2004. *The Global Legitimacy Game: Civil Society, Globalization and Protest.* New York: Palgrave MacMillan.

World Alliance for Citizen Participation (CIVICUS). 2011. Bridging the Gaps: Citizens, Organizations, and Dissociation – Civil Society Index Summary Report 2008–2011. Johannesburg, South Africa: CIVICUS.

Contributors

NICHOLAS ACHESON, Lecturer in Social Policy, Institute for Research in the Social Sciences, School of Criminology, Politics and Social Policy, University of Ulster.

JOHN BUTCHER, ANZSOG Research Associate, School of Politics & International Relations, Australian National University.

JOHN CASEY, Center for Nonprofit Strategy and Management, Baruch College, City University of New York.

GEMMA DONNELLY-COX, Lecturer in Business Studies and Academic Director of the Centre for Nonprofit Management at Trinity College, Dublin.

JOHN A. HEALY, Ph.D. candidate in Business Studies, Trinity College, Dublin and Director of Impact Assessment and Global Learning at The Atlantic Philanthropies.

RACHEL LAFOREST, Associate Professor and Head of Public Policy and the Third Sector Initiative, School of Policy Studies, Queen's University.

BARBARA LEVINE, Adjunct Professor, School of Public Policy and Administration, Carleton University, Ottawa, Ontario, Canada.

CARMEN PARRA, Professor University Abat Oliba CEU.

COLIN ROCHESTER, Honorary Research Fellow in the School of Social Sciences, History and Philosophy at Birkbeck, University of London, UK and partner in the Practical Wisdom R2Z Research Consultancy.

BJÖRN SCHMITZ, PhD Candidate, Centre for Social Investment, University of Heidelberg, Germany.

STEVEN RATHGEB SMITH, American University, The University of Washington.

MARILYN TAYLOR, Institute for Voluntary Action Research and Visiting Professor, Birkbeck, University of London.

EVREN TOK, Assistant Professor, Hamad Bin Khalifa University, Qatar Faculty of Islamic Studies, Public Policy in Islam Program, Member of Qatar Foundation, Doha, Qatar.

META ZIMMECK, Visiting Fellow at the Centre for the Study of Voluntary and Community Activity, Roehamptom University, and partner, Practical Wisdom R2Z Research Consultants.

Queen's Policy Studies
Recent Publications

The Queen's Policy Studies Series is dedicated to the exploration of major public policy issues that confront governments and society in Canada and other nations.

Manuscript submission. We are pleased to consider new book proposals and manuscripts. Preliminary inquiries are welcome. A subvention is normally required for the publication of an academic book. Please direct questions or proposals to the Publications Unit by email at spspress@queensu.ca, or visit our website at: www.queensu.ca/sps/books, or contact us by phone at (613) 533-2192.

Our books are available from good bookstores everywhere, including the Queen's University bookstore (http://www.campusbookstore.com/). McGill-Queen's University Press is the exclusive world representative and distributor of books in the series. A full catalogue and ordering information may be found on their web site (**http://mqup.mcgill.ca/**).

For more information about new and backlist titles from Queen's Policy Studies, visit http://www.queensu.ca/sps/books.

School of Policy Studies

The Multiculturalism Question: Debating Identity in 21st-Century Canada, Jack Jedwab (ed.) 2014. ISBN 978-1-55339-422-8

Rethinking Higher Education: Participation, Research, and Differentiation, George Fallis 2013. ISBN 978-1-55339-333-7

Making Policy in Turbulent Times: Challenges and Prospects for Higher Education, Paul Axelrod, Roopa Desai Trilokekar, Theresa Shanahan, and Richard Wellen (eds.) 2013. ISBN 978-1-55339-332-0

Intellectual Disabilities and *Dual Diagnosis: An Interprofessional Clinical Guide for Healthcare Providers,* Bruce D. McCreary and Jessica Jones (eds.) 2013. ISBN 978-1-55339-331-3

Building More Effective Labour-Management Relationships, Richard P. Chaykowski and Robert S. Hickey (eds.) 2013. ISBN 978-1-55339-306-1

Navigationg on the Titanic: Economic Growth, Energy, and the Failure of Governance, Bryne Purchase 2013. ISBN 978-1-55339-330-6

Measuring the Value of a Postsecondary Education, Ken Norrie and Mary Catharine Lennon (eds.) 2013. ISBN 978-1-55339-325-2

Immigration, Integration, and Inclusion in Ontario Cities, Caroline Andrew, John Biles, Meyer Burstein, Victoria M. Esses, and Erin Tolley (eds.) 2012. ISBN 978-1-55339-292-7

Diverse Nations, Diverse Responses: Approaches to Social Cohesion in Immigrant Societies, Paul Spoonley and Erin Tolley (eds.) 2012. ISBN 978-1-55339-309-2

Making EI Work: Research from the Mowat Centre Employment Insurance Task Force, Keith Banting and Jon Medow (eds.) 2012. ISBN 978-1-55339-323-8

Managing Immigration and Diversity in Canada: A Transatlantic Dialogue in the New Age of Migration, Dan Rodríguez-García (ed.) 2012. ISBN 978-1-55339-289-7

International Perspectives: Integration and Inclusion, James Frideres and John Biles (eds.) 2012. ISBN 978-1-55339-317-7

Dynamic Negotiations: Teacher Labour Relations in Canadian Elementary and Secondary Education, Sara Slinn and Arthur Sweetman (eds.) 2012. ISBN 978-1-55339-304-7

Where to from Here? Keeping Medicare Sustainable, Stephen Duckett 2012.
ISBN 978-1-55339-318-4

International Migration in Uncertain Times, John Nieuwenhuysen, Howard Duncan, and Stine Neerup (eds.) 2012. ISBN 978-1-55339-308-5

Life After Forty: Official Languages Policy in Canada/Après quarante ans, les politiques de langue officielle au Canada, Jack Jedwab and Rodrigue Landry (eds.) 2011.
ISBN 978-1-55339-279-8

From Innovation to Transformation: Moving up the Curve in Ontario Healthcare,
Hon. Elinor Caplan, Dr. Tom Bigda-Peyton, Maia MacNiven, and Sandy Sheahan 2011.
ISBN 978-1-55339-315-3

Academic Reform: Policy Options for Improving the Quality and Cost-Effectiveness of Undergraduate Education in Ontario, Ian D. Clark, David Trick, and Richard Van Loon 2011.
ISBN 978-1-55339-310-8

Integration and Inclusion of Newcomers and Minorities across Canada, John Biles, Meyer Burstein, James Frideres, Erin Tolley, and Robert Vineberg (eds.) 2011.
ISBN 978-1-55339-290-3

A New Synthesis of Public Administration: Serving in the 21ˢᵗ Century, Jocelyne Bourgon, 2011. ISBN 978-1-55339-312-2 (paper) 978-1-55339-313-9 (cloth)

Recreating Canada: Essays in Honour of Paul Weiler, Randall Morck (ed.), 2011.
ISBN 978-1-55339-273-6

Data Data Everywhere: Access and Accountability? Colleen M. Flood (ed.), 2011.
ISBN 978-1-55339-236-1

Making the Case: Using Case Studies for Teaching and Knowledge Management in Public Administration, Andrew Graham, 2011. ISBN 978-1-55339-302-3

Centre for International and Defence Policy

Afghanistan in the Balance: Counterinsurgency, Comprehensive Approach, and Political Order, Hans-Georg Ehrhart, Sven Bernhard Gareis, and Charles Pentland (eds.), 2012.
ISBN 978-1-55339-353-5

Security Operations in the 21st Century: Canadian Perspectives on the Comprehensive Approach, Michael Rostek and Peter Gizewski (eds.), 2011. ISBN 978-1-55339-351-1

Institute of Intergovernmental Relations

Canada and the Crown: Essays on Constitutional Monarchy, D. Michael Jackson and Philippe Lagassé (eds.), 2013. ISBN 978-1-55339-204-0

Paradigm Freeze: Why It Is So Hard to Reform Health-Care Policy in Canada, Harvey Lazar, John N. Lavis, Pierre-Gerlier Forest, and John Church (eds.), 2013.
ISBN 978-1-55339-324-5

Canada: The State of the Federation 2010, Matthew Mendelsohn, Joshua Hjartarson, and James Pearce (eds.), 2013. ISBN 978-1-55339-200-2

The Democratic Dilemma: Reforming Canada's Supreme Court, Nadia Verrelli (ed.), 2013.
ISBN 978-1-55339-203-3

The Evolving Canadian Crown, Jennifer Smith and D. Michael Jackson (eds.), 2011.
ISBN 978-1-55339-202-6

The Federal Idea: Essays in Honour of Ronald L. Watts, Thomas J. Courchene, John R. Allan, Christian Leuprecht, and Nadia Verrelli (eds.), 2011. ISBN 978-1-55339-198-2 (paper) 978-1-55339-199-9 (cloth)

The Democratic Dilemma: Reforming the Canadian Senate, Jennifer Smith (ed.), 2009.
ISBN 978-1-55339-190-6